SOUTH
LIGHTS

The University of North Carolina Press

CHAPEL HILL

SOUTHERN LIGHTS

75 YEARS OF THE CAROLINA QUARTERLY

EDITED BY

Sophia Houghton, Kylan Rice, and Daniel Wallace

This book was published with the assistance of the Blythe Family Fund of the University of North Carolina Press.

Designed and set by Lindsay Starr
in Sentinel and Futura Now
Manufactured in the United States of America

Cover art: Celestial map of the northern sky, ca. 1870,
courtesy of Joseph Meyer and E. G. Ravenstein.

Library of Congress Cataloging-in-Publication Data to come
Names: Houghton, Sophia, editor. | Rice, Kylan, editor. |
    Wallace, Daniel, 1959– editor.
Title: Southern lights : 75 years of the Carolina quarterly /
    edited by Sophia Houghton, Kylan Rice, and Daniel Wallace.
Other titles: Carolina quarterly.
Description: Chapel Hill : The University of North Carolina Press, [2023]
Identifiers: LCCN 2023029864 | ISBN 9781469674568 (paperback) |
    ISBN 9781469674575 (ebook)
Subjects: LCSH: Carolina quarterly. | American literature. |
    BISAC: LITERARY COLLECTIONS / American / General |
    HISTORY / United States / State & Local / South (AL, AR, FL,
    GA, KY, LA, MS, NC, SC, TN, VA, WV) | LCGFT: Literature.
Classification: LCC PS507 .S68 2023 | DDC 810.8—dc23/eng/20230802
LC record available at https://lccn.loc.gov/2023029864

CONTENTS

....

PART III. LOVE   75

PART IV. PLACE   143

PART V. MEMORIAM   161

PART VI. MYTH   209

FOREWORD

....

The life cycle of a story, a poem, or an essay is not unlike the life cycle of a flea. This came to me, unsurprisingly, at my vet's office, when I was bringing my dog in for a checkup. There it was, a giant poster on the wall of the examination room: *Life Cycle of a Flea*, illustrated in nauseating detail. It turns out there are four stages in the life of a flea, and as I waited for Dr. Smith to come check on us I realized the same could be said for a story. Like a flea, a story might begin as an undefined bit of life, full of potential—larval, say—and then grow into something more defined as we writers explore and clarify to ourselves how it all works, its form and meaning and direction. This investigation is the pupal stage. From there, over time—weeks, months, even years (though for the flea it only takes a few days)—the story may mature into what it was always meant to become, complete, as perfect as it ever can or, at least, ever will be—a mature piece of work—in other words, a full-fledged flea. That would seem to be the end of it, and the end of the analogy, but there's one more stage: the flea must make other fleas. The flea must lay some eggs. Only then is its life cycle complete.

In the life cycle of a written work of art, publication and dissemination is not unlike a flea laying its eggs everywhere it possibly can. Publication feels *necessary*. It's less a philosophical question—something about the sound a tree makes falling in a desolate forest—than it is a practical one: What does it feel like *not* to publish? Is this final stage of the life of the work necessary to say it was ever alive at all? If the best and longest part of a writer's life is spent alone scribbling in a room, what's so critical about the comparatively brief experience of publication?

That's like asking a flea why it lays eggs.

For me, and for many writers, quarterlies provide the first and best opportunity to see our work in print, to put it before an audience of any size, to give it life. While some jockey for "the glossies"—the *New Yorker*, *Harper's*, the *Atlantic*, *Playboy*—the reality is that most of us happily begin and just as happily end our publication lives in quarterlies.

Quarterlies are usually published by or through universities and called such because they come out in magazine form roughly three times a year (summers they take off). Online publishing has changed this setup considerably and offered different (though not necessarily better) publishing opportunities. But for the latter half of the twentieth century the only outlet for young, unknown writers was the quarterlies; the same goes for older, quite well-known writers. That's one of the great things about quarterlies: young and old, unknown and well known are all commingled. It's a party. Getting published in a quarterly, then, especially as a newbie, held that secondary frisson: Who will I be published *with*? Whose vaunted company will I keep on the page?

The *Carolina Quarterly* is the paradigm of what a quarterly is meant to be. This I know from experience. In the early 1980s, as I devised my plans for invading the literary universe, the *Carolina Quarterly* was high on my submission list. There were other magazines, of course, but the *CQ* had a special luster. It was edited at the University of North Carolina in Greenlaw Hall, the building where I took my English classes as an undergrad. It was, apart from the personal connection, also one of the most important quarterlies of the twentieth century. I wanted to see one of my stories in it.

Here is what I did to try to make that happen: I typed a story on my electric typewriter, took it to Kinko's, made twenty copies of it, bought forty manila envelopes, slipped a copy of the story into a manila envelope along with a second manila envelope with my return address and postage on it (an SASE, or self-addressed stamped envelope) and sent all twenty copies out on the same day, to all the quarterlies I hoped would finally publish me. When all twenty were returned to me in the SASE I provided, as they usually were, I rewrote the story and did it all over again.

I don't know how many times the *Carolina Quarterly* passed on my stories, but more than a handful. Maybe a bucketful, or a wheelbarrow-full. Because I used to keep records of these things, I know the first rejection was in January 1986, and the first acceptance a mere fourteen years later. Yes, fourteen years. My publishing schedule roughly reflected the gestation life of the periodical cicada. Apparently, I just had to be patient and wait for the next century to come along, because all of that time I had been trying. Along with me, in the Spring 2000 issue of the *Carolina Quarterly* was, among many other luminaries, Ha Jin, winner of the Flannery O'Conner Award, the Pen/Faulkner Award twice, and a finalist for the Pulitzer. I have never won or been nominated for any of these awards, but I was in a magazine with someone who was. That meant something—a kind of conferred prestige.

Southern literature—perhaps this nation's greatest single contribution to world literature—has been nurtured by the *Carolina Quarterly* since its inception. On their own and at their best, quarterlies are collections that embody a moment in time. This book is a selected collection of those collections embodying not just a moment but the arc of the creative life in this country. Seeing all the names and voices gathered in this volume is astounding on both a literary and historical level. As a historical document it's important to know who was publishing, when they were publishing, and what sort of work they were writing. But it's also entertainment, plain and simple; it makes for great reading. One of the virtues of an anthology is that it doesn't have to be read linearly. It's made for bopping around in, opening at random, thumbing through one great piece after another until you find the one you need the moment you need it. You don't have to think another minute about everything the *Carolina Quarterly* has done for southern literature specifically and American literature in general; let someone else take that on. This collection is for the reader. Read this book for the joy collected herein.

I'm so honored to have been published in this quarterly, and so lucky to have had the opportunity to help bring this collection to life. I feel like I was drawn to the *Carolina Quarterly* before I was aware of what I was being drawn to. That this one little magazine was being edited in the same building whose halls I walked as a secretly desirous but (as yet) unpublished undergrad, doing whatever it was I was doing in those lost years, while all that time the *Carolina Quarterly* was just a few feet away from me, doing whatever it is you do to keep literature not only alive but thriving, providing a home to the strivers and the strove, a place for all of us fleas—it was the Dog Star I was following, following even before I knew it was there.

—Daniel Wallace

ACKNOWLEDGMENTS

....

Special thanks are due to Susan Jones for her assistance as we compiled the manuscript for this anthology. Thanks are also due to the Creative Writing Program in the English Department at the University of North Carolina, Chapel Hill.

Above all, we owe our deepest gratitude to the writers who contributed their work to this volume, as well as to the relatives, executors, agents, and publishers who support and carry on their legacies.

SOUTHERN LIGHTS

INTRODUCTION

....

Like the day, the year is a natural measure of time. In contrast to the hour or week, the duration of day and year can be felt in the body, in rhythms of sleep and wakefulness, in steady alternating intervals of dawn and dusk. Days pass and the seasons shift, bringing periods of cornucopia and dormancy, new growth and ripening. The year is a unit for reckoning this earthly rhythm in almanacs and ledgers, figuring how much income, how much was spent, and by the time the earth returns to fruitfulness, the balance book is cleared and shelved, and the next year's book begins.

A quarterly participates in similar cycles of reckoning and replenishment, gathering what's good throughout the year, from fall to fall, recording it for future years to come. Yoked to the seasons, it's grounded in the earth, in its speeds and slownesses, the meter or meting-out of mortal days. In these days we meet: to read the writing in a quarterly is to touch the hand of a workman on the road, ungloved to greet you. You can feel in that touch a losing heat. Just published, printed in its own time and hot from the press, the poem or story in a quarterly is a "living hand, now warm and capable / Of earnest grasping," to use words from the poet John Keats. To read it later, in a retrospective anthology like the one you have before you now, is to come in contact with a chillier grip, a hand from which some of the warmth has seeped, like ink into the fibers of a page.

And yet, as Alan Shapiro observes in the poem that opens this anthology, which collects seventy-five years of prose and poetry published in the *Carolina Quarterly*, "even the coldness on my hands and lips turns sweet / because I think whoever finds me here / might find it, at their greeting, a mortal thing." Shapiro writes these lines anticipating the approach of a host behind a door, someone who has risen from sleep in order to admit the poet to a house in which he hopes to stay the night. Having been abroad so long, the poet is conscious of the coldness of his touch. Here he is, at the threshold of a place of rest, half-imagining that the person on the other side of the door is his mother, "who approaches / when she would find me sleepless at her door, / and till I slept would sing me, Is You Is / Or Is You Ain't My Baby." Perhaps the poems and stories and essays in this collection crave similar comfort, companionship, a long time coming. Or maybe it's the other way around, and we as readers knock, seeking entrance at the outset of this book, our lips both chapped and sweet.

When a poem or story is first printed in a quarterly, the writer's hand is warm in it. Later, the work might be compiled in a book, and later still, collected in an anthology like this one. *Southern Lights* is an opportunity to feel that distant heat across time, a radiance like starlight, which can take many years to reach the eyes of those alive on Earth at any given moment. Collecting prose and poetry from over fifty different writers who have published their work in the *Carolina Quarterly* since 1948, this anthology is a constellation of literary stars, both large and small, new and established. A number of the writers in this book hail from the US American South, but they help map out a much larger, even universal terrain, which makes *Southern Lights* a timeless human document as much as a timely regional record.

In part, this anthology tells a story about the expanding scope (the telescoping-out) of a local magazine—but a brief look at the early history of the *Quarterly* reveals that the ambitions of its editors were far-reaching from the start. Although the *Quarterly* was first established in the fall of 1948 as a campus literary magazine intended to "represent the intellectual and artistic endeavors of students" at the University of North Carolina at Chapel Hill, early editors and contributors were eager to position the publication as an important new presence in the field of southern letters, also indicating their ambitions to participate in "revivals" of literary culture at the national level.[1] Advertisement for subscriptions to the magazine contained in its first issue included an endorsement from the famous local playwright Paul Green, who observed that there is "a great chance for such a publication here in Chapel Hill, the new literary capital of the South." The comment is revealing not only because it situates Chapel Hill as a hotspot for new southern literature but also because it emphasizes the uncertainty or chanciness of the venture. Indeed, from the outset, the journal's financial footing was tenuous. Pitched as a successor to the *University Magazine*, in print for over a century before it was "voted off the campus" due to "political" controversy, the *Quarterly* was at first supported by the student government, which granted the fledgling magazine $2,000 to defray costs of operation during its first year.[2] However, only $800 of these funds were ultimately delivered, forcing the editors of the second volume to "appeal to the citizens of the state and region" by seeking donors and boosting efforts to secure subscriptions. These marketing efforts to sustain the new magazine were savvy, industrious, and farsighted: for example, in its second year, the *Quarterly* launched a campaign to place the magazine in bookstores around the country, far from little Chapel Hill, also sending correspondence directly to business leaders and newspaper editors closer to home, soliciting subscriptions from the wealthy and well connected.[3]

Editorials published in the *Quarterly* in these early years were sober and even a little admonitory, reflecting anxieties about the projected success of the venture that were intertwined with larger questions concerning the state of a nation overshadowed by a looming Cold War. In the winter of 1951, possibly referring to a growing red scare or to the public perception of US involvement in the Korean War, editor-in-chief Lyn Miller explicitly linked the fate of the country and the fate of the *Quarterly*, asking, "When the people of a nation are conscious only of their anxiety, who remains to be concerned with the future of a college literary magazine?"[4] Citing "apathy" as a symptom of these anxieties, Miller observed that "the future of a college magazine is always precarious," in this way echoing her predecessor Harry R. Snowden Jr.'s conviction that "the chances of a literary magazine" achieving long-term stability "are slim."[5] Presumably responding to a lack of interest in editorial participation, Miller foresaw a future in which the *Quarterly* risked becoming a "shell" and a "dull echo" of itself—a fate that haunted early editors, even as they managed to elude it.

Indeed, although the *Quarterly* emerged during a time that editors and contributors deemed "chaotic" and "decadent," envisioning the magazine as an outpost against the decline of a morally dissolute and "self-satisf[ied]" postwar American culture, there was also a sense of excitement underwritten by energetic enterprise on the part of "an unusually large body of mature and industrious students," many of whom had "seen service" in the war.[6] Launched at the height of university enrollments connected with the passage of the Servicemen's Readjustment Act of 1944, also known as the G.I. Bill, the *Quarterly* was staffed by a serious group of hard-working students who laid firm foundations for the magazine's subsequent growth and success.[7] Though they faced steep challenges, the editorial vision was consistently oriented toward the future, even as it remained committed to "Southern Regionalism" as a literary tradition.[8] Writing for the second issue in the winter of 1949, Roy C. Moose argued that American literature had always been essentially heterogeneous, a patchwork of traditions developed organically in the country's various regions and "sections."[9] Having made this claim, Moose situated the *Quarterly* in a broader effort to "develop a genuine Southern Regionalism" that could represent "the modern South with its problems of economics, race relations, and politics." Indeed, Moose concluded, "it is with this new South that the young writers of our region should be concerned."

Over the seven and a half decades that followed Moose's editorial, the journal has evolved, trading an explicit regional focus to become an outlet for national and even international literary innovation. Of course, instead

of seeing this as an effort to shed its geographic heritage, these develop-
ments might be understood as evidence of a changing regional consciousness, an evolving sense of what it means to live, write, and publish in a
southern state. In part, *Southern Lights* offers a portrait of these changes.
Already Moose heralded a changing "modern south" in 1949, and Frank
Murphy observed in 1961 that a "New South" had emerged as a consequence
of dramatic urbanization during the first half of the twentieth century, a
phenomenon that the vast majority of southern writers had yet to register
and develop into a new idiom.[10] In his critique of contemporary southern
writing, Murphy observed the perverse enduring specter of an "agrarian"
past that had been "buried beneath a four-lane super highway, over which
travel each day suburbanite businessmen more concerned with the Dow-
Jones average than with the cotton crop."[11] Perhaps it is this same road that
runs through Michael McFee's "Pearly Gates" (vol. 46, no. 3, 1994), which
recounts a childhood car trip down to Florida. In this poem, McFee remembers how "the rotten mouth of Georgia" seemed to "swallow" him and his
family as they traveled south, an engulfment itself engulfed by "the hungry
sky behind the sky / with its unreachable pearly clouds." In "I Pledge Alle-
giance" (vol. 12, no. 3, 1960), the Black poet Gloria Oden also reflects on the
unreachability or impossibility that characterizes the South as a region,
recalling how, as a child, she had imagined her mother's southern homeland
as an "immediately out of reach box of goodies." Out-of-reach, both sweet
and rotten, a mouth full of sugar and decay, the South appears through the
history of the *Quarterly* as a place of promise and impossibility, a place of
speculation, and so, too, of visions and revisions. Who or what constitutes
the South remains an open question, as much as it did in Doris Betts's "The
August Tree" (vol. 8, no. 1, 1955), a story in which the main character, a
Southern Baptist everyman named Wade Crockett, struggles to assert himself, to name himself and his destiny. "I am what I am!" Crockett exclaims—
abstractly, flailingly—at the beginning of Betts's story. By the end, Crockett
settles for more modest, interconnected terms of self-definition: "I am not
a dog"; "I am not a tree." Crockett can only grasp who he is by responding to
the world around him, coming to terms with his limits in a way that impli-
cates him in an ecosystem of which he is also a part. Perhaps the same can
be said of the South: it is what it is, as much as what it's not. And this is a
source of bitterness and celebration both.

The *Quarterly* is itself not unlike Mr. Crockett: an individual profoundly
marked by limitation and locality but bothered also by the Big Questions. For
that reason, though region recurs throughout this anthology, it is organized

around enduring human themes: Nature, Body, Love, Place, Memoriam, and Myth. In this way, to read this book is to sense a little star ash drifting down to settle in your hair: here you stand in space and time, in a "bare common," feeling your "head bathed by the blithe air and uplifted into infinite space," sensing like Emerson the thrumming continuity of the common with the cosmos, each a fractal of the other.[12]

THE HOST

(VOL. 35, NO. 1, 1982)

Alan Shapiro

....

From the curtained light, inside, they must be moving
slowly out of bed, now that I'm here.
However much time has passed since I've been gone
there's never any hurry in their welcome
though they hear the bell. And no reluctance,
for they come in no time, and are always coming,
friends, or lovers, when I am at the door.
I can hear their soft steps over the carpet
and, in that deepening rhythm, I find myself expecting
an unremembered comfort, as though in their approach
all elsewhere goes till I'm almost nowhere else
but home, and it could be my mother who approaches
when she would find me sleepless at her door,
and till I slept would sing me, Is You Is
Or Is You Ain't My Baby—

                                        her song now in the light
that goes on in the hall, the lock that turns.
Even the coldness on my hands and lips turns sweet
because I think whoever finds me here
might find it, at their greeting, a mortal thing.

PART I

NATURE

I wander toward dawn
And dream
Of staying here forever,
Speaking to no one
If I may.

—ROBERT MORGAN

THERE is a consciousness of dispersion and limitation that filters through this section, where it becomes concentrated into brilliantly specific points of interface between humans and nature. Charles Eaton's trumpet lilies "stir and bend" just beyond the "remote bed of reality" of a nighttime shared; in Doris Betts's "The August Tree," the routine of a passing workday converges with the cyclicality of natural time to reveal our small "position in the Scheme of Things"; Robert Morgan waits for a loved one in the shadows of the river; and in the destruction of a rosebush and the killing of a crow, Wendell Berry presents images of grief, its ever-present bloom. In this section, feelings distill into the "secret textures" of life touched by and growing out of the land.

THE SWAN

(VOL. 1, NO. 2, 1949)

Charles Eaton

....

In the distance a swan breaks the air, twisting under the palm shade
Like an orange-fanged white serpent, striking from the pure nest of its
    own body.
Then the wind unmoors the current, and the webbed feet braid

The water with a lustrous jet ripple. Though the sinuous arc
Of the neck and the silver breast open and feather the air, the black eyes
    glint cruelly.
And no one knows whether evil or innocence drifts from the slowly
opened arms of prophetic dark.

Whether evil or innocent, no one knows. But the soft fan-float
Of the wings draws a train of fascination across the afternoon,
And even the fingers of the water would reach up and stroke the
    irresistible white throat.

TRUMPET LILIES

(VOL. 1, NO. 2, 1949)

Charles Eaton

....

Over the valley shines the morning star
Blown pale by the dark wind of night.
From our bed, through the window, far
From the touch of the hand, we see the silver trumpet lilies
    stir and bend
On vague stalks of mist. Only the light
Is whispering between us the lonely aftermath. That
    it should end
So, with a distant vista of lilies, is only the final part
Of passion: the perfection missed: the contemplated
    and intended purity.
There is no one among the lilies to blow the music
    as pure as the sound should be.
On the remote bed of reality we lie, our lips sewn
    with dreams and the terror of the awakening
    heart.

THE AUGUST TREE

(VOL. 8, NO. 1, 1955)

Doris Betts

....

There were a number of things in the world which irritated Mr. Crockett, but worst of all was the suspicion that he was being constantly and objectively categorized.

By this, Mr. Crockett meant that somewhere whole hosts of people were thinking of him as though he were synonymous with only a part of himself—as though he were merely a small businessman, or a Rural Box Holder, or a Baptist, or an alumnus of Crabtree High School. Whereas, in truth (he would think indignantly) he was not one but all of these; and it made him angry to suppose, for instance, that the mechanic at Fitchley Motors thought of him only as The-Man-with-the-Fifty-Chevrolet-that-Rattled.

Because Mr. Crockett had grown so acutely and angrily conscious of this danger of being thought about too simply, he had taken to explaining himself to absolute strangers; and for this reason they often looked on him with dark suspicion. It was as though he felt bound to give, at least, some clues to the man within.

As, for instance, when a worker approached him for the Cerebral Palsy Fund, Mr. Crockett could see himself clearly reflected in the waiting eyes, twin pictures of a balding man already labeled: Possible Donor. And Mr. Crockett, seeing himself so simplified, would remark in a cross voice, "I have a farm out from town. Crossbreeding Brahmans and Angus. Very interesting." And then he would rare back in his chair, frowning. There! his look implied. *That* should have settled the dust.

Or a great longing would come upon him to walk up to absolute strangers in the street and say to them loudly and rudely, "I am what I am!" and see what they would say.

Or once when Reverend and Mrs. Grimley called on him and everyone in the room was suddenly busily occupied being Minister, Minister's Wife, Church Member, it was Mr. Crockett who burst out irrelevantly, his eyes popping from agitation, "Once I stole four dollars!"

It was a lie, but it bathed his soul with reassurance. It reminded him that he was himself and that he was inviolate.

And Mr. Crockett considered himself an educated man though there had been only two years of technical agriculture at his uncle's expense; he was educated because he read books and asked questions and had some conception both of his capacity and of his ignorance. He had been to Shakespeare and to Plato and Saint Luke, and he thought it ought to show in him a bit, like a highly tailored suit. If only he had taken up some other enterprise instead of the one his uncle left him.

For Mr. Crockett was in the septic tank business. He cleaned them and installed them, in strict conformity to Board of Health regulations; and he had a well-drilling rig on the side. It was a good business, he often said defiantly to his wife. It had paid well. Sometimes Mr. Crockett was even able to tell himself that through his efforts rural life in Prince Tyler County was becoming more sanitary. It was becoming downright hygienic.

But at other times Mr. Crockett's position in the Scheme of Things frightened him by its smallness. He would wake at night, surprised to remember his unimportance.

At that time he would picture himself, coming round and bald into the final Glory, an insignificant pinpoint of a soul; and hearing that majestic roll of the voice of God saying to him, "And what did you do all your life, Brother Crockett?"

"I cleaned out . . ." he would begin, stammering "Sir, I cleaned up . . ." But here he would stop, appalled at what he had been about to say. He could not say *that* word. Not to God.

In his younger days, it had seemed important to Mr. Crockett to acquire the very tags he now found so disagreeable—to be a Businessman, a Baptist, a Husband and Father; to have the things his parents had not had—the soft mattresses and the white bread and the indoor plumbing.

Old Mr. Crockett had sharecropped, and he himself had picked the cotton that was not half theirs and slopped hogs and hoed weeds; his uncle had built the septic tank business and produced no heirs; another uncle had worked in a sawmill all his life, all his life turning trees to dust.

His mother (she had outlived them all) was thin as a pencil with eyes that looked as though they had grown that way from seeing through stone walls. It seemed to Mr. Crockett that both his parents had warred all their lives with the soil and the sky and captured nothing; they had only worked and eaten and slept and now and then the land—as though it relented—gave up to them a few spindly things, enough for molasses and flour and a tinseled motto for one wall, a motto that he could see even now as though it were still hanging in his head, "The Lord is my Light and my Salvation. Whom shall I fear?"

Who indeed? Only the very air about them; only the unfriendly earth and the hostile seasons.

So when Wade Crockett thought of the unpainted boards in that long ago house and the splinters and the cold and the homemade whitewash on the hearths, he would feel he had come far and done much after all.

If only it had been by some different road, banking or law practice or setting bones; and if only he could be sure that he was—after all—different from his parents, that he had won more at less cost. For he was not really sure of this. Sometimes it seemed to him he moved around the same tired circle, and it was only wider somewhat.

And whenever Mr. Crockett thought about all these things in the night with his tubby little wife sleeping soundly beside him and a branch coming and going against the house, he would clasp and unclasp his hands and turn on the mattress as though it were a heap of stones.

"Frances?" he would whisper finally, desperately. "Frances, are you asleep?"

Frances Crockett would slow her snoring, catch her breath in surprise, and then be gone again into those dreamless regions he could not quite reach. He had almost pulled her out; he had almost made her lie beside him and be aware of dark and space going out forever on all sides.

But then she escaped again; she began breathing in and out and out and in; and all the time the branch was going up and down with a terrible regularity against the wall.

Mr. Crockett would turn onto his back and stare up at the ceiling a million miles away. He would think to himself, I am all alone.

It was an August morning and the sky as blue as cornflowers but Mr. Crockett was in a bad humor for all of that. He thrust his tongue under his upper lip and brought the razor down as gently as he dared and then stretched his jaw out of shape and got the whiskers there.

He thought, for perhaps the hundredth time, How ridiculous this is! Every day as long as I live, scraping the hairs away.

"Hurry," Frances called. "They'll get all soggy." She had poured him a bowl of cornflakes for breakfast and was as anxious as though she were serving crêpes suzettes to visiting diplomats.

He said, giving himself a hard look in the mirror, "I'm rushing as fast as I can." He put the razor down and frowned crossly at himself and pulled his own nose.

"You've been there half an hour," Frances called.

He did not answer her. He leaned his chin into the glass and blew, so that the steam hid his face completely. Then, like a child, he made two holes in the fog and let his eyes show through.

"I'm coming," he said again, not very loud. He watched the man hiding behind the steamed-up face and thought to himself that at just this hour all over the world thousands of men and women were scraping off old faces and painting on new ones and getting ready to walk out into the daylight as though they were real, as though they were themselves. He could picture them all before thousands of identical mirrors in thousands of bathrooms, stretching the smile across the teeth, reddening the mouth, plucking the hairs from the nostrils, smiling and frowning a time or two to see if the whole thing fit.

He sat on the toilet seat, miserable.

"Are you coming?" It was Frances and from the sound of her she was starting up the stairs, puffing. He turned on the water, loud.

"Sometimes," Frances was saying, a little out of breath, "Sometimes I can't imagine what you do in there all the time."

No, nor I either, he thought, holding the shaving brush idly under the faucet. A few of the hairs washed loose and went down the drain. A thousand more of those, he thought, and I'll have to buy a new one. He was as tired as if he had worked all day.

"I'm coming, Frances."

He opened the bathroom door right in her face and the two of them looked at each other, surprised. Then he smiled. He loved her, really; after all these years he loved her; the thought continued to amaze him. It was as though he owned something infinitely precious and now and then would take it out and cup it in his hand and say to himself, surprised, "Why it *is* mine, after all."

He put his hand out now and slid it around the neck and underneath her hair. "I'm coming," he said.

She smiled at him.

When Mr. Crockett came downstairs he saw that Teena was still at the breakfast table and he set his face and shoulders cautiously, like a soldier going into heavy fire. Teena was his only daughter; she was sixteen and she was a little hard to take sometimes. Teena made him feel like the never-mentioned member of the family who one day escapes from the backroom and appears in the parlor before company, drooling spittle and making meaningless noises.

Mr. Crockett nodded to Teena now, trying to look as inoffensive as possible and as though he would not disgrace her.

Frances frowned over his shoulder as he sat down and finally took up the spoon and prodded his cereal critically.

"It's like wet rags," she sighed.

"Fine, fine," said Mr. Crockett absently, eyeing his daughter. Teena was altogether hidden behind a book ("The Rubaiyat," he read with his lips, mispronouncing); and sometimes hands appeared on each side of the cover and, as if by radar, located toast and butter and pulled them out of sight.

Mr. Crockett said cautiously, "Good morning, Teena."

There was a mumble and a crunch of teeth that he accepted for reply.

He sloshed the cornflakes around and finally ate a mouthful or so. They had all the flavor of wood shavings; he tossed on a few more spoons of sugar hopefully.

Suddenly Teena lowered her book and he saw that her eyelids were droopy, which was a bad sign. Teena wrote poetry, huge scrapbooks full about Nature and God and Unrequited Love, most of it over crackers at 2 a.m. in pitch blackness, and it made her weak-eyed in the mornings. It seemed to Mr. Crockett an inconvenient method, but Teena said it was soulful.

"Night is very soulful," she said. "Naked."

Now, dropping her book abruptly and drooping her eyelids from the night's long and soulful composition, Teena said, "I don't suppose you saw the moon last night."

"No," Mr. Crockett admitted, feeling gross and insensitive. He gulped cereal, hastily, and then—trying once to reach her—said, "I heard the tree. The one that rubs on the house whenever the wind blows."

Teena looked contemptuous. It was evidently *not* the same thing.

Frances said, sensing a storm, "Have some more cornflakes, Wade," and he had some, feeling resigned. All my life, every crisis, he thought bitterly, eating more cornflakes.

In spite of himself, he smiled.

Later, as he was driving to work, Mr. Crockett thought about his daughter with envy. It was all worked out for Teena right now; she knew her function in the Universe. Teena was the Socratic gadfly. It was for Teena to prod the sensibility of man, to cry "How sad!" or "How beautiful!" or "How noble!" for him in all the right moments and for all the best causes. Her poems had all the superiority of youth, that smug conviction that until this precise moment in time no man anywhere had reached such depth of feeling or known such tragedy, or expressed either quite so well.

Mr. Crockett, sighing, left the highway for Lawson Street, waved at Mr. Elmo and Bobby, thought that he almost wanted to be as young as Teena himself, to be that raw and receptive to experience, to touch everything as though it were newly made for his hand.

But that was too long ago to reach. While he waited for the traffic light, he saw a cat go up a tree and come down again, looking dissatisfied.

He drove finally under the wooden sign that said Wade M. Crockett, Septic Tanks and Well Drilling, and parked the car (which was a Fifty Chevrolet, and which did rattle). Someday (he thought, just sitting there with the motor running), someday when she was older, he might really be able to talk to Teena. Someday perhaps he would even tell her about that tree that scraped at his house in the night like something longing to come in, and about that sense of utter isolation that flooded his bedroom with the dark. It wasn't that night was soulful (he thought now with sudden clarity) but that it was limitless; it took the edges and corners off things so that the yard and the street outside were the same, and the walls of houses shut nothing in and nothing out, and on all sides the black went out for a million miles.

Mr. Crockett turned off the motor suddenly, trying to laugh at himself, a foolish fat man sitting absently in a running car, making abstract arguments with his daughter.

Ivey looked up from her typewriter when he banged the screen door and walked into the unfinished outer office where the calendars hung on one bare wall and the four straight chairs lined up against the other.

"G'morning, Mr. Crockett."

"Morning, Ivey. Going to be hot."

She nodded and three tight curls on her head leaped up like watch springs and settled back again. Mr. Crockett watched, fascinated. Sometimes when this happened he expected it to twang.

"Mail come?"

The nodding and leaping took place again. "August bills. Eight checks. Circulars. It's on your desk."

"All right."

"My sister's going to have another baby." This was announced with the same tone as the morning mail.

"Which one?" he said, being polite.

"Ruby. The youngest. This'll be her second baby."

"That's wonderful." He said it automatically the way one says "That's terrible," about illness, and "That's tragic," about the death of a child.

"Kids are a lot of trouble."

"That's right, they are."

Her look accused him. "But worth every minute of it!"

He began to edge toward his own office. "Oh yes. No question about that."

"Bet you wouldn't take anything for Teena."

"Not anything." He was into the other room now and at the roll top desk, relieved.

Getting past Ivey in the mornings was like running a daily gauntlet. So far as Ivey was concerned, the world was sharply divided into two classes, the Unhappy and the Married. Ivey wanted dreadfully to be Married. Mr. Crockett sometimes felt that what Ivey actually wanted was a bit more elemental than this, but he looked away from her carefully when he thought it. He felt disrespectful, as though he had been caught peeking down her blouse (which, goodness knows, would have been a great waste of time). He began to look through the bills now, frowning.

"The work crew get out?" he called.

"Eight o'clock," said Ivey. "Huey's sick."

"What's the matter with Huey?"

"He says it's a hernia."

Mr. Crockett snorted. "Huey doesn't know."

"I guess not. That's what he said, though."

Ivey had a very sharp voice as though she had overused it and finally worn all the softness off. Even when she stood next to you she seemed always to be calling into other rooms; and she wore also a sharp perfume that went out from her like darts on all sides.

Suddenly, there at his desk, Mr. Crockett had a picture of himself trying to talk to Ivey about whether a man was important in the world or not, and whether it mattered if the dark were friendly or indifferent to him, and how there was a tree at his house that went up and down and would continue to go up and down until it aged and rotted and crumbled away. He could hear Ivey relating the amazing thing to one of her three married sisters, what Mr. Crockett had said.

"And he's got such a nice family, too," Ivey would say, inclining her head so that the curls wobbled, expectantly.

"Gee," they would answer. "That's a shame."

He sat at the desk chuckling until Ivey asked him what was funny.

"Nothing," he said. "Nothing really."

At noon, when the crew came back and banged into the outer office and stood there dirty and sweating as though to accuse him by their weariness, Mr. Crockett went to his office door and nodded to them.

"Everything OK?"

"Hot as blazes," Huey said. "Hottest August on record."

"You feel all right?"

Huey gave him a look of disgust which meant he did not feel all right, as any fool could see.

Pete said he was going to knock off for lunch.

"Can I be off this afternoon?" said Huey. "I got to see a doctor, that's all."

Mr. Crockett said Huey could be off.

"Who's a good doctor?" This was to everyone.

"Critchett," said Pete. "At the Clinic. When I had kidney trouble . . ."

Huey said hastily that he thought Critchett would be fine and began to tell them all how bad he felt before Pete could get started on his kidneys. They all went out the door, Huey's complaints carrying them along.

Mr. Crockett said he thought he might go eat himself, and Ivey made some joke about that sounded like a cannibal; until he had to stand and smile and smile like an idiot, his face cracking, while she laughed about it.

He escaped to the car finally and gripped the steering wheel as though he were thinking of pulling it out. I don't see why we bother, Mr. Crockett thought. Talking to each other. It seemed to him then that the space between people was no less than that between star and star, and that most conversation was no more than the tossing of this or that small thing across the miles.

He drove down Lawson Street and onto the highway and nodded to Mr. Elmo again and almost ran over a cat, which might or might not have been the same one he saw that morning. When he got home, he found lunch on the table (Frances was having her hair done) and the morning mail at his plate for him to read. There was a mimeographed letter from the Church Building Committee and a card from the neighbors, who were in California, and a letter from his mother, who still lived in incredible discomfort on a Georgia farm and would not have plumbing.

"Let me alone," his mother always said grimly, as though she were proving vast truths by pretending there was neither electricity nor good heating systems in the world. He took up her letter and read it first.

His mother wrote that he should hold to the Lord and not let Teena take up with bad company and that he must be careful how he spent his money, because the world was full of thieves. He smiled at her; she was not suspicious really; it was only a way she had of making herself heard.

Mr. Crockett ate some lima beans and stirred his coffee and read the letter again, thinking about her.

He could almost see her writing this particular letter, hunched over the kitchen table with her shoulders as sharp as plowshares, making the word just so, every loop on every letter neither too large nor too small; and lifting her pen at the end of every word so that there were no unnecessary flourishes.

And he thought of his mother, as he had thought so many times before, *They will never kill her*.

And by "they" he meant everything from cancer to automobiles; he felt she would go on living until she had literally worn out every joint and fiber in her frame and then only the body would go; and somewhere her skinny stubborn spirit would prevail.

That comforted him somehow, the way as a child he had been comforted by knowing God had not been born and would not die.

It seemed to Mr. Crockett, thinking thus, that he was almost upon something then; he had almost laid hand on it. It was an idea, a thought, a Something that scuttled just away from his grasp, like an animal not yet willing to come close.

He shrugged, folded the letter, grinned, drank the coffee. And suddenly he saw his mother as he had once seen her, standing in the hail that was slicing all the plants, standing with her face up into the pellets angrily, and crying aloud, "Stop that! Stop it, I say!"

There! Almost he had caught hold of the thought a second time and he stood up in his kitchen, holding his coffee cup like a doubtful torch, and said to himself, I almost knew something important then.

It gave him a feeling of vicarious importance himself, like a returned soldier who forever tells neighborhood children, "Once when Pershing passed I touched him with my hand."

When Mr. Crockett got back to work, he learned that Huey had been put to bed for three days, and he drove out to see him and advanced him part of his wages.

And later he sat down to write his weekly copy for his ad in the *Lamberville Gazette* and he could think of nothing original to say on a hot August afternoon. He wrote down finally, "We do the best work we can," and set it in. He was oddly pleased about it, as though he had invented some clever slogan.

And now and then that day he remembered his mother, remembered the spindly petunias she had grown in an old tire in the yard, and how she had lavished more care on them than on the cotton; and remembered the day his father died, how she had gone about the house canning and baking and stewing all the things he would never eat again, and pressing all his clothes, as though each wrinkle were a blot on his memory.

He balanced the books and made the bank deposit and went out to talk with a man who wanted time to pay his bill because crops had been bad. He knew about crops. He knew how it was to wait for a cloud like a man's hand that might mean rain, and wonder if it would come in time.

He was already tired when he drove up to his house that evening, and there were two dogs on his lawn, a bitch and a male, doing just about what one might expect of them. Mr. Crockett saw a lady passing stone-faced in the street and looking carefully away; and he sat at the curb in his own car for a minute and watched them lurching all across his yard.

From the living room window Teena called, "Daddy, can't you do something?" and he said, grinning, "Looks like they're doing all right by themselves," and Teena giggled as though she thought there might be life in the old boy yet.

The dogs went off into a hedge and threshed in the leaves.

Still Mr. Crockett did not get out; he sat there reaching in his mind for that thought again and suddenly he had it; and it was so simple he could have cried. I am not a dog, he said to himself, softly, and that was all it had been all along.

He got out of the car, disappointed, and started up the walk toward the house with the tall door and the big windows with the limbs against them.

Then he thought again, I am not a tree.

It did not comfort him now, but he thought someday it might. He thought this might be the beginning of his knowing why it mattered to dig deep clean wells and pay fair wages and go on loving his wife and touching her hair in the mornings. It was as yet a thought no more than smoke, but he thought someday it would mean something to him and he was not so tired as before.

Teena said from the window again, "Will you help me fix my bookcase?" and Mr. Crockett said he would.

He kicked once at the tree outside his window as he passed, but not unkindly, more as a gesture, more to show that he could.

THE BROTHERS

(VOL. 8, NO. 3, 1956)

Wendell Berry

....

I. The Crow

Me and Brother came across the Crandels' house on our way home from the pond. We hadn't caught any fish. Not even a bite. Mrs. Crandel's grandson that comes up to see her from Louisville was setting on the grass in the front yard, playing with a pet crow. Old man Crandel had caught the crow before it was big enough to fly and give it to him. The boy was all cleaned up and had his Sunday clothes on.

When we came by he walked over to the fence and looked at us like we was dirty or something. "Hi," he said. He talked city talk.

"Hidy." Brother said. "What's your name?"

"What's yours?" the boy said.

"Puddin-tame," Brother said.

"Mine's Carol," the boy said.

"Carol. That's a girl's name." Brother laughed and I did too.

"Would you like to come over and play with me?" the boy said.

Play, he said. I bet he never did any work in his life.

"I'll let you ride my bicycle if you will," he said.

Me and Brother climbed over the fence.

"Where's the bicycle?" Brother said.

"On the porch."

We went over to the porch. The bicycle was a right new one. And he had a BB gun too. That kid's got all kinds of stuff.

He got the bicycle down from the porch and rode it around in the yard. It was painted green and the sun shined on the spokes of the wheels when he rode it and it was pretty. I wished I had one.

In a little while he got off and gave the bicycle to Brother. But Brother couldn't ride it, and it turned over with him. I tried it too, and it turned over with me.

"Let me try it again," Brother said.

The boy said, "No, you can't. You might break it."

He caught the pet crow again and we went over and set down under a big locust tree.

"That's a mighty fine crow you got there," Brother said. "Can I look at him?"

The boy said, "You can if you be careful not to hurt him. Grandfather is going to let me take him home."

"Sure not. I won't bother him," Brother said.

Brother put the crow on his shoulder and rubbed his feathers. "Say," he said. "I bet you don't know much about crows."

"Not much," the boy said. "Grandfather says they'll eat about anything, and if you split their tongues they'll talk."

"I can show you a little trick about crows," Brother said. "You want to see it?"

"Yes," the boy said.

Brother motioned to me to come and help him. He got a dynamite cap out of his pocket and a piece of fuse about as long as your finger. The boy came up real close and watched Brother stick the fuse in the cap and crimp the cap against a rock. He is the dumbest kid I ever seen.

"Here," Brother told me. "Hold his tail feathers up." He winked at me and I knew he had a good plan. Brother is a fine planner.

I held the tail feathers up and Brother poked the cap in the crow's bunghole.

"Got a match?" Brother said.

I give him a match and he struck it on his belt buckle.

"Now you watch," Brother said. "This'll learn you a lot about crows." He lit the fuse and pitched the crow up in the air. The crow kind of fooled around for a minute, like he was getting ready to come down right in the middle of us. And me and Brother got out of the way. Then he looked around and saw that little ball of fire following him, spitting like a mad tomcat. He really got down to business then. I never seen a crow fly so fast in my life. He was aiming to go right off and leave that fire. But it caught up with him right over old man Crandel's barn. Blam! And feathers and guts went every which way. Where the crow had been was a little chunk of blue sky with a ring of smoke and black feathers around it.

Me and Brother took off over the fence. When we looked back the boy was still standing there with his mouth open, looking up at the place where the crow had busted. The tears was running down alongside his nose. He looked sillier than hell.

II. Birth

After breakfast, Daddy went to the barn, and me and Brother went to the garden and picked a mess of beans and dug a wash pan full of potatoes for dinner. Brother dug the potatoes with the grubbing hoe, and I picked them up and busted the dirt off of them and put them in the pan. I always like to dig potatoes. It's sort of a surprise. In the spring you plant one potato in the ground, and then along in the summer you open the ground up and there's a whole hat-full of potatoes, all from that one little dried-up, dead-looking one you planted in the spring. And it's like a miracle. You can't tell how it happens, but you know it will—just as sure as you plant that one potato and it rains on it.

We took the beans and potatoes to the house and put them on the kitchen table. Mother was dressing a chicken on the back porch. She was singing. She sings all the time when she works, because she says it makes her happy to think about me and Brother eating what she fixes.

When she emptied the dish pan over the yard fence, the live chickens ran up to eat the guts of the dead one. They had a real scramble, fighting each other over their brother's guts. But chickens don't know who their brothers are, so you can just laugh and not get mad at them.

Then Daddy came up to the porch. He was sweating, and there was blood drying on his hands. He told mother to call Doc Lawrence, that the heifer was trying to have her calf. The heifer was in trouble, he said.

He turned around and started back to the barn. Mother went in the house; then she stuck her head back out the door and said, "You boys stay away from that barn. You've got no business out there."

We gave her plenty of time to get on the telephone, and went to the barn.

The heifer was lying on the floor of the driveway. We could see one of the calf's legs sticking out of her. She breathed real slow and loud.

"Hadn't you boys ought to be at the house?" Daddy said. Then he took a bucket out to the well and went to washing it, and we knew it was all right to stay.

We waited; and before long Doc's car came dusting through the gate and stopped in front of the barn.

Doc got out. "Well, hello boys," he said. "I see we got plenty of help."

Me and Brother said hello.

Doc grinned over at Daddy and said, "What's the trouble, Ralph?"

"Heifer calving, Doc. She can't have it and I can't help her."

Doc opened the trunk of his car and got out a pair of coveralls, and put them on over his regular clothes. He pumped some water into the bucket and washed his hands.

"What're you doing that for?" Brother said.

"Because they're dirty," Doc said. He flung the water off of his hands and started in the barn. "Well, let's have a look at her."

He kneeled down behind the heifer and gave a little pull at the calf's leg.

"It's turned wrong," he said. "It's trying to come out backwards. We'll have to turn it around."

He pushed the leg back inside her, then put his arm in and pushed. Then he put his other arm in, and pushed with one arm and pulled with the other one. He gritted his teeth and squinched his eyes up.

"Damn," he said. "If this ain't a tough one."

I sat down by the heifer's head and rubbed her nose. Her breath grunted out hot against my leg. I said, "Does it hurt you bad, Jeanie?"

Brother was leaning over, watching Doc. "What're you calling her Jeanie for?" he said. "She ain't got no name."

"Her name's Jeanie," I said.

Doc got the calf turned around and pulled the front legs out.

"At least we got it aimed right," he said.

He looped a chain around its ankles and pulled. Then Daddy caught hold of the chain and pulled, too. They sweated.

Her breath grunted out and blew a little clean place on the floor by my knee. Her eyes was rolled back in her head. It hurt her awful. I rubbed my hand on her face.

"The slut," Daddy said. "Got herself bred before she was a yearling."

Doc grinned and winked at Daddy. "I bet she's thinking it went in a damn sight easier than it's coming out."

They quit pulling and rested a minute, wiping the sweat off. Then Doc went to the car and got a block and tackle. They fastened one pulley to the calf's feet and the other one to the bottom of an upright. Daddy got a log chain out of the stripping room and they chained Jeanie's feet to an upright on the other side of the driveway. Then they pulled again.

The calf's legs came farther out, and then the head came out. After that it wasn't so hard any more. They pulled faster, and the calf slid out on the ground.

"No wonder," Doc said. "He's half as big as his mammy is."

They stood the calf up and dried him off with some sacks. Daddy unchained Jeanie's front feet so she could rest easier. She was awful tired.

But in a few minutes she heaved herself up and started licking the calf. He stood all quivery and drawed up in a knot and let her lick him for a long time. Then he went around to suck. His back end could not follow his front end too good, but he made it and started sucking.

Doc laughed. "I don't blame him. I'd be hungry too." He started back to the well to wash his hands again. "He's all right now. When they come out hungry they're all right."

He finished washing his hands and took off the coveralls and pitched them back in the car.

"Send me a bill," Daddy said.

Doc grinned. "Don't worry."

Daddy said thanks a lot, and Doc got in the car and drove away.

Me and Brother helped Daddy gas up the tractor, and then went out behind the barn. It was getting pretty hot by then. The dust was thick on the bare ground around the gate, and our tracks caved in as quick as we made them.

The day before we had caught a black butterfly with all-colored spots on him. He was the biggest prettiest one I ever did see. We had him fastened in the top of a rotten post that was hollowed out inside. A flat rock was on top of the post to keep him in.

Brother lifted the rock up a little to see if he was still alive. And he was. I looked in, too, and he was setting there in the bottom of the hollowed-out place with his wings quivering.

I said, "Brother, you reckon his mother ain't looking for him?"

"I don't know," Brother said. "Do you think they care about each other?"

I looked back in the post at the butterfly. His wings was quivering like they was wanting to fly but he wouldn't let them because he knew it wouldn't do him no good. I said, "Yes, I think they care."

Brother knocked the rock off and he flew out. And his wings was shiny black in the sun.

III. Death

The day our mother died, Daddy cut down the rose bush by the front door.

Our mother had planted it and watered it with water from the well. She said when she saw it bloom in the spring it made her feel like winter never would come back again.

He came around the corner of the house with the double bit axe over his shoulder. And he cut the rose bush down, with the people watching in the front windows, and the preacher in his black suit standing on the front steps, watching.

He cut the rose bush down with one lick, all of its stems with one lick. He swung on the rose like it was a big tree. But he did not stop when he cut the rose bush down. He kept swinging the axe into the ground where it had grown. And every lick he hit he drove the axe head into the ground up to the helve.

Then he was sweating. His shirt was wet, and the sweat ran down his face around the corners of his mouth and dripped off of his chin. And the preacher was pulling on his shoulder, saying, "Don't Ralph. Come on in the house, Ralph."

And Daddy just kept swinging the axe into the ground, saying, "Ah. . . . Ah," every time the axe went town. The preacher could not budge him. He just stood there, swinging the axe into the ground like he was cutting a big tree, with the people watching out the windows and the preacher pulling his shoulder, until he had chopped the stems of the rose bush up in little pieces. When he got done there was a big torn up patch of black dirt instead of green grass where the rose bush had been. Then he laid the axe over his shoulder again and went to the barn and put the axe away, and came back to the house and cleaned up and said hello to the people.

The preacher came out of the house again and told me and Brother we had better go upstairs and clean ourselves up. "You must be quiet," he said. "Your mother has gone up to Heaven."

"We know it," Brother said. "We knew it before you did."

We were going up the stairs and Mrs. Simmons opened the hall door and said, "Do you boys want me to help you get dressed up?"

Brother said, "No ma' am."

"Do you know where to find everything?" she said.

"Yes ma'am," Brother said.

We went upstairs to our room and poured some water in the wash pan. The sun came through the window curtains and made their shadow on the floor. When the wind waved the curtains the shadow on the floor waved.

"Let's both wash at the same time," Brother said.

I said all right, and we set the wash pan on the floor and kneeled down on each side of it to wash.

Brother squeezed the soap and it flew out of his hand and splashed water on me. I splashed water back at Brother. Brother laughed and I did too. Then Brother was snapping me with the towel, and I was sloshing water at him out of the wash pan.

I looked up and there was Daddy behind me. He caught me by the shoulders and held me clear off the floor and shook me. He shook me so hard I saw all of the room at one time. First it was me that was shaking. Then it looked like it was the room shaking. It looked like it was going to fall apart. He held me still and looked at me for a long time, then he put me down again and went out the door.

I sat on the floor and kept from crying until I started to feel better.

"Did it hurt?" Brother said.

"No," I said.

I got up, and we put our clothes on and slipped down the stairs and out the back door.

We went down the hillside to the hollow below the house and sat down. The sun was hot, and after we sat still a while we could hear the bees working in the clover up the hill behind us. And away in the woods a woodpecker beat on a dead tree.

"If Mother was here, he wouldn't pick on me like that," I said. "I'll bet she wouldn't let him."

Then Brother started to cry.

I said, "Don't cry, Brother."

But he wouldn't listen. He got up and ran down the hollow, crying, until I could not hear him anymore.

I laid back on the dry leaves and looked up at the sky. There was a buzzard floating up there, high over the woods. "Buzzard, you can't have my mother," I said. "Don't get my mother, buzzard."

After a while he sailed away, and then there was just a cloud in the sky, and the woodpecker knocking the dead tree away in the woods.

A NIGHT "LANDSCAPE"

(VOL. 13, NO. 2, 1961)

Lawrence Ferlinghetti

....

In the lower left-hand corner
of an album landscape
I am walking through a dark park
with a noted nymphomaniac

We are talking as we walk
of various villainies
of church and state

The moon makes hairless nudes

An alabaster girl upon her back
becomes a body made of soap
beneath a wet gypsy

We are talking as we walk
of various villainies

Suddenly we rush
through a bent gate
into the hot grass

one more tree
falls in the far east

WINTER SUNSET

(VOL. 17, NO. 3, 1965)

Robert Morgan

....

Late sun
Burns over treetops
Driving rays of ice
Through limbs,
Tips the snow
With fire.

In the shadows by the river
I wait for my father.
Tired, happy, I wait
In the bitter cold
To go to supper.

A crow flaps out of the pines
Into the sunset.
The house across the river
Flashes gold
From its windows. The sky flowers
Red, then purple.

I wait at the edge of the trees
Thinking of sleep. The air suddenly—
Smells heavy
With food and darkness.

FIELD AT NIGHT

(VOL. 17, NO. 3, 1965)

Robert Morgan

....

I walk at night
Under a soft burning moon
Under pines.
I walk in a field of long grasses
And feel the secret textures under me
Out of the wind.

It has been a long day; far
From the rising sun and mist
I wander alone
And hear a distant train: the night
Lets down the noises to me, separately,
In rhythm.

Pools of darkness
Whirl before my eyes, the hills
Turn in all directions.

I wander toward dawn
And dream
Of staying here forever,
Speaking to no one
If I may.

WINTERSONG

(VOL. 17, NO. 3, 1965)

Robert Morgan

....

My uncle's pasture
Has a single oak at the top of the hill.
At twilight I walk there alone,
Where cattle have stood all day
Waiting for sundown
While I watched them from the window.
It is six o'clock,
A winter evening, clear
With purple sky
And stars.
It is Christmas Eve:
I long for a quiet stable
With straw.

A LEAF FOR APRIL

(VOL. 36, NO. 2, 1984)

Frannie Lindsay

....

Again the world floods over with practice gardens:
clover and loose
magnolia. Their petals are scattered
decks of debts we count between each other, a guess
paid gently back.

This morning, running, I added my steps
by twos, the road behind me
winding open. Snow on the ends of the air: this wind
we softened with afterwishes, feathers of breath
flown off in random desires. Two riders
passed me on a white tandem, clicking their silver
clock-spokes. The snow was

dust stitches dropped from the loom
where we counted our whispers. And now the loom after all
is of weeds, but abundantly
ours to blow apart. Ours: the knots
of hyacinth climbing untied from roots
and slipping into bloom. In this late snow I gather
two brown-spoked leaves.

They are stem-holds, spare rungs that rustle
uphill. The riders have left a melting
treadle and floss marks of tires to follow. This is their story
expanding toward you or away: at its heart,
that decision. One can go on
waiting for them, their intricate gear-tick unlooping
the hill's incline. Or choose

this one brown leaf
and let the other slip back onto the air. It's greener, perhaps,
when lost
so completely to mind. Amnesia's a casually deft
ambition: it acquires a weakness for us. So there's a leaf, perfectly
missing, a mark in a book where I keep
my guesses. Clover, fiddlehead fern waxed flat, I'll lose them

or find them wherever
I scatter your heart: my scraps of whoever-she-is, trick dreamer
riding behind us, feet hardly touching the pedals. Instead, the coasting
shoe of bare white, the cheek flashed raw with a hazard of wool
flown back in the light, and the wink a quietly misplaced
stitch. Or only this

breeze that wakes a petal to all she has
yet to touch; your hands
floating each magnolia back into its wind arrangement.
You finger-and-tell, you end
the story in gossip: the front rider
unweaves her into your arms, you hold for me pieces
of brown lace or maple: this leaf I am left to
dare turn over.

THE PEOPLE IN ANSEL ADAMS' LANDSCAPES

(VOL. 58, NO. 3, 2008)

Michael Chitwood

....

Aspen Grove, North Rim

GRAND CANYON NATIONAL PARK, ARIZONA, 1947

It's dark back in that shade, but someone's in there. Clank of metal helmets or scabbards. De Soto? Cortez? Who's in there? Come on out. There are archipelagos, shortcuts to the spice trails, Cities of Gold and Fountains of Youth, there's a whole New World, ripe, namable. We'll make maps.

Mount Moran, Autumn

GRAND TETON NATIONAL PARK, WYOMING, 1948

In that aspen grove, Henry Clay and Mickey Mantle are playing mumblety-peg with a bowie knife.

Old Faithful Geyser

YELLOWSTONE NATIONAL PARK, WYOMING, 1942

Behind the blast of mist, Cotton Mather, Brigham Young, Billy Sunday and Billy Graham are tuning banjos for a tent-meeting hootenanny.

Mount McKinley and Wonder Lake

DENALI NATIONAL PARK, ALASKA, 1948

In the deep shadows on the other side of Wonder Lake, William McKinley and Ava Gardner are roasting wieners over a campfire. Their lithe green sticks keep them from getting burned.

Stream, Sea, Clouds, Rodeo Lagoon

GOLDEN GATE NATIONAL RECREATION AREA, CALIFORNIA, 1962

Robinson Jeffers, way out, way way out, is swimming naked, basking now in a back float, his white belly honoring the sun and he's humming. Could a man be happier, slick as a seal?

Tenaya Creek, Dogwood, Rain

YOSEMITE NATIONAL PARK, CALIFORNIA, 1948

On the right bank, just behind that spray of dogwood blossoms, that's me, soaking wet, thinking of my grandmother's doilies, how she'd wash and iron them and then let them bloom again in the old homeplace's living room.

Mount LeConte, Autumn

GREAT SMOKY MOUNTAINS NATIONAL PARK, TENNESSEE, 1948

There's a pine in the foreground. At its base, his back against the trunk, his moccasined feet propped on a rock, Daniel Boone is thinking of settling down, maybe getting a town named after him, maybe becoming a legend and taking it easy.

Grounded Iceberg

GLACIER BAY NATIONAL PARK, ALASKA, 1948

In a johnboat, behind the iceberg, there's a priest, a minister and a rabbi.

Tree, Stump, Mist

NORTH CASCADES NATIONAL PARK, WASHINGTON, 1958

Behind the stump, whimpering, writing to his mother, Henry David Thoreau complains about the food on the trip, his wet feet, his scratches and chafes, the chiggers, ticks and biting flies. He wishes he were home by the lamps in the evening, his mother singing, his vellum laid out before him.

Stream and Tree Trunks, Autumn

GREAT SMOKY MOUNTAINS NATIONAL PARK, TENNESSEE, 1948

Just down the left bank in back of that . . . is it a sycamore . . . A. P. Carter and Charles Wright are playing checkers on a blanket. It's a picnic. There's potato salad, ham and scratch biscuits. Nothing like biscuits and a picnic for enjoying the shade.

The Tetons and the Snake River
GRAND TETON NATIONAL PARK, WYOMING, 1942

Across the river, in that stand of trees, Henry Ford and Ernest Hemingway have set up camp. They've got chairs, ovens, wine racks and a portable billiard table that Thomas Edison invented. One car is completely dedicated to guns. They have a crank Victrola and Henry has put on a recording of Appalachian Spring. Its simple tune haunts the bend in the river.

Forest, Beartrack Cove
GLACIER BAY NATIONAL PARK, ALASKA, 1949

In back of that central tree, the one that for the viewer is the apex of the classical triangle of composition, Ansel is taking a leak. He set up the shot, had to go and a companion tripped the shutter. Nearby he wrote in his journal, "Imaginatively inclined, I felt Alaska might be close to the wilderness perfection I continuously sought."

PART II

BODY

The weight on my hip
wants to return to the earth, spill
over the ledge of bone.

—SHARON HASHIMOTO

THIS section explores how the body can be made foreign by the world through which it moves. Sharon Hashimoto locates this foreignness in the betrayal of gravity, which pulls from her the safety of employment. Marianne Gingher captures the irreconcilability of a young body that refuses to grow. Kalamu ya Salaam's "Worth More than a Dollar" reckons with race as the body of his narrator becomes a site of profit, and in the process the joyful freedom of movement converts into the "quiet stillness" of lost pride. Joyce Carol Oates measures the universe in heartbeats. In these ten pieces, the body communes in frequencies beyond language, anatomizing the "laughing riptide" of what cannot be forgotten.

LOVERS' BODIES

(VOL. 22, NO. 2, 1970)

Joyce Carol Oates

....

always
the profane heavy beat
of someone's affection—
radios in kids' cars speeding
narrowly in the street

always flags of all sizes mourning
dead leaders, or fathers
in gusty front yards of narrow streets
or cemeteries blotched with geraniums
always the damp pulsing of flags
the fluttering of rotted cloth

and the beat
of something growing—
filling in holes
filling in eye sockets—

the visible universe
collapses
and repeats itself
in our bodies:
all visible things
repeat themselves
into permanence

FOUR WEEKS UNEMPLOYED

I Fail the Water Department's Lift and Carry Exam

(VOL. 43, NO. 1, 1990)

Sharon Hashimoto

....

My cheek feels the rough touch—
burlap hugged close in my arms.
A man repeats the warning:
Lift with your legs, not your back.

Burlap hugged close in my arms,
I raise 30 pounds of soil to the table,
lifting with my legs, not my back.
The shifting sack has no bottom.

How to raise 40 pounds of soil to a table?
I balance the weight on my hip.
The shifting sack shapes a bottom
on the ledge of bone. I stumble—

unbalanced. The weight on my hip
wants to return to the earth, spill
over the ledge of bone. Stumbling,
my breath collapses like skins of small balloons

wanting to return to the earth, spilled
of their air. At 50 pounds, my body knows its limits.
My breath collapses like skins of small balloons
holding everything together. But I can't escape

beyond a body's limits.
I want a job, a secure position
to hold everything together. I can't escape
the words of my mother and father:

You need a job, they say, *a secure position.*
Late nights, I fell asleep listening
to the words of my mother and father.
When did they let go of their dreams?

Late nights, did they fall asleep listening
to each drop of rain breaking against the roof,
remember how the sky let go of its dreams?
I pulled the illusion of warmth close to my body,

folded myself into rain breaking against the roof.
My cheek feels the rough touch
of burlap. *Two minutes to finish,*
a man repeats the warning.

NIGHT DRIVES

(VOL. 44, NO. 2, 1992)

Edward Falco

....

At three a.m. I leaned against white tiles in my narrow box of a shower and let hot water stream hard on my stomach easing night cramps while you were someplace else for years by then, miles from all the promises from places so deep the air as we spoke like air before a storm that almost hum that skin-slight vibration.

Light off-white tiles, I'm lit up bright as a movie screen. Outside dark quiet rural homes cricket's nightsong. When the pain won't stop I get in my car and drive past dorms where now even students have called it a night, past neat rows of houses, out onto gravel roads that fall through woods. I turn up the music, turn off the lights.

That went on for a year, waking like that, under the surface urgent, it scrabbling up a slick wall acrid opening onto. Word scraps going bad and bubbling up the throat grit black. He did this she did that. He said. She said her words his words stored in cells twist in sleep words become pictures that tell the truth lying if need be: that's not her body you're shoveling dirt over or him mutilated on the side of the road, just a stranger you're crying near when you wake as if something's alive inside your body, something deep and just under the skin.

WORTH MORE THAN A DOLLAR

(VOL. 50, NO. 1, 1997)

Kalamu ya Salaam

....

Otis Johnson was sweating. The concrete was griddle hot. Otis' scuffed, black leather shoes were clean although unshined. The plastic, hot sausage bucket he used as a kitty had twelve coins in it: three quarters, five nickels, two dimes and two pennies. He'd been hoofing on the sidewalk a long time, too long for just a dollar and twenty-two cents, thirty cents of which he had used as startup money in the kitty.

He stopped dancing. None of the passing tourists seemed to notice the sad stillness of Otis. People flowed around him without breaking stride and without even the slightest modulation or hesitation in their conversation. Otis could have been litter on the banquette: a candy wrapper, an empty plastic beer go-cup, anything someone no longer wanted; that's how he felt as people stepped around him.

For a moment Otis had been so absorbed in his inner turmoil that all he heard was the replay of Hickey's effective pitch from when they had danced as a team.

"Thank ya, thank ya, ladies and gentlemen, boys and girls. You are enjoying the best tap trio in the world. Him is June-boy, I'm Hickey and that's Otis. We can out-dance anybody on this here street. We is called the New Orleans Flying Feet. For our next number we gon show you how good we is and we would appreciate it if you would let us know how much you like what you see. When we finish our show, just drop in a few coins before you go. All we ask, as we dance so pretty, is that you reach into yo pockets and (all three of them would join in together, execute a spin and end with their arms outstretched and their fingers pointing to the bucket Otis' mama had given them) FEED THE KITTY!"

Then they would go into another routine Otis had choreographed for them. It was full of hesitations, hops, spins, shuffles and jumps. Since June-boy was fastest he always went in the middle. Otis went first, he'd get the people clapping. Then June-boy would have them goin' "oooohhhhh" and "aaaahhhhhh." Then Hickey would step in with his feet beating like drums. Nobody on the street could tap out rhythms as powerfully as could Hickey, whose short, stocky frame was surprisingly agile.

When they stopped, everybody would be clapping and then would come the showstopper. Otis' cousin Marsha had told him: always save your best stuff for last. Otis thought what would be best was a dance that didn't use no singing or hand clapping, only the music they had inside themselves. So Otis had worked up a secondline routine that the Flying Feet executed flawlessly.

They would start off dancing as a team, every move the same, right down to their finger movements, bugging the eyes and sticking out their tongues, shaking their heads and going "aaaAAAHHHHH." Then they would go into the solo part. Two of them would break and stand back to back, except they stood about two feet away from each other and leaned back so that it was really shoulder to shoulder, and they would have their arms folded across their chests. They would be looking up like they was searching for airplanes, and of course they would be smiling. The third person would be doing a solo, any solo he wanted to do, except that it had to be short. Then after all three had done their solo, they would link arms and high kick, end with some spins and jump up clapping. Then Otis would dance with his mother's umbrella that June-boy had artistically decorated in the same way he had painted the kitty-bucket. June-boy would go through the audience with the kitty-bucket silently soliciting gratuities. And, of course, Hickey worked the audience asking them to give what they could to "keep the Flying Feet flying."

Afterwards, they would divide up the money and they would sit in the shade to rest. Hickey always said, "Divide the money up on the spot and ain't nobody got nothing to say about how much they got."

Usually they did pretty good. Ten or fifteen dollars apiece, twenty on a really good day. Once they had made twenty-seven dollars apiece with eighty some cents left over which Otis gave to June-boy and Hickey since June-boy, who was good with numbers, kept excellent count of their profits and Hickey did all the talkin' that encouraged the people to give.

They had worked that way for six Saturdays and, even though it was hard work dancing for five or more hours, they had made good money. Then Hickey's old man left his mama, and his mama decided to move to Houston by her cousin.

Otis knew how badly Hickey must have felt. Otis had never known his father. His mama said that the man who was his lil' sister Shaleeta's father and who came around all the time, frequently staying the night, wasn't Otis' father.

Anyway, without Hickey it just wasn't the same. June-boy couldn't talk hardly at all and Otis couldn't talk like Hickey, so the money fell off drastically. Nobody could hustle the crowd like Hickey.

"Don't be fraid to give a dollar, don't be shame to give a dime. If you can't give nuthin' but a smile and say thanks, we 'preciate that too, cause we out here dancin' just for you. Now if you could spare a quarter that sho would be right swell, and if you could give a bill instead of silver that would really ring the bell. But whatever you give we appreciate it each and all, all we ask is that you FEED THE KITTY Y'ALL."

When Hickey did it, it didn't sound like begging. It made people laugh and they would give. And of course it also helped a lot the way June-boy, who was real small and reed thin with big eyes and a bigger smile, carried the kitty bucket around staring up into the faces of strangers, silently pleading for their financial support. So when June-boy got sick and Otis tried going out on his own, he would be lucky to make four or five dollars a Saturday.

Dancing on the street used to be fun when all three of them were together, but now it was neither fun nor profitable. In the middle of his dance, Otis abruptly stopped, turned away from the street, stood stone still for two whole minutes, and then brusquely snatched up the kitty bucket with the dollar twenty-two in it and started walking away.

He didn't know why, but today when he was dancing for tips he felt like he was doing something he shouldn't be doing. In fact he felt almost as bad as "that dollar day," which is how Otis always referred to the incident.

"Look at them lil' niggers. They sho can dance." The man laughed as he jovially poked an elbow into the arm of the guy standing next to him. It was a raspy, albeit almost silent, mouth-wide-open laugh of amusement.

June-boy had heard what the man said and was sheepishly walking away from him. With a familial pat on the shoulder, the laughing man stopped June-boy. In one fluid motion, the man went into his pocket and pulled out a small wad of bills held together by a gold money clip which had "R. E. T." floridly engraved on its face.

Rhett, as he was affectionately known by both friend and foe, peeled off a dollar bill and dropped it in the bucket, "Here you go, young fella. Y'all dance real good."

June-boy looked at Rhett's mouth. Rhett was smiling. It looked like a smirk to June-boy. June-boy looked away, first at the dollar in the bucket, then at the other people standing around.

Otis reached into the bucket, pulled out the dollar, crumpled it in his small fist, and threw it at Rhett. The money hit Rhett in the waist and fell at his feet. "We can dance but we ain't no niggers."

Rhett was stunned. He looked at the man he had hunched moments ago. "I didn't mean nothing by it. They kind of touchy these days, ain't they? Even the little ones." Rhett kicked the knotted dollar toward the boys and walked off chuckling.

The small crowd that had been watching dispersed quickly and quietly. One guy dropped three quarters in the bucket and said, "Wish y'all luck. Don't judge us all by the way some old redneck acts."

Hickey was livid. At first he had looked around for something to throw at the guy: a brick, a can, a bottle, a stick, anything. The only possible missile within reach was the dollar bill. After the first flush of anger, Hickey turned from staring at the stranger's back, and refocused his attention on the money lying on the sidewalk. As Hickey moved toward the dollar, Otis stamped his foot atop it.

"Naw, we don't need no redneck money. I ain't gon let nobody buy me like that." Otis snatched up the dollar, walked over to a nearby trash can and threw it in. "Come on y'all, let's go." And they started walking home, heading out Rue Orleans. Otis was so angry, he simply halfheartedly waved and didn't even verbally respond when his friend Clarence, who was standing by the hotel door, said to him, "What's up, lil' man?"

As the frustrated trio exited the French Quarter, crossing Rampart Street and taking the shortcut through Louis Armstrong Park, they argued about the money. Hickey was still angry. "Boy, I wish I'da had me a brick. I woulda bust that sucker all up in the back a his head. I woulda kicked his ass good for true and it wasn't gon be nuthin' nice!"

June-boy responded, "Yeah and then what? The police woulda put us in jail for fuckin' with a tourist." June-boy walked over to one of the benches in the Congo Square area and sat counting their take for the day.

"They'd had to catch me first."

Otis ignored Hickey's verbal bravado. Silence reigned as June-boy finished the count.

"How much we got?" Hickey demanded, obviously still agitated.

"Twenty-six dollars and fifty cents. That's eight dollars and some change each."

"Yeah, and if Otis wouldn't've been so stupid and throwed that dollar away. We could of had nine dollars apiece."

Otis spoke up, "You was mad enough to kick him but not mad enough not to let him kick you by putting a dollar in the kitty while he calling you out your name."

Hickey quickly retorted, "Way I see it, Otis, we had earned that dollar, and we shoulda kept it."

June-boy divided up the money and gave each one his share. They rose from the bench and continued walking toward the projects. Nobody said anything for half a block. Finally June-boy broke the silence, "Aw shit, it's over nah, let's forget about it."

Otis tried not to say anything more, but the words were burning his throat. "Money don't make it right." Neither Hickey nor June-boy said a word.

When Otis got home, the pain his mother saw carved into her son's furrowed brow was not on account of what the white man had said but on account of how June-boy and Hickey had reacted. Otis told his mother what the white man had said but didn't tell her that Hickey and June-boy wanted to take the money.

"Otis, you hear me. I don't want you going back out there. We don't need the money bad enough to have people mistreating you while you trying to earn honest money."

Otis knew that it was his mother's pride speaking, but he couldn't wear pride. They couldn't eat no pride. He had bought the taps for his shoes. He had bought the jeans and some of his T-shirts. He paid his own way to the show. He even helped buy pampers and things for Shaleeta. That little money he brought home was plenty. "Mama, I can take care of myself. I'm alright. I got sense enough to stay out of trouble and sense enough not to let nobody misuse me."

Shirley Johnson looked at her son and smiled at how grown up he was acting. Just then Shaleeta had started crying. "I'll get her, mama," said Otis, glad for the opportunity to end the conversation before it got around to his mama asking what did June-boy and Hickey have to say behind what went down.

Otis picked up Shaleeta, held her in his arms and began dancing to the music coming from the radio which was always on either B-97 if Otis was listening, or on WWOZ, the jazz and heritage station, if Shirley was listening. OZ was playing Rebirth Brass Band doing a secondline number.

As the crowd flowed around him, Otis started feeling sick. He left the corner they had held down for over two months now.

After walking two blocks in ruminative silence, he passed Lil' Fred and Juggy dancing on their corner. Otis waved at them. He knew they wouldn't wave back because there were five white people standing around them.

Suddenly it dawned on Otis what had so upset him about the dollar day. Otis stopped. He looked back at Lil' Fred and Juggy. They were black. He looked at the people they were hustling for money. They were white.

In his mind Otis surveyed the streets as far back as he could remember. The results stung his pride. He had never seen any white kids dancing on the street for money and he had never been given money by any black tourists; indeed, most of the black tourists would walk by quickly without even looking at the youngsters mugging, clowning, and cutting the fool on the sidewalk. Only black boys dancing. Only white people paying money.

Otis looked at Lil' Fred and Juggy grinning at the white people as the dancing duo held out their baseball hats seeking tips. Otis shook his head. Is that how he looked when he danced? While turning away from the image of his friends hustling on the sidewalk, Otis spied his own face reflected in the sheen of the brass hotel door held open by Clarence the doorman.

A well-dressed couple walked past Otis and Clarence into the hotel. Otis was eleven years old and dressed in worn jeans and a Bourbon Street T-shirt. Clarence was forty-two years old and dressed in a white uniform which incongruously included sharply pressed short pants with a black stripe running down the side.

"What's happenin' lil' man?" Clarence genially greeted Otis.

Otis was frightened by what he saw. He saw his young face in the door and he saw Clarence's old face beside the door. Was this his future?

They had always told themselves they were hustling the white people. But that dollar day had started him thinking. Fred and Juggy across the street, clowning for tips had brought the thought to the surface of Otis' consciousness. And Clarence patiently opening doors, bowing, and servilely smiling a "welcome" made it clear as clear could be. Clear as that stinging, unforgettable southern drawl that constantly replayed in Otis' head: "Look at them lil' niggers. They sho can dance."

Otis walked resolutely out of the French Quarter, vowing never to work there again.

GREETINGS FROM THE PITUITARY

(VOL. 51, NO. 3, 1999)

Marianne Gingher

....

"Do trees ever get depressed?" Typo asked suddenly. "I'll bet they do. Think about the weeping willow. Think how sad it would be to be a tree." Gravely he closed the book he'd been reading, *The Call of the Wild*. His mother, Abby, sniffed the book's raggedy, grubby elementary school library binding. She was driving him to the endocrinologist's for another round of hormone testing.

"Why would it be sad to be a tree?" she asked.

"It's always sad for superior life forms to be dominated by inferior ones. Trees are superior in every way to humans, and yet they can't get themselves out of the bulldozer's way."

They'd nicknamed him Typo because, for twenty years, his father had suffered writer's block and he, the child, had been conceived accidentally. On a rainy afternoon, when Bill ought to have been writing, he'd distracted himself and banged out a human being instead of a poem.

"How is a tree superior?"

"It knows how to make its own food, right inside its own body—we animals can't do that. It doesn't need money. It doesn't need school because it's born knowing what to do. It doesn't cause wars or commit crimes. It doesn't cry when it's hurt, and it never sleeps, and it never feels ashamed."

"How do you know a tree never sleeps?"

"A superior life form would never need to sleep," Typo said. "A superior life form would make the most out of every second it was alive."

"Have you been studying trees at school?" Abby asked.

"No," he said. "We've been dissecting things. Next week we're going to dissect a woman."

"Oh?"

"But I study trees when I ride my bike in the park. I study everything, and I like to give myself tests. The other day, I tested my sense of smell to see if I could smell snakes in the woods. I could smell them all right, and so I didn't take the short-cut home."

"What did they smell like?"

"Jumbly."

Abby nodded. "Yes," she said, "it's almost spring." She said this as if to imply that, Yes, since it's almost spring, *of course* you can smell snakes in the woods. Because Typo's lies weren't the same as other people's. They had the eager, persuasive allure of an amusement park, twirling with possibility.

"I like to identify smells," he said. "A dog's tongue smells like boiled weenies. A cat's tongue smells like okra."

Abby smiled. She would probably smell a cat's tongue now. She would have to.

"Ever heard of anybody named Wax Paper? There's a new girl at school named Wax Paper. It's her real name, too. Nobody believed her but me, and now we're friends. It's not a nice name. But Wax Paper herself is nice. She's in fourth grade, and she wears high heels to school. She got them at the dump, they're silver. Her dad's a garbage man and he rides her to school in his garbage truck. It doesn't stink like regular garbage trucks because they take it to the car wash every day. She rides standing up on the bumper, and, on the way to school, she helps her dad collect the trash."

"You can ask her over to play one day."

"Are you joking? A *girl*?"

He had no friends. He was the shortest, frailest boy in the second grade. He wasn't in any percentile on the pediatrician's growth chart. He weighed forty-six pounds fully dressed, with shoes. He wore an expression of suffering insightfulness on his face constantly, his tall forehead rumpled like a rug by the colliding forces of fact and fancy rough-housing in his brain.

"Am I going to have to take the hormone shots?" he asked.

"Not if you don't want to," Abby said. "Dr. Blackwood thinks it's possible you have a problem he can't treat. Your Grandmother Klingon is very short. Maybe your stature is just the luck of the genetic draw."

"Maybe if I would eat more?"

"Maybe."

A few weeks earlier, Typo had pilfered money from Abby's purse, then turned himself in to the police. She'd overheard him on the telephone, directing a lieutenant to their house, and she'd intervened. But Typo didn't want to be absolved; he wanted arrest. "It doesn't matter when I pay the price, now or later, but I will pay it," he'd told her, forlorn.

"Everything's fine, darling. Nobody's mad," she'd said softly, stroking his back, feeling the ratchety little spine and the sharp angelfish fins of his shoulder blades.

"God's mad. God's going to send me to that middle place for all eternity—Pituitary." She'd almost corrected him. But in a canny way, for him to envision an afterlife of glandular stasis was appropriate. He would be punished not only for stealing but for not growing as well. God would stunt his prying, slithering little fingers the same as his height. Maybe Pituitary was where she'd end up, too, with a shrunken heart the size of a raisin seed.

"Wax Paper says her father pays her to eat," Typo said. "Not with money. They're too poor. Wax says that he pays her for eating green vegetables by doing back flips. For every green bean she eats, Mr. Paper performs a backflip. One day she ate thirty green beans, and Mr. Paper did thirty backflips to pay her. He used to be an acrobat, so it was no big deal to him."

"I used to be good at cartwheels," Abby said. "But I couldn't do a backflip if you paid me."

"I wish I knew how to do backflips," he said. "I'd do them all the time. When the gym teacher made us run laps, I'd run backflips. Wouldn't that be neat? Mom? Which would you rather be: mean and alive—or good and dead? Think about it. Take your time. I can't really decide myself. See, if you were mean and alive, you'd be living and breathing all right, but you'd be causing trouble. On the other hand, if you were good and dead, it would be a waste. Right, Mom?"

"Gosh, I don't know, honey," Abby said. It was a difficult question, although, in a way, she felt as if she'd already answered it. Lying to Bill about having had the flingette, she'd already chosen to be mean and alive, hadn't she? It was a terrible, pathetic lie, maybe the worst lie that a wife could tell a husband, because if it had been true, it would have been the worst truth.

Why had she told it? *To see what would happen next.* What a little kid thing to do, like wanting to lose yourself in deep woods. Briefly, the lie had made her feel young and breathless with a roaring heart and bony skinned knees and dirt under her fingernails. The lie had been easier to tell than to admit to Bill that she was afraid to grow old with him. All lies were a form of postponement.

"Are you daydreaming like I do, Mommy?" Typo asked.

"Oops, sorry. What was your question?"

"Would you rather be mean and alive or good and dead?"

"Mean and alive," she said with resolution.

Typo grinned with his tiny white seed pearl teeth—he hadn't lost a single baby tooth yet. "Good choice!" he congratulated her. "Because as long as you're alive, there's always hope that you'll change for the better, right? Meanness can switch to goodness any second, right?"

She nodded. But she wasn't certain she believed this anymore. Her friend Babs had warned her that lies propagated faster than coat hangers in closets. A lie hated to be single, so the faster it found a mate—or a harem—the better. Next came the wedding of the lies, because a lie, superficially moral, recoiled at living in sin. After the wedding of the lies, look out. Lies never, under any circumstances, used birth control.

Abby guided the cranky old station wagon into Dr. Blackwood's parking lot and rolled up beside a Mercedes sedan. She noticed that her inspection sticker was overdue. She could hear the muffler—which Bill had tied on with picture hanger wire—snuffling. When she turned the key to shut down the engine, the car continued to clunk and buck, and the hood shuddered.

An elderly, neatly dressed woman stood beside the Mercedes, touching its hood ornament protectively. She'd watched Abby park, wincing as the old Buick finally quieted, then she slid back into the Mercedes. Its motor turned over with the velvety efficiency of beaters in cake batter. Abby watched the woman repark at what she deemed a safer distance. As she left her new parking spot, the woman looked at Abby as if Abby now owed her a favor.

"Which do you think is the strongest in the world—meanness or goodness?" Typo asked.

"Meanness," Abby said with conviction.

"Gosh, Mom, I sure don't." His voice sounded high and bright, like the sunny tweet of a songbird from the planet she'd fallen off when she told Bill the lie. Tears stung her eyes, but she blotted them with her fingers. She turned towards Typo and swept him up in her arms, feeling resistance in his jumpy, incessantly curious little bones.

Why was he never quite with her, even when he was?

"Another question Mom. Has a spider ever gotten caught in its own web? Would it eat itself if it did? Could a person eat themselves to survive? I mean, if you were trapped on a desert island with no food, would you live longer if you didn't eat or if you ate yourself, a little at a time, every day? Mom, how many calories do you think are in a hangnail? Mom? Have you ever stood in front of a mirror for so long that you didn't recognize yourself anymore, and all you seemed to be after a while was a pile of moles and teeth and nostrils and hair follicles, and the parts of you didn't add up to any whole person? Too many questions at once, right?"

LIVING BREAD

(VOL. 58, NO. 1, 2006)

Karen An-hwei Lee

....

She walks four miles in hot weather for coconut palm juice, chrysanthemum tea, iced coffee, fish cakes, green papaya stewed with carrots and tomatoes in lime sauce, sour lemongrass soup, seafood curry with green shell mussels, po pia tod with chili sauce, and carries it all home in brown paper bags.

In some places, says the blind woman, trees are planted to bear bread since their flesh is to be eaten. Cassava root, let's say, and the breadfruit tree, though cassava must be boiled until no traces of cyanide remain, and raw breadfruit is bitter. Trees break water and light into bread for us, breathing freely before the end of photosynthesis. It's not bread, however, until broken again by hand or machine. Blood of unfermented fruit. Ground carob pods without red flowers.

THE LIMBLESS BOY OF A MAYAN MOTHER

(VOL. 61, NO. 3, 2011)

Adriana Páramo

....

I. No Ordinary Party

Today is Carlitos' first birthday. We gather at a parochial community hall adjacent to the Guadalupe church in Immokalee, Florida, where an army of caseworkers have volunteered their culinary skills to help celebrate. It's a Mexican fiesta. An array of salsas *picosas* and homemade nachos fill the center of the white vinyl-covered table. Mexican aromas meander through the hall from the kitchen to the cement benches outside the front door. It smells of fried beans, rice, and a medley of pork, chicken and beef seasoned with chili powder and garlic. Women sit in plastic chairs placed next to each other against the walls. Some have their babies on their laps; some have them in American-made baby strollers and car seats. The men stand outside. They don't like to hang around women and babies. They chat, laugh, and tell jokes in Amusgo, a Mayan dialect that only they understand.

Spirits are high, but there is no music, or a piñata, or balloons. There are no noise makers or cone hats. No lollipops or curling ribbon eggs in coordinated colors. There can't be any of that. Carlitos is not a regular baby. He was born without limbs. His body is a perfect rectangle of flesh and bones topped by a perfectly round head of soft hair. He giggles a lot, more than a regular baby. Francisca, his mother, a teenager who screws her nose when she laughs and looks more like a Mayan doll than the mother of a deformed baby, sits in one corner of the room with Carlitos glued to her chest in a kangaroo-style baby carrier.

The party guests have been carefully chosen. They are farmworkers from the community, mainly from Guerrero, the Mexican state that Carlitos' parents are from, and they all have babies. Sick babies. The unspoken theme of the party is solidarity. The caseworkers want Francisca and her husband to feel that they are not alone, that other mothers have also given birth to extraordinary babies like Carlitos and that this is a safe place where the deformed, the underdeveloped, the handicapped, the feeble are all beautiful children.

Across the dinner table from me is Cristina. Her shiny, black hair is gathered at the back of her head in a braid so tight that it makes her brown eyes slant a bit. Juanito, her baby, is five months old and, like Carlitos, he is no ordinary baby. He was born with a cleft lip and palate and some other issues that, if I want, she says, she'll tell me about later. Cristina gulps a hungry mouthful of fried bean dip as she motions for me to walk around the table.

Juanito is asleep inside his stroller. Half of his small face is at peace; the other half, the one with the cleft, is at war. A deep trench interrupts the course of his upper lip, separating it into left and right halves. The trench disappears into his left nostril. His mouth is closed, yet I can see his pink tongue somewhere behind his gums.

This is no ordinary party. There is an American journalist who traveled deep into the Mexican mountains to show Francisca's parents pictures of their deformed grandson. There is also a photographer, who is pointing her camera at Carlitos from every possible angle. The woman shoots while Francisca feeds him, when he is strapped to a barrel-shaped device that allows him to be upright, when he frowns inside his straitjacket-like apparatus, when he giggles, when he cries, when he spits his food. The photographer doesn't ask for permission, she just shoots. Francisca and her husband, Abraham, hold the baby and smile for the camera, once, twice, and many more times, until Francisca stops smiling and Abraham leaves the hall to join the other men outside.

In one corner of the hall, with dark bangs covering her eyes and a t-shirt covered in food stains and dry breast milk circles, sits Rosa and her three-month old baby boy, Camilo.

"He's a little sick," Rosa tells me when I touch his tiny fingers with mine. She cradles Camilo in one arm and with the other lifts his shirt. A pink scar splits his tiny chest in two.

"Heart problems," Rosa says, as she shakes her bangs on the baby's face, cooing into his breath. Camilo coos back.

If a Mexican woman by the name of Sostenes hadn't gone north to the Carolinas to work, she would also be at the party with her fourth son, a boy named Jesús. She was Francisca's neighbor and coworker at the Immokalee farm where they picked tomatoes. Sostenes left because Jesús was born with Pierre Robin Syndrome, a condition in which the lower jaw is exceedingly small and set back from the rest of the skull, and the tongue is displaced toward the back of the throat. When he was born, Jesús was at risk of swallowing his own tongue and dying of asphyxiation at any time. Sostenes had never heard of such a thing. It was best to leave Florida just in case she got pregnant again and the air, the water, or the food in Immokalee once more warped the life in her womb.

And had Maria not lost her baby, she would also have been at the party. She lived in the same migrant labor camp and worked for the same produce company as Francisca and Sostenes. Two months after Carlitos was born, Maria gave birth to an underweight baby boy with no nose, no ears, an underdeveloped heart, and malfunctioning lungs. She initially named him Jorge, but his underdeveloped genitals looked more like those of a girl, and so he was re-named Violeta. Jorge, Violeta, died a few days after being born.

II. Francisca and Carlitos

In the months following the party I made several attempts to locate Francisca. I wanted to interview her, but she is a nomad like the other farmhands: constantly changing telephone numbers, constantly on the move, leaving no trace.

When I finally located her, we had long telephone conversations. I explained to her that I was a writer. That I wrote about women working in the fields. That I would like to sit down and interview her. She liked my Colombian accent, she said. I liked her sparse Spanish and that she made me repeat everything I said. As we got to know each other better her initial reluctance to receive me at her house faded away, until one day she agreed to meet. Before she gave me her address she sought reassurance about my intentions.

"You're not a reporter, right?"

"No, I'm not."

"So you don't work for a newspaper or a magazine, no?"

"No, I don't."

"You know I can't talk about the lawsuit, right?"

"Yes, I do."

"So, you won't ask?"

"No, I won't."

Francisca comes to the door dressed in a beautiful red *huipil*, a woven, rectangular tunic that covers her arms, front and back. Her mother is an artisan, she explains after I compliment the intricate white brocade. Half of her straight, lustrous hair is up in a capricious bun, the other half rains softly over her back. She's barefoot. She has soft skin, vibrant eyes, small fingers, and plump feet with traces of different shades of polish on her toenails. Her head is constantly tilted, as if she is curious or surprised all the time. I have to remind myself that she is not simply a teenager; she is the mother of Carlitos, the baby without limbs.

We sit on a large couch with the baby propped between us. He smiles and gurgles, looking in his mother's direction. If Carlitos had arms, he would probably be marveling at the sight of his own hands, grasping and releasing fistfuls of air, drawing invisible shapes in space, tugging at his mother's *huipil*, pressing the flashing buttons of her cellular phone. But he doesn't have arms. Not even stumps long enough to support prostheses with which he might one day embrace Francisca in a robotic hug. Not even that.

Francisca places a reassuring hand on Carlitos' tummy as she starts her story. She was born 19 years ago in the town of Huehuetonoc, a remote Amusgo village in the state of Guerrero where weaving is a way of life. Her mother is one of the best artisans in town and her father grows rice.

The TV is on. Francisca is watching an episode of *Tom and Jerry* dubbed into Spanish. The mouse and the cat on the screen are more interesting than talking to me. "What is it that you are again?" she asks me without taking her eyes off the TV set. I remind her I'm a writer. I write books about women. She chuckles at the explosives that the cat has thrown into the mouse's house. I ask her if we could turn the TV off. She grabs the remote control and presses the mute button. The word BANG appears on the screen. A hairless cat with charred whiskers wobbles away from the mouse's house. Francisca is delighted. "Bad cat," she says, wagging her index finger.

When she was fifteen, a boy named Abraham arrived in town. He told Francisca about fantastic places that she had only dreamed about: Acapulco, Mexico City, and many others she could not pronounce because they were in *El Norte*, the sweet north, a grand nation where people earned loads of dollars, drove big cars and did not make their own *huipils*. One sweltering night Abraham and Francisca eloped. He was full of lust, she of fear of spending the rest of her life sitting at the loom.

Francisca finally switches the TV off. Carlitos is growing restless. She lifts him up above her head.

"What's going on, baby?"

She throws him up in the air and catches him midflight. The room is filled with Carlitos' laughter. With every one of his belly laughs, he exposes eight uneven baby teeth. There are no legs kicking in delight or hands outstretched trying to touch his mother's face. But he is happy and his joy catches me off guard.

"Abraham takes me to Acapulco. There, he has many girlfriends and I cry," Francisca says.

It takes me a while to get used to Francisca's present-tense narrative about the past. Her rudimentary spoken Spanish is devoid of past and future tenses, her vocabulary limited. I wonder how effectively Francisca and her American lawyer communicate through their interpreter, who I know doesn't speak Amusgo.

Francisca's relationship with Abraham was choppy from the start, full of infidelities on his part, and framed by relocations, long separations, and silent breakups. Francisca's worst fear was to be left to grow old in Huehuetonoc, a place where the future is mapped out on Mayan brocades. So when Abraham and his brother paid a coyote, a human smuggler, $1,500 each to cross the border into the US, Francisca waited nervously for her turn to take the leap too.

"I tell him, 'if I don't see you in four months, don't ever come back for me. I find another man.'"

Abraham heeded her ultimatum. Three months and three weeks after crossing into the US, he wired his coyote $1,600. Three weeks later, Francisca was in North Carolina, where she picked tomatoes alongside Abraham for 12 to 14 hours a day. When the harvest was over, they traveled south to Immokalee, Florida, where another produce company hired them to harvest tomatoes.

"Did you live in the company's camp?"

"*Sí*. The name is Campo Rojo. There, we live with four other people," Francisca mumbles, biting her fingernails. I take a good look at her. Carlitos has fallen asleep on her lap. Her knees are drawn together, her two big toes touching, the balls of her feet apart from each other. She looks like a distracted teenager. She looks like she is waiting for something.

"In Campo Rojo, each of us pays $35 per week. I think it's too much because the house is dirty, hot, and full of bugs and leaks," she says.

Then she found out that she was pregnant.

"Were you happy?" I ask.

Francisca shakes her head. No.

"Abraham has many girlfriends and too much drinking on weekends. Sometimes he's drunk for days and I don't see him. That's why I can't be happy when I know about the baby."

They drifted apart but remained together. Abraham drank more and Francisca worked harder.

"In August I go to Naples to see the doctor for pregnant women and he put his thing on my belly."

I stop writing. "He put his thing on your belly?" I ask, looking at her over the frame of my glasses.

She covers her mouth with one hand, then the other, then both, laughing through her fingers. Carlitos rises and falls on her lap. His rectangular body wriggles.

"No, not the thing you're thinking," Francisca says, shaking her hands in the air. "The thing that lets you see the baby on the TV. An ultrasomething..."

"Ultrasound?"

"*Sí, un ultrasonido.*"

"Did the doctor see anything wrong with the baby?"

"No. He only says the baby is fine. I'm happy." Francisca wraps a lock of hair around one finger, holds it in place for a few seconds, then lets it go.

"When I'm eight months, the doctor puts his thing again on my belly." She says it once more, this time for effect. I smile.

"The doctor says it's a boy. That's good news. Abraham doesn't want a girl. A boy is better for everybody. I'm very happy. Maybe a boy makes Abraham a better man. Maybe he stops drinking now that he is going to have a boy."

"Did the doctor tell you anything about the boy's legs and arms?"

"No, he says that the baby has to come out straight away because he's sitting down."

Francisca doesn't remember much of what followed. Just how a wave of heat hit her face, how she felt dizzy and wanted to be left alone. The doctor said something about an incision across her belly. The baby had to be born immediately. She cried in the doctor's office, in the hallway, looking out the hospital windows by the elevator, in her sterile room, on her bed, falling in and out of a chemically induced dream.

By the time Francisca woke up, she was no longer pregnant.

"The baby doesn't breathe when he comes out and he is in an incubator where all is warm with a light bulb and he is alive," Francisca says.

She crosses her legs, forgetting that Carlitos is on her lap, and the baby tips over. I instinctively reach for his underarms, but Francisca's expert hands go for his waist.

"He falls a lot," she says, rubbing his head although he didn't hit anything.

"How does he fall?"

"Oh, I don't know. Sometimes I forget where I put him and he falls. Just like now," Francisca tells me between noisy kisses that she stamps on Carlitos' face.

After Abraham arrived, a nurse took them to see their baby.

When Francisca was wheeled into the incubator room, her eyes got wet with tears. Newborn babies were wrapped in blankets inside rows of glass boxes. Some of them were covered in wires, hoses and gauze patches.

"Poor babies," Abraham said.

"Poor mothers," Francisca whispered.

They passed tiny, pink babies with emaciated legs that looked like red frogs, the kind of thing Francisca had seen only in Guerrero. The nurse stopped in front of a little glass box. The baby inside it was smaller than the others, even the ones that looked like red frogs. He had translucent tubes sticking in and out of his nostrils and mouth.

"That's your baby," the nurse said to the young couple.

"Can I hold him?" Francisca asked.

The nurse lifted his body out of the glass box. She cradled him in her left arm, and began to unwrap his body with her free hand. As the incomplete baby emerged from the blankets, Francisca gasped, and Abraham took a step back.

"Who wants to hold this handsome guy?" the nurse asked in her most cheerful voice.

There was nothing handsome about him. Francisca winced, closed her eyes and turned away.

"That's not my baby," she said, containing her tears. "This is a monster, not a baby," Francisca's eyes moved back and forth between the nurse and Abraham. He agreed. He demanded to see their son.

A translator joined them. Her Spanish was impeccable, her message loud and painfully clear. That rectangular baby with no arms or legs was their son. Did they want to hold him? No. No. No, they didn't. How could they?

"For a long time I can't hug him. I can't even look at him. I pray that love for my child comes to me but I feel nothing for months."

"Did anyone explain to you why Carlitos had been born this way?"

"How? Nobody knows. Some people say it's the pesticides in the field, all the white powder I breathe when I'm pregnant. The doctors ask if there are other babies like Carlitos in our families. *Dios mío!* How can they ask such a thing? We have never seen anything like that."

"What do you think?"

"Me?" Francisca asks. "*Yo no sé casi nada de nada.*" She knows almost nothing about everything.

"That must have been very hard for you, Francisca," I say. She looks away. I have embarrassed her.

"Do you want to know the truth?" Francisca murmurs, her torso bent forward as if she were about to tell me a secret.

"I tell the doctor to let Carlitos die. It's better. I suffer, he suffers, Abraham drinks. Life is nothing but trouble and sadness since he's born."

She had numerous sleepless, lonely nights, during which she prayed in Amusgo. She asked for a miracle, for legs one night, for arms the next, for silence, for peace, for love, for death. She got none of it. She held Carlitos in her arms, waiting for love to fall upon them like a shroud.

"And Abraham?" I ask. "What did he say about his son?"

"Oh, I don't know," she says, shoulders shrugged up to her ears, nose scrunched. "Nothing. He says nothing. He only drinks and disappears every weekend."

"When did you start loving Carlitos?"

"What do you mean?" Francisca asks. She says she doesn't understand me. Her Spanish is not that good, she says.

"Do you love Carlitos?"

She sighs and looks at Carlitos propped between us on the couch.

"I don't know. I want him to have at least legs. Or at least arms."

Francisca's eyes tear up a little. At 10 she was toiling in the bean fields of Huehuetonoc. By 13 she had become a weaver. She turned 16 somewhere between Mexico and the US. Her feet were swollen after days of following the coyote through the desert, her legs cut and bruised from falls in the dark, her eyes bloodshot from sleepless nights. She was still watching cartoons every Sunday morning when she found that she was pregnant.

"Are you going to ask me about the lawsuit?"

"Not unless you want to talk about it." She seems satisfied with my answer but doesn't say anything. I give it a timid shot.

"I know that your lawyer filed suit against your ex-employer. The suit holds the company liable for medical and hospital costs, lifetime care costs, disability, disfigurement, pain and suffering and mental anguish, among other charges. I also know they are talking about millions of dollars and that the company is fighting back with everything they have."

Francisca seems surprised that I know so much. "What else do you know?"

"I know your lawyer is very handsome and that his office is in Coconut Grove." Francisca bursts into a fit of giggles. She places her hands on her cheeks and tells me she doesn't know whether the lawyer is good looking.

"I don't look," she says blushing. After the giggles subside, Francisca asks me what else I know.

"I know that the lawyer is trying to prove that Carlitos' deformities are linked to your ex-employer's documented recklessness with pesticides and I know that without the testimonies of the other two mothers—Sostenes and Maria—the relationship is going to be difficult to prove."

Francisca is now looking at me attentively. Most of what I say she is either hearing for the first time or has heard before but is just beginning to understand.

"I also know that the study of the effect of those chemicals on pregnant women can take many years."

Francisca bites what's left of one fingernail and asks me how I know all that. I tell her that I read it in the newspaper.

"The newspaper in English?" I nod. "What else have you read in the newspaper about me?"

I tell her that I saw the pictures of her relatives in Huehuetonoc that the American reporter took on her trip to Mexico. "Did you see the pictures?" I ask her.

"They just come, take pictures, ask questions, and leave. I don't know how they find my family in my village. The pictures are nice? Is my mom in them?"

It dawns on me that the reporters who wrote about Carlitos never bothered to share the final result with Francisca. The photographer who shot pictures of Carlitos at his birthday party published them in the local newspaper but Francisca never received a copy.

"What is your dream, Francisca? What would you like to do with your life?"

She wants to study, she tells me, love Carlitos a bit more every day and live far away from Abraham.

"Don't you love Abraham?" I ask.

"I never love him. I don't know what's wrong with my heart, but loving? Loving is the hardest thing to do."

We fall silent for a few seconds. Francisca reaches for the remote control. *The Pink Panther* is on.

{HONEST} RANDOM {CAUSED BY DESIRE TO DE-CATEGORIZE} SELF

(VOL. 64, NO. 2, 2014)

Felicia Zamora

....

"When all else fails . . ." I say to myself. When all else fails I go to the thesaurus. When I go to the thesaurus to discover religion and get sidetracked by porn, I lie about this action. I lie about this one too. Deciphering is the easy—all the rest breaks, breaks, my concentration lacks luster; bees honeycombing in my: {you want to say *bonnet, cleaver me*- no} heavy cranium. All shade in these gelatinous tendrils: shady as shady goes. {Head stroke here.} I twitch at being told what to do. {Insert term: *micromanage*. Do not insert an emoticon. I am sad I know what *emoticon* stands for.} Yoga classes— out. Pottery—out. And yet, pushback from curiosity . . . journalistic ellipsis remind me of how I tell stories. Did you hear the one about my brother and me getting kicked out of swimming lessons? Over and over again. I dream of drowning. My subconscious wastes away on fear and more fear. Over and over again I tell this story. Polite fosters energy loss. "Swimming privileges revoked . . ." I think I make a guttural sound. What is in me is the truth. What is in the truth is me. What the mind tells the body; what the body tells the mind; what the body tells the body. Sticky lies of on lips. {I taste my own fear of drowning.} Aren't we all: synchronicity? A stream of consciousness: then there's this: what's wrong with tubing in the shallow bodies? {Very Midwestern: *tubing*.} Always, a thing held in; a thing held back. Constraints beg {disobedience} {perhaps a lullaby tuned to Lady Gaga}: eyes on this page hold contempt for the words written {"lullaby tuned to Lady Gaga"}. {No, not yours, mime.} Lack of sound {em}powers. {Say *nonverbal* here.} The mime isn't bad at her job; she's just chatty. Remember when "gaga" was a baby's term. I don't recall starting from anywhere; self-help books tell me I'm lucky to be here. What does *lucky* look like? Oh, the alliterations roll now. Language: a vestige I tote under my arms, in hopes the clouds pass. Language: I burden you, then turn to you for redemption.

GLARING PATTERN BALDNESS

(VOL. 67, NO. 2, 2018)

Alicia Mountain

....

Does it afear you,
the ways in which my blood leaves me
                                    and yet I live?

Moonspeak, a pitch too high
                for your body / propriety,
                                    a pitch too low.

What sense to be culled
from overheard revelry—

        that we are not dying in cycles
        that we are so much   iron   and   saltsea
so much laughing riptide with disregard.

You need not
drown in this blood, but you might.

CRYPTOZOOLOGY

(VOL. 68, NO. 1, FALL 2017 / WINTER 2018)

Kathleen McNamara

....

My spine is hooked on an invisible line, and every few minutes I feel a sharp yank on the barb.

"Yanked by what?" says Josh, rolling tobacco muck between his gums.

"A cloud-dwelling fisherman. Or Earth's magnetic fields. Or my ex-wife's voodoo dolls. Take your pick."

He suggests sciatica. It's July in North Pole, Alaska: the time of year when the sun winds a tight circle above us, tracing a halo. We're stationed in Fairbanks, and Josh and I run errands before softball on base. We've seen three foxes this morning, hunting along the highway. Josh swears it's good luck: "No way we'll lose to the medics." He pounds his fist into the mitt. I want to agree, but I'm distracted. When we reach the post office, I almost crash my truck into a metal candy cane welded to the ground by the entrance sign.

"Son of a bitch." Josh braces himself against the dashboard, whistling. Spits brown sludge into a Styrofoam cup wedged between his thighs. "Don't kill me yet. Give the terrorists a shot." He's grinning: a joke.

Inside, our crush Swayzee works the counter. We bet she can't be older than twenty-three—Josh's age. She's got hair like ropes of spaghetti always caught at the side of her mouth. She asks everyone who isn't there to buy stamps if they want to buy stamps: manager's orders. Now I've got five books of them stashed next to the dishwasher.

We watch her kick a plastic crate toward the new guy in a delivery uniform. "All of these are addressed to Santa," she says. "We get like a hundred every morning. Then another hundred in the afternoon. Old man likes reading them." The old man is a member of the city council who changed his legal name to Kris Kringle. He runs Santa Claus House and dresses in a red suit year-round—sitting in his Santa throne among thousands of miniature Santas, and train sets, and elf statues, and frosted plastic trees glistening with tinsel, all slapped with price tags. Makes a killing whenever the tourists pull in.

"Next." A ringing in my ear makes it hard to hear, and Josh nudges me toward Swayzee, lovesick goon-smile plastered to his face. She pops her gum and looks us up and down as if to say she has ten thousand better ways to spend her time. Reminds me of my ex-wife, Brenda, who I loved the way all the country songs said I should. I give Swayzee the notice I found in my mailbox—insufficient postage—and she comes back with a care package from my mother in Oregon. Mom started sending them when I was still a kid, just landed in Afghanistan, and never stopped. Said she did it so I wouldn't forget what we were fighting for. First time she sent one, I wrote her a thank-you note: "It's good to know I'm fighting for Girl Scout cookies, sunscreen, beef jerky, and handheld video games."

"No," she responded, "you're fighting for freedom." For a while I liked the sound of that. We both knew the real reason I enlisted: I enlisted because on my eighteenth birthday, I purchased a Ford Mustang with a seventeen-and-a-half-percent interest rate. I grew up on welfare with four brothers and one parent in a house with a cement floor. I needed the signing bonus.

"Can I interest you in a book of stamps?"

Josh raises his hand like a schoolkid, frog-eyes glazed with longing. "Me. I'll take one."

Swayzee talks into her computer screen: "One customer transaction at a time." I pay the difference, and Josh buys the stamps, lingering at the counter even though she's looking past him.

"Bye, Swayzee." Josh waves.

"Next."

We stop for lunch at the Dream Palace. It's against Army rules, but I'm Josh's CO, and we figure an afternoon show can't be as raunchy as late night. Josh convinces me: "Everyone knows they have the best fried chicken."

I park in back, where the American flag airbrushed on my tailgate won't be recognizable from the street, and where moose lope through the mud like they're curious about the girls inside.

Inside, they're blasting Journey's greatest hits while Goldie Rush climbs a pole, burlesque tassels on her nipples. She's a nice girl; she'll give you half a free lap dance if you show her your military ID. Says it's her patriotic duty. Second half is twenty bucks. A redhead named Diamond greets us at the velvet-curtained entrance.

"You two again?" Diamond has a pre-emphysema voice. After her third kid, she retired from the stage and started waiting tables. She holds out menus and points us to our seats, but when I pull out a chair to sit down, I'm frozen. In my back, I feel pain like walls cracking. A claw has crawled up my spine: seizing bone, ligament, muscle.

"What's wrong?" I can read Diamond's moving lips, but I can't hear her. All I can hear is shrieking tinnitus, sharp enough to mute "Don't Stop

Believing." Then it's gone, and so is she. Josh leans forward in his chair, slides me a menu. I sit down carefully.

"I know a chiropractor you can see. Went there myself. And sent Goldie to him once, when she threw out her back. Look at her now." He nods toward stage. Goldie has a gold-dusted leg wrapped around the pole. She spins upside down, hair dangling to the floor. Her face turns plum with blood and gravity. "And she's in heels." He grins, like he's the one invented strippers.

At the softball game, when I throw from third to first, it feels like my arms are toy arms. My spine is a joke-spine, coiling from dirt, attached like a wire spring. The ball clunks into a dugout, and the batter advances to second. "Son of a bitch," screams Josh, chucking his glove in the air. We lose 6–4.

That weekend, I follow Josh's directions until I reach the end of a dirt road. I leave my truck and set out on foot. Blooms of spotty red mushrooms have sprouted from summer moss, and I walk through clusters of aspen until I find a clearing. Josh said the guy worked miracles on his back after he flipped his car: "He popped shit back there I didn't know I had." My back needs miracles too.

I expect more than what I find: an RV propped on cement blocks in knee-high grass, HOCKAM CHIROPRACTIC painted on the siding. You can hear the rush of the Tanana through the woods.

"There's something wrong with my back," I say when Hockam answers the door. He's got a wind-caked face: features like knots on tree bark. "I can't turn my head to the right." I demonstrate my limited mobility. "When I try, I hear a loud ringing in my left ear."

He rubs his palms together, motions for me to get on his table, then starts testing pressure points. "How's this?" he says, "Or this?" I tell him fine, no problem. I can handle it. He turns me on my side, and I focus on the wood-paneled wall above his desk. He's got an oversized POW MIA decal next to an embroidered patch that says, "Vietnam Veteran Agent Orange Victims" over the outline of a copter raining toxic clouds. Surrounding it are photographs of a young man at various stages of growing up: a mule ride; a Little League portrait; pimpled at the prom with a date and a yellow rose in his lapel.

"That's my son," says Hockam, rolling me onto my gut. "Best damn short-stop in Alaska." I tell him we could use his son on base.

"We have slow-pitch softball in the summer. Yesterday, we lost to the medics. Not a good look for those of us who have been in combat."

He grunts. Silence unnerves me, so I tell him that since I got promoted to sergeant, first class, I don't have to live on base, and I moved out to that fishing lake over by Santa Claus House. When I want to scream, he instructs me to imagine pain as a white flame melting to liquid between my vertebrae.

"Some knot. What'd you do to yourself?" But I can think of too many answers. Perhaps I did it to myself during months of humping gear through Kunar Province and then digging trenches for the outpost in the Valley of Death. Or maybe it was from hauling stones and timber we bought from locals who didn't want to be seen talking to us, so we could build walls that were supposed to keep destruction out but invited it instead. Or it could have happened sometime during those endless nights when the bleating of any lost Korengal goat had me reaching for the M16 and pointing at the shadowy lines of the Abas Ghar ridge, guided by moonlight reflecting off the river.

"It's probably from working out," I say. "Lifting weights." But I doubt it. I hate exercise.

"You know a Bigfoot lives at that lake of yours."

"I did three tours," I say. I'm not sure I heard him right. "Afghanistan and Iraq."

"Whatever you want to call her: the Yeti, Sasquatch, gigantopithecus. When I was a kid in Arizona, we called them Mogollon Monsters. It's all the same species. They're very advanced beings."

"Is that so?" I don't want to laugh at a man who has his hands on my neck. Some of the nerve endings back there are fried, and at moments when I know I should feel pain, instead it comes to me mushy and dull, like I'm made of omelets packed in plastic.

"I've been here ten years, and I've seen her three times. She's blonde." I assume he means blond fur, but he says that Bigfoots have hair, not fur, same as us. I hear a sound in my spine like kelp being ripped apart. When I sit up, my blood feels carbonated. "Read this," he says, handing me the *North Star Gazette*. A photo of an enormous footprint dominates the front page. "Spotted her picking through trash outside the old mining hotel last week. Ran off before they could get a picture. You can hear her sometimes in these woods. Screams like a twenty-foot woman getting branded with a hot iron."

"No kidding." I nod and smile. "You were in Vietnam?" I ask, but he doesn't answer, except to say the session costs fifty bucks. I pay him.

That night, I wake up every time the dog stirs. The ringing in my left ear crescendos then subsides, and when I fall into a half-sleep, Blu's tail between my feet, I dream about bodies. I walk the streets of a city that is Kabul and

Fallujah and Fairbanks, one block leading to another. Everywhere I go, I see meat hanging on hooks outside storefronts, slabs of meat woven together like quilts and then laid out to dry on the sidewalk. In the dream, I cough and pull vertebrae out of my throat. One after another they appear, like I am a magician performing a trick with a rainbow scarf, except there is no audience. The bones belong to different species of vertebrates: one is an elk Josh and I shot last fall; another belongs to Red, our family husky who choked on a golf ball when I was nine and playing catch with him; two others are the remains of young Afghan sisters who died when an IED exploded outside their home, collapsing its stone walls. The bones fit together like a puzzle, and before long, I am wearing this skeleton lei around my neck, roaming the street in uniform. I pass the Dream Palace, and Mai Thai Restaurant, and sometimes the stores are not stores, but piles of rubble, with blankets of neatly trimmed meat covering destroyed brick, like every broken room is a child, and someone has tucked them into sleep.

When I turn a corner, I find a deli. Inside, our softball team sits at a table, eating sandwiches. Josh says we're about to head back into Korengal and need energy because we have to carry all the ruins in the city to the mountains and use shattered concrete and fragments of meat to rebuild our outpost, and even though none of the guys on the softball team were with me out there with the Second Platoon, it makes sense in the dream, I think, because I feel that same unslakable thirst I remember from that time in my life, and because I can hear that electricity I felt in Korengal whenever I had to run five hundred yards from where the trees ended to our firebase, my feet jumping bullets like popcorn. Josh offers me a sandwich, and I take it. It's raw and cold, and it bleeds in my mouth, and I notice then that I'm not the only one. All of us stand around as blood drips from our mouths. Someone jokes that we are vampires. When I examine the sandwich closer, I can see that between bread, slathered in mayonnaise, is a beating heart, pumping blood from severed arteries, its juice dripping down my arm. I ask Josh what we're eating.

"We caught a Bigfoot," he says, with a red smile. "Bigfoot is the most tender meat you'll ever find in your life." He has a toothpick and stabs at blonde hairs between his teeth. Then someone who is supposed to be our CO appears from behind the deli counter in a bloody butcher's apron, wiping a cleaver on his knee. His face is hidden behind a surgical mask.

"In war," he says, surveying his room, "it's very difficult to say who's responsible."

We nod, holding up our sandwiches like pints of beer. "Hear, hear," we say, digging in.

At the dugout on base, I tell Josh about Hockam's Bigfoot. "That's the craziest shit I ever heard," he says, practicing his swing. Josh is twitchy. No fat on him. Joined the Army three years ago, and they still haven't sent him overseas. "I've had enough of these drone strikes." He flexes the bat in his arm. "Just wait till they unleash us. How many CKs did you get again?" I don't want to answer. Instead, I rub my head to remind him that before the war, I had hair. Then I take the bat. At the plate, I try to rip the ball when it comes toward me, but I miss. Aluminum slams my back, and I fall into dirt, feeling pain so alive that it seems to have a sound only dogs can hear, clanging the skeleton of an instrument in need of tuning.

"I'm fine," I say, but for a while I can't move, except to taste chalk lines between my teeth.

When I finally flip over, a sergeant major who's been watching the game stands over me.

"We can't have you like this." His voice is familiar. He's the CO from the dream, the butcher who's in charge but not responsible. "Help me get Sullivan to his feet," he calls, and then I'm surrounded by the arms and legs of the US Army, men who call themselves my brothers, lifting me higher and higher until I'm upright and can pretend to walk.

"You're fine, Sullivan," he says. "But I'm ordering you to Bassett." It's the hospital on base. He's got a bat in hand, reflecting the sunlight. It looks like the cleaver from the dream.

"In war," I say, as clouds spin, "it's very difficult to say who's responsible."

"Somebody drive him there," yells the commander.

The x-ray film shows families of tumors clumped around my spine like lupine buds. "Your chiropractor may have popped one," says the doctor.

"He's not my chiropractor. I only went to him once."

"It looks like you have about two dozen in there. Could be neurofibromas. Or could be metastasized. Tell me about your other symptoms." As grim reapers go, he's remarkably cheerful. "We should probably look at the rest of your body." I start to talk, but the room is fading in and out, and my voice sounds like the voice of someone on television, a rerun of a sitcom, the volume turned down, and when he says he's sending me to a radiologist for a CT biopsy, I nod and say thanks, even though color has evaporated from the room. He starts looking in my eyes and ears with a scope, sometimes saying "huh" in a way that worries me. After a while, he asks if he needs to arrange a ride home for me, but I tell him I have Josh. Josh is sitting in the waiting room hunched over the glossy pages of *Military Spouse*.

"How'd it go?"

"I'm dying," I say, and he laughs.

"In the mood for fried chicken and the afternoon show? Goldie's on." I tell him I need sleep. Somehow, in the commotion of my public failure, my shirt ripped, so I go to my office to change, but all I have in there are combat uniforms—desert, forest, night. The angles of the room seem off: the ceiling's too low, and it's tilted. I put on desert. Once-rectangular windows are now trapezoidal. I order Josh to let me drive myself home, and he goes back to his cup of tobacco sludge. In the truck, I watch yellow stripes wobble and shift on asphalt, floating. I end up at Santa Claus House. I want to sit on Santa's lap, but he's a thin Santa, and I'm not thin. Plus I'm in uniform now, with my name sewn to my chest, and a bus of tourists has just arrived, and people are lining up to meet him. I walk between plastic evergreen limbs that fill the store: branches loaded with fruit-shaped glitter bombs and epileptic lights. On a shelf next to a nativity of cats—three wise cats offering gold, frankincense, and purr—and an animatronic Rudolph, I find a Christmas Collectible™ diorama of a baseball diamond, the tableau of a game underway. Santa's fielding both teams. He's pitching; he's at bat; he's stealing third; he's selling peanuts; he's trying to catch a fly ball in center. Elves cheer in the stands. It's too heavy to hang on a tree, too small to sit in the yard, but I'm suddenly overcome by the feeling that all will be right in the world once it's sitting over my fireplace—that it will be like the first Noel, when angels sang, or that Frosty the Snowman will spring to life, or that it will make it true that a fat man like me could fly across the world in one night on a magic reindeer, spewing gifts like comet dust.

But when I go up to the counter to pay, I have to wait behind the tourists. It's Swayzee standing at the register. At first, I wonder if I'm hallucinating, but no, it's her: straw-blonde hair caught at her lip, boredom in her eyes. "You work at the post office," I say, when it's my turn. She looks up, and I can tell she doesn't recognize me, or if she does, she doesn't care.

"Uncle Sam says you gotta make a living." She's eying the uniform, smirking. "Thirty-six fifty." While I pay, a tourist taps me on the shoulder and asks for a photograph. I smile for the camera. He gives me two thumbs up.

"Thank you for your service," he says, in labored English, shaking my hand. He goes back to his family, showing them the picture, and they laugh about something in a language I don't recognize. Swayzee wraps the baseball game in tissue paper, hands me a bag that says SANTA CLAUS HOUSE.

"Merry Christmas," she says.

"It's July." Already the magic seems broken.

She rolls her eyes. "You're the one who came in here."

After the biopsy, I don't hear from the doctor for three days, and I assume then that I'm going to die at thirty-three. I don't know what I'm going to say to my mother. When I call her, she asks me if I like the care package she sent. I say yes but it's still sitting on the kitchen counter, unopened.

"I sent those sour candies you always used to ask for when you were deployed," she says. "You still like them?"

"Those were for the kids," I tell her. "Local kids." She sounds disappointed, so I add that yes, I still like them. Light in the room dims, then brightens, then dims again, and I have to sit down. Now that I know I have tumors, I feel them at every movement. They chafe when I reach to turn on a lamp; they cut like gear teeth when Blu tugs his leash. What I thought was a spider bite that wouldn't heal behind my knee now seems to vibrate when I walk.

"You don't sound so good," says Mom. "Are you sure everything's okay?" Blu is barking at a squirrel outside, and the walls around me have a pulse, so I tell her I'll talk to her later. Then, because I can't tell my mother the truth, I call Brenda, except I never get to the part where I'm dying because Brenda has a new husband now, and she says she's sorry but she doesn't want to talk because she doesn't know who I am inside since I refuse to tell her what I did over in Afghanistan to earn that Bronze Star while she sat at home waiting for me and watching the war on television. I tell her I'm sorry too.

"For what?" she asks, expecting more.

When the doctor calls and tells me to stop by his office, I'm there in an hour. I've been rewriting my will, crossing out every mention of Brenda, so ready to give up that I almost don't hear him say the tumors are benign. "We've concluded you've got neurofibromatosis," he says. "Your case is actually rather mild. The ringing in your ears? Those are acoustic neuromas. We should remove them to prevent permanent hearing loss, though you should expect them to return. Tumors are also what's disrupting your vision. It's a genetic disorder. It'll probably worsen as you age." I guess I'm relieved. Then I'm not relieved.

"And Sullivan," says the doctor, "I don't recommend looking at pictures of neurofibromatosis online. Like I said, your case is mild."

"Thanks, doc," I say, but when I'm home, the first thing I do is turn on my computer. What I see are images of people whose insides seem to be pushing out of their bodies, trying to escape.

I call him. His secretary or someone says he's not available, but I wait. Finally, he answers. "You didn't tell me I have 'Elephant-Man Disease.'"

"Well that's not the word we use," he says, catching a laugh. "No one's going to sell you to the circus—you're a war hero." He clears his throat. "Anyway, technically your neurofibromatosis is a different type than the Elephant Man's."

It doesn't reassure me.

Between the diagnosis and the surgery, I forget to count time. Instead, I count moments of pressure, when it seems like all sensation in my body is compressed into a single point for a prolonged moment, and all the feeling I've ever witnessed in life is collected in me and piercing my consciousness through one disc in my spine. When I have the surgery, doctors remove every tumor they can find. Afterward, my hearing works, and the world is no longer floating or misshapen. I'm fine again, except that the area on my neck that seems made of scrambled eggs has expanded, the lifeless flesh marching south.

I miss the softball championships while I recover. When I'm back at work, summer and fall have ended, the sun has left the northern hemisphere, and each day is so short, it rotates from dawn to dead of night, blanketed in snow. Doctors tell me I'm doing well, but when I can't sleep, I find myself sitting on the freezing porch with Blu, watching auroras and following the grace of shadows as they slip through moonlight. In those moments, when I hear the wind howl in complete sentences, I think of Hockam. Ice cracks on the fishing pond, and I'm sure it's her, reaching through aspen with her tree-branch arms, her enormous blonde hands coaxing me closer and closer, until I want to slip under the frozen surface, into the ink of her glacial home, and become one in the chorus of monsters. But then Blu is behind me, nipping my ankles, and I wake to find that I have been sleep-walking in a sub-zero forest: foot-numb, frosted, brought back to consciousness by a dog. The shadow is a moose, nosing for food, its enormous wooden frame lumbering through the snow. It bellows as if to say, *there you are: man in hiding.*

When spring arrives, an unusual heat comes with it, and layers of permafrost begin to melt. Someone finds mastodon tusks that have been frozen in ice for a hundred thousand years. I'm devising a war game for the unit, pretending north Bolivians are fighting south Bolivians over water. Then Josh gets transferred to Texas. I hear he's deploying to Syria, and I'm lonely, and one day I go to the post office trying to work up enough nerve to ask Swayzee on a date, but she's not there. Instead, in the newspaper vending box in the lobby, I see the front-page story of the *North Star Gazette*: a teenager walking home at night, hit by a car—dead. They run his prom photo, his baseball stats. I recognize the yellow rose.

"We had him cremated," says Hockam when I knock on the door of his RV and find him unraveled and gray as a dishrag. I don't know why I'm visiting. I barely know him, but I can't stop myself. "We scattered his ashes in the Tanana and watched him float downstream." Hockam has newspapers and fast food wrappers and smashed cereal boxes stacked up inside his RV. His chiropractic table is strewn with dirty clothes. "And at that very moment," he says, "that blonde Bigfoot emerged from the trees, very solemn-like. She sang a magnificent song for him. It didn't have words, just sounds. Ethereal sounds." He slumps onto his table. "I know you don't believe me," he says, crying into his mouth. "But other people saw it too."

I pat him on the back. I'm not good with feelings, but I tell him I understand what grief can do to a person. Then I tell him how, in Afghanistan, we used to carry sour candy in our packs, to give to children when we showed up at their homes to question their fathers. Two sisters in the Korengal village used to fight over the green ones, so I always made sure I had a handful when we arrived at their house, and while we pressed their father for intel, the girls stood with their mother by the hearth, pointing and giggling at each other's green mouths. After we gave them candy, those girls weren't afraid of us anymore. "That meant a lot to me," I tell him. "To be seen as human. To be trusted."

"What's that got to do with anything?" asks Hockam. He's sitting on a pile of used towels. I don't know the answer. It's just a story Brenda liked, probably because I never told her the ending.

A few weeks later, I drive toward the Arctic Circle with Blu, fishing tackle loaded in the truck bed. But my ear starts buzzing again, and the check engine light flashes red. The steering wheel locks; I can't figure what's wrong, so I get towed back to base. My truck is a specialty model, and the mechanics tell me the parts must be shipped from Detroit. In the meantime, the Army gives me a Humvee to use. I don't much like the way it rattles when it turns, like its bones are loose, but I bring it home and park it in the driveway. That night, rinsing dishes, I watch from the kitchen sink as rain slows down outside the window.

You probably won't believe me, and I don't blame you, but what I'm about to tell you is true. I'm loading the dishwasher, and I see a hairless animal crawl out from under the hood of the Humvee. He's ten inches tall, walks like a human, and looks right at me, holding a rusty screw in his jellyfish hand. He has pointy ears, a wrinkled elfin brow, and a blue vein popping from his forehead. The look on his face says he's been messing with shit in there—you're right, the bones are loose, his eyes say. I don't know any other word to call him but gremlin. He grins: a yellow, triangulated smile, mouth crowded with disease. Blu watches through the sliding glass door, his ears back, his teeth bare. I'm not crazy. The creature walks toward us.

"In war," I want to say, as he gets closer, a wave rising in my throat, "it's very difficult to know who's responsible." But he's staring at me, holding the screw in his amphibian hand, tap, tap, tapping the glass.

"Excuse me." His voice is the voice of a salesman of Bibles or dictionaries, like a recruitment officer reassuring the mother of a teenage boy who still has hair that all is well at boot camp, like a manager at a car dealership who sees a young man looking at a Ford Mustang and says *she's a beauty, don't you think?*, offering his hand to shake. "Did you lose something?" He drops the screw on the porch.

I'm fiddling with the lock on the door. When I slide it open, he's gone. I wonder then where the little monster came from: if he was a virus picked up on base, or if he was a gift from the Taliban that had shipped overseas undetected, or if, somehow, he had once been part of me, until he crawled up my spine like a ladder, out of my throat while I slept, like a ribbon of magic scarves, eager to infect the world.

One day it was a stone house, and the girls loved green candy. The next day: a child's elbow under rubble, another string of bones you are supposed to wear like a trophy. You have your weapon over your shoulder, candy in your pocket, the assurance of American dollars in the bank. Your mother says they wrote your name in the paper when you got the Bronze Star. You get letters from your childhood mailman, your dentist, your third-grade teacher: Thank you for your service. It's what you say when the rest is unspeakable.

There you are, whispers the night, the gremlin, the Bigfoot of a midnight sun: *we've found the man in hiding.*

PART III

LOVE

It is hard not to feel tenderness towards this world even as I suspect that I have been all wrong about it.

—KRISTEN CASE

IN these stories and poems, love and desire are coded with radiance, reverence, revulsion, and revision. Joyce Carol Oates and Rilla Askew meditate on ill-fitted, ill-fated companionship and the "sheer boundless energy" that keeps two people burning toward an unhappy end. Oates's narrator wonders if, once circumstance is stripped away, love is essentially "friendship," "simple dependency," or "ravenous, sheer appetite." In this light, we're left to wonder about the limits of love. Similarly, Faith Merino confronts the "distant tidal pull" of a past and unequal relationship between a girl and her teacher, the significance of which reveals itself once the narrator crosses "the liminal hang of childhood and into adulthood." Kristen Case's stunning piece, "On Certainty," offers a latticed canopy of history, philosophy, and self-recognition through which—as in all of the following pieces—the only certainty is a question about "what is possible between people."

FROM HELL TO BREAKFAST

(VOL. 21, NO. 1, 1969)

David Wagoner

....

Leaving the night upstairs
And minding their manners,
They sit down at the table.
For what they are about
To receive, God, make them grateful
And good enough to eat.
What made these appetites?—
Tomato juice for vampires,
Heaps of scrambled eggs
While the rooster is still crowing.
And what's the use of letting
The night into the morning?
Stir sugar and cream in it.

Their eyes are the right colors
Except at the corners, their clothes
Are as cool as the season,
She put her face on straight,
He had a close shave, but they seem
To remember someone screaming.
Was it next door? In the street?
She dreamed something was burning
In the oven, a midnight snack
No one would dare to eat.
On stumps like a veteran,
Something walked in his sleep
Like himself cut down to size.

Give them their daily bread
And the daily paper. Hundreds
Were screaming if they had time:
Some fell or were pushed, and some
Ran smack into it
Or woke up behind bars.
Thousands coughed up their souls
In the night, and two got in
On the wrong side of bed
And cured their love like meat.

They both may be excused
If they wipe their mouths. Look,
No hands across the table, no
Holes in the walls, no windows
Scattered across the floor.
It could have been worse, and they
Could have been worse than it.
They have each other's names
On their shopping lists. In the doorway,
A brief passage of arms,
And they're off, they're off and running.

MUSTARD SEED

(VOL. 24, NO. 2, 1972)

Rosellen Brown

....

The baby is in her carriage for the first time. Under her fist-tight head is a fancy pillowslip, lace all around, with a satin stripe like Miss America's, announcing her name before anyone asks. It is not Molly Dugan's style, rather a gift of her mother, whose way of making the best of things tends toward the grandiose in exact proportion to her misery.

Molly looks at her baby and thinks again, yes, a child can come as though by Parcel Post. A knock at the door, she's yours, given like a gift. Fairy tales are full of that, children delivered from hand to hand, prizes, forfeits, always someone's to give ... She has signed a paper that says I am sane. *Promises* I am sane (which in the first place is not sane). Says I will apportion my moneys into two piles, a small one for myself, a tall one for this child's shoes and cereal. It's a contract, she thinks, stamped, sealed and filed somewhere, and I have married a daughter.

Whom no one would marry. Or rather, whom someone married and then, taking a long, long time about it, gave a second thought to and began to itch all over (in a manner of speaking). Molly is maneuvering the carriage through the narrow inner door, thinking of the back of Verne's head. How deadly the fit of his head to his neck, as though someone had tried to do a complicated joining job with too few screws. The first time she came near him from behind and touched his shoulder, he had jumped. It made her feel good, charged in a way she wasn't at all used to. "Your neck looks so tense," she had said shyly, feeling a tentative need to bend and unbend her fingers, the way they feel when she approaches a bread-board full of dough waiting to be worked to smoothness. That was the way everything had felt with Verne: new energy that she had only dreamed of, glimpsing it in others, had moved jerkily through the channels she had always suspected were there. There were no huge surges of desire, no hashing insights and sudden weakness; better, since she was a skeptical woman, and seasoned in her skepticism, not that young, a solid two-footed resounding weight of certainty. Yes, this is good, it is right. This sober man makes sense to me. So she had said quietly, seductively (but he could ignore the seductiveness without embarrassing her, she played it that safe): "Your neck looks so tense, can I massage it for you? Help it relax a little?"

Verne, poor Verne, all strung together with catgut and chicken wire. He had moved his chin warily, cocking it all the more tensely to challenge her. But she was standing so close to him that he must have felt the waves of hopeful warmth coming off her flowered shirtwaist. He bowed his head and she lay hands on his flesh, swarthy and firm right under the close-cropped hair. (All this was a few years ago when hair had to be banked neatly in back—when she cut it for him, their little economy, it was all but impossible to do it well. Now, last time she saw him, he was his short-haired self under such a weight of longish hair she might have thought it a wig. If he were a different man.) So, misleading her, he had done this sort of thing: she kneaded and pressed, she patted and prodded, all the way down his resistant shoulders and back, and she had felt his constant, persistent tension disintegrate. The tendons or whatever they were, muscles? softened and then the slackness of his back was full in her hand, as though she had subdued it. Verne had eased himself around slowly so that she was in the crook of his arm finally and had kissed her with his hard mouth. He hurt her so often with his mouth, not out of unappeasable passion but with that same insistent tautness that couldn't really feel her there. His kisses were more teeth than tongue. Because he was just so much less hard than a stone she could soften him into her arms but look. Molly, look, she finally had to say to herself, what you love in him is what you can do to him, against such odds. How you cozy him (briefly) into human positions. How you can feel like a woman who sings and smiles sleepily with your hair across the pillow, who can make him feel or pretend to feel he needs you. What you love is you, for want of him. She had married a man with a ramrod up his ass. Once upon a time, before she met him, she would not have said "ass." Now that there is color in her speech and in her clothes she would say it, and more, but that irony didn't make it any less of a ramrod.

Molly is pushing the carriage through the front door. She gets the front wheels down the doorstep onto the welcome mat and stops. Good God, how do you get a carriage down the steps with a baby in it? She had arranged Carie Lyn so carefully, as though for an ocean voyage . . . She looks around, flushing, to see if anyone has been watching. Molly has fair skin, freckled like a lawn full of clover. It prickles now, carbonated. She is about to think the worst thought she knows, it gathers in her exactly as her migraines do, a twitch of imminence before she even knows it's there. She is pushing it away almost with her hands, her breath held, averting her eyes from herself as the quick dumb tears press forward. Who says, who says, any other mother would know (it breaks through, a shout of pain) would know better? How would she know, any other, any real, how will I do this, this is not my baby who ended in a bottle, what difference does it make whose baby, she walked out holding him (the ones who don't make it, the nurse said, are more often him's) stiffly away from her white cotton cleanness like something unclean, unnatural as the pain, in a labelled jar my bulbous clot of a child, unchild, the best in me purple, blue, brown, red, like something that exploded. Where do they bury the little yolks that are not even corpses, do they burn them back to ash-flecks the size of sperm and egg, or flush them down, or chop them up in a bowl? She asked and the nurse, making out the death certificate in her name, patted her arm as though she were insane.

She turns her close-cropped head against the door frame but does not remove her hand from the cool carriage handle. Her tears seem to make their way like an underground spring up through inches of dirt, the rigid silence she has enforced on herself since Verne made her weep that one last time, turning his purie marble eyes on her. "No we will not, no, what the stinking world does not need is a child who smells like we do. You and me, separately and together." Did he celebrate the death, the non-life of that one, then? Did he wish it? *Did he cause it?* Were all the children of his stone body stone? Or was she, old flesh, just past its prime, so rotten inside she could not warm anything growing there but her own death?

Molly jerks the carriage up the doorstep again, brakes it, very carefully lifts the baby out, Carie Lyn Dugan swathed in the softest pink and white blankets, and—suddenly casual—rests the bundle on the hall floor, sleeping face up, and rackets the carriage down the cement steps, one-two-three. She marches back, picks up the baby who stirs with a comfortable moan, and before she has blinked her eyes open, has her deep under the carriage hood again, the CARIE LYN pillow ("Really dear," her mother had said, seizing on a focus for her disapproval, "they had to special order this! Couldn't you have picked a more everyday name?" Always different, Molly, is what she was thinking, of course; always up your own tree, alone) pressed to the back, all sweet sixteen ruffles flapping down Cobden Avenue. Sometimes these days, mood alternating with mood, she frightens herself a little. It is like living with a stranger.

The carriage takes some getting used to. It makes unwieldy turns and overcomes curbs with an effort; she needs to learn various subtle pressures of the heel of her hand, wheels up–wheels down maneuvers. Teaching French to indifferent fifteen-year-olds is easier, she thinks, and this time smiles.

She is waiting for a green light, standing between a man and a woman, and color creeps to the top of her cheekbones. She's heard her friends talk about the embarrassment of walking down the street for the first time in a maternity dress—what is it, the night-secrets you are giving away, or the way your private image of yourself hasn't begun to catch up with the single public image you've become? The woman turns to look at her absently, and her pink powdered face softens at the sight of the carriage, a mouthful of sugar gathering behind puckery lips. Molly stands very straight, the way she does when a truck-driver toots his horn and whistles, looking hard at the light as though it might dare to change unnoticed.

She must look like a nursemaid walking someone else's child. A little old-ish for the young mother's stance . . . Dry skin, creases bannering out from the corners of her eyes, a rack of bones at the shoulders of her sun-dress. Slender or skinny, neat or parsimonious, brightly dressed in an orange and purple cotton, or desperately ingenue? But of course she was even thinner at seventeen—there is some settling of firmness, gravity's if not her own, to make her less transparent now. And, wanting to be invisible, her clothes ten, fifteen years ago were always gray or brown, thrift-shop style. But no woman a good few years over thirty should be alone unless she has a very fine view of herself or she will falter terribly (she's thought this more and more) between a cool view of what she is and a fevered view of what she's always wanted to be . . .

An absurdity. Molly Fry Dugan, B.A., M.A., French with honors, divorcee, WASP, dreamer of adolescent dreams, keeper of her own body, gratefully knowing it is in better hands now than it has ever been before, her canvas shoes on large feet, her long legs attached to a pale and hollow trunk that no one seems much inclined to want to come near or look at in light or darkness (Verne having said that her small wan nipples were like owl's eyes, sad and round and too lonely to be helped . . .) that Molly Dugan is wheeling, jerk-ily, a borrowed carriage with (it is becoming apparent) an incipient squeak; the carriage containing the delicious curled body, all new cells. some never sloughed yet! of the baby she found by irrevocable legal means in a basket one day at her body's closed gates. An absurdity.

She is walking in a fog of humiliation, bumping into the dangling car-riage basket every few steps, she is so out of phase with her own stride. This is not the way things were supposed to be! It is all falling apart, falling down, ashes, ashes, can she keep the baby alive a day? It awes her that people, teen-agers even, who can't pass her French exams, seem to manage to keep such tender bones attached. Can you be mortified before yourself? Yes, she sees it, if you spend enough time alone, you make a good enough audience and judge. She wants to go and cry behind a tree, like a kid who has to pee.

The trailblazer, ladies and gentlemen, the historic landmark case whose name was in the evening edition, the first single woman in the state of Virginia to be allowed to adopt a baby alone, is standing on Cobden Avenue, corner North Street, covering her prickling eyes with her hands, having forgotten how to set one foot before the other. She is flushed, sweat pokes down between her unuseful breasts. At a standstill, swaying, her face is in her hands.

There is no one in the world who can tell her anything she needs to know. Every problem from here on in is her own. Alone up her own tree. Right, mama. Right again. Her friends are so put off by her "strength" she can barely talk to them, she has put such distance between herself and their conventional lives that the more they admire her the more she understands how much they'd been pitying her all this time. Her parents are too angry at her, underneath their cowed silence, to say a single word. Not even congratulations or good luck, which, though unhelpful, as though she were launching a yacht, would at least have been a sign of hope and reconciliation. Just that presents arrive, cold in their white frothy wrappings: some kind of peace gesture easy for her mother, the way she's seen food stand cooling on the table between certain friends and their parents. Demilitarized zone.

Carie is stirring, protesting because the carriage has stopped. She is thrusting her head from side to side like a turtle. She has, or will have, the head of a little blackberry. Though the hair is still thin there are very tight shiny curls laid one above the other, blue-black, purple-black. Her skin, a light pinky-brown when she was born, is darkening now day by day; at the folds of her elbows, behind her knees, the places her mother drips the tickly water from her cloth, for fun, she is very dark, graying towards black, just as you might expect in shadowy places. Molly is not dismayed at how much browner she is turning, but she feels guilt in exchange for her curiosity: Who is this stranger? (Hey lady, she is your daughter. We hereby give her to you because she is—even to you who intend to love her—strange, if not ugly. To the state she is worthless, less even. A burden. Therefore she is yours for the asking. If you can give her some worth, fine, though not so much it will ever come home to the state to roost. And keep the little bastard off the welfare rolls, will you?)

So Molly begins to move again. Cobden has narrowed by now and gotten a bit patchy, and the carriage rides the waves of broken sidewalk like a small ship. Every now and then she rams the front wheels against a protruding square and it nearly bounces out of her hands. It's a bad time of day to be walking here—school must be just over and the sidewalk is awash with teenagers. This end of the street the stores are random and grubby, many of indeterminate nature, every face is Black, and the children are exuberantly at home. Girls go past her in clots calling out to their friends walking across the street. Most of them are clutching their notebooks to their chests in that crook-armed protective hug no boy has ever needed. She feels herself in a jungle of legs, long legs and such high asses, and all sharply dressed in the tiny skirts and ponchos and overalls-tops of the exact moment. These girls, that boy rushing past in his rust-colored pants, running—outrageously right on him, with gold moving fast down the sides like racing stripes—some of them have such distinctive features and figures you know you could find their mother tribes in Africa, they could go join hands with their ancestors and show their inheritance around, these great-great-grandchildren. (Why was that—when you've found a child's eyes in her mother or his height in his father, you feel you've found the source. But when you see the miraculous construction of bones on some Black children, back you go to their lost tribe, why? As though their only real parents were free, the lucky ones who never saw a slave-ship?)

Carie Lyn, what will she look like, the young women from Kinshasa, from the Ivory Coast? Will she be short and round, yielding early to fat no matter what spinach her mother feeds her? Or will she have those narrow wire legs that bend and straighten and bend again they are so endless, and her little rear tucked way up tight and sassy? Verne had once told her—her good liberal decent math-teacher husband from Fond du Lac, Wisconsin—that girls who looked like that were all chippies (his word: a little cuter than he meant, but he liked to hide from threats. He must have had one once). Maybe they would meet again in fifteen years and Verne would have to think, Molly has raised this little whore, well, could that really be? Maybe he would reconsider his certainty about narrow long-legged Black girls . . . Maybe, more likely, he would think it made a lot of sense, yes, Molly who had so lustfully prodded him into her bed, guilty of his guilt. But walking on this street among these girls and their noisy boyfriends, she feels neutered, pathetic in their eyes. Not a soul has noticed her but she is holding firm to the slick bar of the carriage, slowed, waiting for them to blow past like a summer shower.

Carie Lyn blinks, her eyes open. They are still looking inward. Gross shadows draw them but not Molly's smile, yet, not the tumult of her people, anyone's people, on Cobden Avenue. The mother who bore her—her other mother? her real? her unreal?—was a few, but not so many, years older than these high school girls. Her father might have been anyone, no record will ever bear his name: he was a magic wand indifferent (presumably) to its power. Would they be angry if they knew their daughter was going to grow up crosstown in a white lady French teacher's house, with soulless food and pottery on the shelves, Mozart on the phonograph? Their daughter? But there is no such person, there is no "they." Her skin is a question of physical substance, pigment, her culture a matter of chance. A baby this new lies in the light of her beholder's eye.

Boring! Boring! She's been through all this a hundred times. Still, when Molly sees two young men making good time down the block towards her, one in a blue dashiki, one in a gorgeous robe that seems to have caught the glow of some sun setting, she tenses, her freckles drowned in a flush. They near her, both have hair that stands out all around electrified, and eyes focused keenly on something. She is knocked down, in her mind, she should be, her baby snatched and carried away under the extravagant robe, and she is left without a word in her mouth. Give our sister a home, a name? What, you still get to own slaves? You get to steal our children, come back to show them off in lace with your name on them?

They had barely talked about any of this when she held her stiff and proper discussions with the agency. So little that was real had dared to sit between them in those social sessions, they had been more like teas with her maiden aunts on their porches in Old Lyme, than legal confrontations. The point was (there might just as well have been a notice on the wall commanding it in the name of the governor) she was to be all petitioning gratitude and maternal anticipation, and they the bountiful horn out of whose miraculous mouth her child was born to her. The Miriam Waddington Home As Cornucopia. Her particular fears did not appear in the pamphlets they were constantly handing her; those dealt with laughably remote questions like "Should we tell our child that he is adopted?" and "How much does resemblance matter—if we are blond, should our child be blond?" To discuss her guilt in the face of men in dashikis would have been to bring a family of slime-green frogs to the conferences and set them free on the interviewer's glass-topped desk. To say, yes, they are right! I know they are! and who, in this fairy tale, would have won this child (f., blk.)?

Molly pushes the carriage up to the wall that stands at the dead-end of Cobden Avenue. Across the street where the bus turns the corner is a bench with an Alpo dogfood sign peeling off its back in great scrolls. She makes for it gratefully, feeling like an armadillo whose armor has been baked and buried in sand. Carefully she brakes the carriage and peeks inside at Carie, who is looking up lazily, back at the edge of sleep. Someone's long lashes she'll have; they are curled so tight they look mascara'd. Molly smiles—because one does? Because babies drink in smiles with their milk and grow on them? Because the smile just comes, she sees the soft curve of chin, the eyelash shadow on her cheeks and wants to smile?

Molly doesn't want anything, only a cold drink and sleep, her tight folded life with no more shame in it but what she cares to admit to herself, however much at a given time, and nothing owing anyone. She, who had come out of the divorce court like a bull into the corrida, energetic, vigorous, newly discovered, unfulfilled survivor of that dreary marriage exempted from the need of a man to make her life around, she sits in a clump on the hot slatted bench thinking, wouldn't Verne laugh? Wouldn't he enjoy the sight of it, my child, nearly my child, here within my grasp finally, why don't I pick her up, paralyzed, do I smile, don't I, if I do why do I, Molly get a doll (is what he said), get yourself a doll with detachable sexual parts for your every mood, and a whole wardrobe of arty clothes you can run up yourself, and spare a real child your grip, because you grasp too tight, lady. No matter how tame your pointy little face and your old dun hair, your fingers on the world are not gentle. You are hungry after starving yourself too many years. Those years weren't my fault, why should I pay you for them? Just because I came too late, don't you bludgeon me. Your shoes wear down in a week, your hair grows fast and crooked, you chew up your pencils like breakfast toast, you go around walloping pillows to get them to sit straight, you swim like a life-guard without stirring up the water but you make waves in the bathtub, you look like a mouse but you are noisy as a cat in bed and make scratches on my shoulders and I. Cannot. Stand. It. You looked to me like an ordinary decent woman like my own sister who was glad to have a man and live out of danger finally. I don't know what you are always nattering about. Molly thinks, crossing her legs, uncrossing them, crossing them again, looking around suddenly as though she has done some unseemly thing (she has never thought this before, not dared out loud). And you could not give me what I wanted. What does quietness have to do with ardor? Some people have to grow up secretly alive . . . You railed at me for every breath I took because you didn't breathe. You could never fill up the empty place in me but . . . dumb blind Verne with your insulted sex, what did it have to do with sex? At the end of a day you've lived together you go to bed together—that seemed plausible. But Verne was made for mounting corpses, he lived his life like a necrophile. Sex is blank, transparent, the sheets are a tabula rasa that you fill with your living. And I am still alive, at least for a while . . .

She stands, looks into the carriage, feeling ruthless anger. From the car-riage hood hangs a narrow gold chain that bounces back and forth like a bell-pull as she lowers her head inside to tuck the pale blanket tighter than it needs to be. She has hung it there herself, a mustard seed like a cat's eye, a slit of deep yellow for luck, her wish for Carie Lyn out of a legend neither black nor white. Once a mother whose child had died went to the wise man weeping and he told her, "Good woman, go knock on the door of every house in the village. And where there has never been calamity in that household, never been the death of a loved one, bring from that fortunate house a mustard seed." When the woman returns to him foot-weary and defeated, overcome with the sorrows of the world, her hands (of course) empty, he tells her that she has proved once and for all that the only wisdom is to live with no love for a human and therefore no fear of pain.

When Molly hung the mustard seed from a tiny red pin stuck in the carriage roof, she had told herself, this is a fool's wish. It is Verne's dead hand, his curse of detachment. He, who else, was the wise man who counseled the noble path that is wide enough for one only; the path he is taking. But this is the mustard seed that comes from the house of joy, she had insisted to herself, frowning to make sure the logic was on her side. This is the impossible prize.

Lifting her head from the carriage the chain tangles in her hair. She has to cross her eyes to work the reddish strands out of the links, finally she tears a few to unhook the charm from her head. She closes the tear-shaped glass bead in her hand and holds it half-protectively, half as if to leech some of its resolution from its small folded core. She is looking idly down the street where dozens of wooden stoops slouch in front of the matched houses. Children dodge up, down, around, dark as tree-bark. Two boys very near her are scrunched down right in the drainage ditch that runs along the street, their feet dug into its swampy canyon sides. They must be playing hide and seek, the IT is counting in a sing-song voice out of nowhere.

The calls blend and separate and blend again, like the sounds of civilization—she will always remember, with her whole body; she tenses right now in a kind of echo of old panic—the time, at nine, when she told her mother she was not staying in the summer cabin, called her a death-dealing tyrant (under her breath), rushed out slamming the screen door, and lost herself, desperately, in the real woods. She had been crying silently for half an hour, her legs scratched and bitten to the knee, cold evening air rising from the ground in waves, no trail, no light of any clearing over the treetops. She still dreaded going home to the quiet that lay like a pale chenille bedspread over the summer, muffling every noise. But she had prayed to her imaginary best friend Veronica, who was half-magic, half-girl, and had never had parents—and had spun around to pick a direction, stopping where she thought she divined a slight pull. Ready, if it didn't lead her anywhere, to lie down and wait to be destroyed. By ants, by bears, by wind or hunger or loneliness, she had brazened through the underbrush quivering for hate and love of the lost world, when she heard voices, this very same rising and falling under the open sky, and one high shout as they finished up the count: "80–90–100-here-I-come-ready-or-not, anyone-around-my-base-is-IT!!!"

She had stood still, at the brink of the woods, staring at them as though she had just stepped out of a spaceship. How they ran and circled, tagging someone OUT. How they touched each other violently, casually, hard.

DECEMBER

(VOL. 35, NO. 2, 1983)

Joyce Carol Oates

....

Driving haphazardly south along the Ocean Highway, Robert would like to tell Naomi about an incident that had taken place in his life approximately twenty years before. But she has asked him not to talk—she wants to concentrate on the view. And twenty years is so very long ago, in fact before her birth, it would probably be an error in strategy to speak of it.

He had been alone at Cape Cod one midsummer day. He had signed on for an eight-hour ocean excursion in a chartered "pleasure" boat, bound for an indefinite point some fifteen miles out in the Atlantic. Whatever abrupt gaiety, or curiosity, or self-conscious loneliness, or simple boredom had attended Robert's uncharacteristic decision, he cannot now recall, no more than he can recall, except by a pitiless effort of will, that young counterpart "Bob Ashby": but he remembers clearly the buoyant shadowless day, the short-crested waves, the flock of noisy gulls that followed the boat, the air of exuberance and adventure that gradually subsided as the boat plowed along. Then, suddenly, they were going through an area of manic turmoil in the water that extended for approximately one mile. Along this broad strip fish were feeding, thousands and millions of fish, savagely feeding, so that the ocean had become a swath of frenzied activity of a kind Robert had never before witnessed.

It was explained to the incredulous passengers that this area was a plankton path or field. Small fish were attracted to it in the millions; and this unusual concentration of small fish naturally attracted larger fish, which preyed on them; and these predators, yet larger fish. The classic food chain, Robert thought, standing at the rail. He was unnerved and a little sickened but he forced himself to observe. (For didn't he conceive of himself as having been placed in the world to be instructed, to uncomplainingly absorb the world's lessons, however disagreeable; didn't he intend to learn as much as he could, if only by way of his own recoiling and disgust?) Here, spread out before him, was a region of unfathomable appetite: foaming, churning, flashing, quicksilver with the eel-like bodies of fishes, a threshing as of sheer boundless energy itself, incalculable. The food chain, Robert thought calmly, giving a name to the spectacle, "classic," he thought, fighting down a sensation of fairness, wonderfully accelerated, abbreviated, as if for his instruction. Convulsive life devouring life. Fish devouring fish. Robert's fellow passengers exclaimed, and took photographs; the "captain" with his bullhorn was professionally hearty; only Robert seems to have been gravely shaken by the sight. Perhaps if it hadn't been so wide a swath, so without visible limits, perhaps if the jaunty white boat hadn't cut right through it . . .

Robert recalls a woman close beside him, at the rail. But he must be mistaken. He hadn't yet married Charlotte, he wasn't yet in love, all that lay before him. There could have been no woman at his side to stroke his arm, to distract him, to soothe and comfort him.

Commiseration is what we require, Robert would like to tell the girl beside him, who has been turned away, staring out the window at the ocean, for the past half-hour. Commiseration, not lust. But the danger is that one will be mistaken for the other.

It's cruel to refer to Naomi as Robert's "teenaged mistress," since she is nearly twenty years old, and she is Robert's "mistress" only intermittently, and unreliably. But Robert doesn't feel that it is a point he can explain to his wife.

Ten days before Christmas Robert takes her on a drive along the New Jersey coast. He cannot determine if the drive is aimless or carefully plotted. He isn't desperate, he doesn't intend to push her, to bring pressure on her. Atlantic City, Ocean City, the toll bridge at Corson's Inlet, Seven Mile Beach, Stone Harbor, Cape May, Cape May Point. . . . He had picked her up in New York City that morning at a brownstone on East Thirteenth. He hadn't been angry with her. He felt no anger at all.

In Cape May they quarrel briefly. Robert would like to check into an inn or a motel, Naomi wants to get to the ocean, to the beach, as quickly as possible. Robert argues that since they intend to stay overnight at the Cape, they should probably take a room now. Naomi says she doesn't give a damn where they stay. It's nearly four o'clock and the sun will be going down soon and she wants to walk. We don't even have an hour, she says. Her voice is husky and calm but Robert knows she is very angry. Her skin is a luminous dead white, her eyes appear to be all pupil. He doesn't dare touch her or even to suggest a drink. He says, Well—we'll have the morning, won't we?—and the next day. We can stay here as long as we want, no one knows where we are.

Oh shit, says Naomi, beginning to laugh. Listen to him. Again.

She zips up her bulky quilted jacket, she pulls her black woolen cap roughly down over her forehead. Robert drives along Beach Avenue past the old Victorian hotels and parks at the deserted snow-swept boardwalk. Folly, he thinks. The sky has acquired an Arctic pallor, the chill merciless sheen of mother-of-pearl; there are massive snow clouds about to eclipse the hazy sun. Folly, he thinks, but he feels strangely invigorated. The wind is from the northeast and the ocean air is damp and fresh and it's a relief to have elicited some emotion, some feeling, from Naomi.

Come *on*, she says, poking him, suddenly playful. We've been trapped in this car for hours.

She is bright, nervous, elated, very beautiful. Suddenly very beautiful. The skin is stretched tight across her sharp cheekbones, her dark eyes are glistening, she's all elbows, knees, long uncoiling legs. Robert thinks of his daughters, his son, when they were small children, but he doesn't think of them for long. Naomi scrambles impatiently out of the car and winds a long beige lambswool scarf about her neck. She puts on red mittens, children's mittens, and slams the car door. In her tight knee-high leather boots she looks like a springy colt about to run wild along the beach. Robert is left behind to lock the car doors.

They hike along the water's edge at the foot of Congress Street. The wind is colder than Robert has anticipated, and razorish, making his eyes water. Naomi exclaims excitedly about the waves, the fresh air, the El Greco sky. She seizes Robert's hand and they stride along swinging their arms, very much like lovers. Robert regrets the fact that the boardwalk and the beach are deserted, except for an elderly gentleman walking his dog some distance away: consequently no one sees them, no one envies these heedless young lovers, taking a romantic December walk in Cape May. Folly, Robert thinks, grinning, squeezing Naomi's hand hard,—fate.

That morning at seven she telephoned him. After twelve days of not having answered his calls. He was lying in bed awake, he was lying in bed thinking of her, of what he might do to her if they were in the bed together, when the telephone rang, and he reached out to answer it. He didn't even think his hand was shaking.

Naomi pulls away from him, trotting so close to the splashing surf that her jeans are dappled with wet. She's a tall girl, as tall as he, maybe even a little taller in those classy yellow boots. If only people would let me alone, Naomi often says bitterly, then I'd be fine. When she says this she might be referring to her problem with drinking, or her problem with drugs, or her problem finding a reliable friend, male or female, whose aim isn't simply to manipulate her. So far as Robert can tell she doesn't refer to her parents, whom he knows. She rarely speaks of them at all and only in the past tense.

Robert lowers his head against the wind and the freezing ocean spray. The air is invigorating, the walk is a superb idea, his pulses too ring with excitement, perhaps he will live forever. At that moment the cloud bank shifts and the sun glares, broken on the waves, eerily beautiful, blinding.

He paws his pockets but doesn't find his sunglasses—they've been left behind in the car.

Come *on*, Naomi shouts. He has rarely seen her so excited.

His breath comes in thin little vaporous clouds, his heels sink through the sand's brittle crust. Cape May in December, an exhilarating northeast wind, icy ribbons underfoot, sharp-eroded little gullies in the sand, seaweed and debris and dead fish battered to anonymity. Bob Ashby, forty-six years old, striding along the Atlantic with his teenaged mistress, wearing his outdoors jacket (the green and black plaid zip-up with the sheepskin lining, which he'd worn while doing chores about the house and lawn) and the funky Irish hat his youngest daughter had given him for Christmas last year. It was shapeless, funny, droll. It had no pretensions. Naomi likes it: she liked hats on men.

Robert catches up with her and slides an arm around her shoulder. He kisses her sportily on the lips but the gesture is forced and ungainly; their teeth strike together; Naomi winces and laughs. Her lips are luxuriantly cold, icy cold, a pleasure against Robert's overheated skin. Hey, he says as she turns away, I love you, but she doesn't hear, the surf is too noisy, the wind blows his words away. The set of his jaw is tense but she doesn't see.

Jesus don't talk about *that*, she once said. He had been hinting lightly that she should move in with him, now that he had leased an apartment.

No one is walking on the beach, no one is on the boardwalk, traffic on Ocean Avenue is light. Robert can see wind-whipped Christmas decorations, mainly tinsel, arcing over the street. He can see the prim elaborate facade of the old Washington Inn, numberless windows, Victorian carpenter's lace and fretwork, white clapboard badly in need of paint. It was one of the famous old Cape May hotels, built in the 1890's, during the short-lived era of the Cape's fashionable notoriety. Horse-racing, gambling, yachting, any number of suspect pleasures. . . . Driving through town Robert said, I thought you'd like Cape May, it isn't only the off-season here but the off-century. Naomi did like it. She had never seen the town before, hadn't even known this part of New Jersey existed. Stately melancholy faintly absurd old houses, inns, converted gambling casinos, all quaint verandas and gingerbread trim and vast porticos. Naomi leaned forward and looked from side to side as if she were memorizing everything she saw. Robert could feel the tension in her slender body: it might have been something she had taken in a restroom (they had stopped once or twice for drinks on the way down), one of the tiny off-white pills that lifted her spirits, or it might have been her genuine excitement about Cape May town: she retained the impulse toward extremes, toward enthusiasm or repugnance, characteristic of young children. Her heartbeat was often rapid for hours at a time, the surface of her skin dryly warm, even burning; she sometimes appeared to be thinking with her entire body, tense, strained, finely trembling. It was Robert's fancy that her temperature was always a few degrees above normal but he had no real basis for saying this.

That's the Chalfonte, one of the famous hotels, Robert said, why don't we get a room there?—unless it's closed for the season.

And then they'd had their little quarrel. But it hadn't lasted long, no more than three or four minutes.

Robert had brought his family to Cape May just once, some years ago. Andrea had been about thirteen then, which meant that Molly would have been ten, Bobbie nine. The children had been disappointed because there wasn't an amusement park, there wasn't an arcade of shops and booths, only one movie house in town, playing Disney's *Aristocats*, which they'd seen before. They had been frightened of the jellyfish washed ashore all along the beach.

(In fact there had been a virtual invasion of jellyfish that August. Stingings were common, Robert himself was probably stung while swimming but he didn't want to make a fuss about it. It was part of the amiable fiction of the Cape that the huge gelatinous creatures with their many tentacles did not exist, or, if they did exist, were not important. What are these ugly things, Robert asked a beach attendant but the man smiled and shook his head and said he didn't know. Are they dangerous, do they sting?—are they poison? Robert asked. The attendant said he didn't know but of course it was best to be cautious and to avoid them.)

Charlotte had certainly been frightened of the jellyfish, but she hadn't complained. She was accommodating, unfailingly amicable, one of the sunny souls of the world, it was impossible not to love her. She never swam in any case. The surf was too cold and too rough. She waded, she splashed with the children, she lay in her one-piece floral swimsuit on a white beach towel "soaking up the sun," reading a magazine, or half-drowsing with a straw hat over her face. She didn't complain about Cape May or about Robert's restlessness though there was an air of reproach in her voice when she said to Robert, Why can't you be happy and relax, we're going to be here for a week. Robert said, as he often did: But we could have been happier somewhere else.

The first time Naomi spent the night with Robert she told him in her droll uninflected voice about certain friends of hers who had "disappeared."

This was in September, before Robert had moved out of his house. There was a boy she'd gone to Europe with junior year in high school, he was a freshman at Columbia when he made plans to hitch-hike to San Francisco, and as far as anyone knew he'd started out . . . but he disappeared en route. His relatives in San Francisco waited for him but he never arrived. His family called the police of course but they never found him and had no "clues to his whereabouts." He just disappeared, Naomi said. For a long while she didn't speak and Robert was so struck by her expression—it was brooding, it was bemused, it was envious—that he couldn't think of a reply.

Then there was a girl in her dormitory at Middlebury, she'd disappeared too, the summer before sophomore year, she had been riding a bicycle along the lake in Evanston, Illinois, where her family lived, and she never returned home. No trace of her either, Naomi said slowly.

Though there was no logical transition it seemed fitting that she tell him about a boy she'd known, in fact she had been living with him for a while after she'd dropped out of Middlebury and came to New York, he did some dealing in drugs, mainly pot but cocaine too when he could get hold of it, and this boy, he'd taken a year off from Columbia where he was studying politics, he lived on Broadway just above the University, this boy made some enemies and it was really a mistake, Naomi said, still in the same subdued uninflected voice, because one time they broke into the apartment and wrecked everything and the next time (this was a few weeks after she'd moved out, it was a scene, she said, she couldn't handle) they killed him. They stabbed him to death, the body was in the apartment for three days in the heat, only because somebody downstairs picked up on the smell were the police called . . . They actually killed him, Naomi said with an air of faint wonderment, picking at her front teeth with a fingernail. It seems funny, I mean . . . when you think of . . . When you think of how . . . Her words trailed off into silence. Robert studied her angular face and saw, with a small prick of despair and elation, how certain frown lines between her marvelous thick eyebrows were already deepening.

Don't make faces like that, he has heard his wife say, to one or another of his daughters.

Robert fell in love with Naomi Merrill, the Merrills' older, "difficult" daughter, two years before, at the Winter Concert given by the high school chorus and orchestra. He and Charlotte had attended the concert with the Merrills, in fact.

Do you remember the Palestrina you sang, Robert has asked Naomi, the "Exultate Deo"?—do you remember the Vivaldi Psalm?

He hadn't fallen in love precisely. During the candlelit procession he had felt, staring at Naomi Merrill's lovely shadowed face and sly winking eyes, a gripping seizure in his chest and belly and groin, an extraordinary sensation that had left him short of breath and disagreeably shaken. It wasn't love. It wasn't even desire.

The candlelit procession was one of the traditions of the Winter Concert, his fifteen-year-old daughter Andrea and her friends talked about it excitedly, two by two they filed from the rear of the auditorium to the stage, the girls in their high-necked ruffled white blouses and long wine-colored velvet skirts, the boys in dark suits and ties. Robert and his wife sat with the Merrills, casual friends of theirs, companionable acquaintances whom they saw several times a year. They had craned their necks waiting for Andrea. She was a plump-cheeked almost pretty girl with brown eyes and honey-brown wavy hair, a manner shyly appealing, like Charlotte's, and Robert was proud of her, and loved her very much, and felt distinctly uneasy that, as the candlelit procession continued, girl after girl and boy after boy, some of the illuminated faces, like that of the Merrills' daughter, possessed of a heart-stopping beauty, he had in a sense forgotten her: her childlike pretty blandness flowed past his rapt gaze, his hungry pulses leapt at other faces, other hooded winking shadowed eyes.

Of course in recent weeks and months he has exaggerated the incident. He has revised it, embellished it. For though Naomi recalls virtually nothing of the music of that evening (she'd been very bad about rehearsals her senior year, she had come close to being expelled from the chorus) she does remember the tremulous candlelit procession. The blurred sea of adult faces, her parents' among them, the Ashbys' among them, turned toward her and the other members of the chorus.

Robert sat with his wife and the Merrills, on the aisle. So that he could see the procession—so that he could see his daughter—close up. The odor of damp wool, damp leather boots, the red splash of poinsettias on the stage, a murmurous approving admiring uncritical audience, parental pride, parental anxiety. In his former life Robert had felt a great deal of anxiety. When the children were young, in particular. He lay sleepless in bed, his mind crackling as if with static electricity, his ghost-self prowling the upstairs, checking one bedroom and then the next, Bobbie's room and then the girls' room, again and again, compulsively, mechanically, checking to see if they were covered, if they were asleep, if they were safe. Only if he were absolutely convinced that they were safe, that they were breathing, did he allow himself to sleep.

I should have been a woman, Robert once said, in a jocular bewildered tone, to a friend of his with whom he played squash in the winter,—so that I could cradle and comfort the kids as much as I'd like. So that I could nurse them, I suppose. Have you ever felt the same way?

Robert does not remember his friend's reply.

Robert has fallen into the habit of catechizing himself, since he spends so much time alone. Is love simple dependency, he wonders. Is it friendship. Is it ravenous, sheer appetite?—that nothing will finally satisfy?

Are you in love with someone else, Charlotte asked him carefully, not long before he moved out of the house. You can tell me if you are. I think we should talk about it, if you are.

But he was too unprepared, too frightened, to tell her. At that time.

My skills at impersonation are breaking down, Robert tells Naomi, who does not grow restless when he drifts into one of his monologues, so long as he doesn't begin to interrogate her, or to speak, however lightly, however casually, of her moving into his apartment. "Making conversation"—"drawing people out"—"passing the time of day": I seem to have lost my ability to do it overnight. It didn't atrophy, the way a skill like playing piano or swimming would atrophy, Robert says, running a hand through his hair, laughing, bewildered, it just disappeared overnight. It died.

He remembers so many amiable postures, so many evidently successful impersonations. It astonishes him that he managed them so adroitly. That he wasn't bitter or cynical. That he didn't wink as he shook hands, or screw up his "handsome" face in a lewd grin.

The friends and acquaintances and business associates who formed a circle of sorts to define him, to contain and control and define him, whispered that he had gone off the deep end, pitied Charlotte and his children, professed to feel concern for him. Of course Bob Ashby isn't the first husband to behave so very strangely at this time of his life and career, but. . . . The embarrassing truth was that he found them boring. Exquisitely boring. The round of dinner parties, the round of cocktail parties, the holiday season, the business luncheons, his wife's family, his own family, the complaints and enthusiasms and gossip and medical surprises, the entire texture of that life, that imposture. I think of it as my own failure, Robert confesses to Naomi,—I mean my failure to continue the impersonation. But it all broke down. It died overnight.

Those things happen, Naomi says.

Two years after the Winter Concert at the high school, when Robert had certainly forgotten his friends' daughter (they chose to say little about her other than the fact that she'd decided to "take some time off" from college, she was living in New York, no she rarely came home to visit), she had approached him in a restaurant on the New York State Thruway. She was with a skeletal pale-haired boy in overalls, both were carrying knapsacks, both were charmingly though a little too defiantly high, their smiles elastic, their eyes childishly bright. Mr. Ashby, is that you Mr. Ashby, d'you remember me, it's Naomi, d'you remember?—Naomi Merrill?—I was a year ahead of your daughter in high school, maybe two years, d'you remember? You and your wife know my parents—

Of course he remembered, after the first shock wave passed.

Naomi lies in his arms and sobs herself to sleep, her knuckles pressed against her mouth. She tells him again about the boy who was killed (not, evidently, the boy she'd been hitch-hiking with—he was just a friend she had met on the Thruway coming down from Canada); she tells him about her dance lessons, her "unreliable" but "very charismatic" dancing instructor, a middle-aged Hungarian woman; she tells him about her "story to herself" about disappearing.

What do you mean? Robert asks.

It's just a story I tell to myself, Naomi says.

What kind of a story?

I tell it to myself, I sort of see it, you know, as if it was a movie, or something on television, Naomi says vaguely. Just that I disappeared. I was gone. And they couldn't find me, there was no trace of me. That kind of thing.

But where did you go? Robert asks. Where do you go?

Oh I don't know, Naomi says, suddenly shy. It's just some crazy sort of . . . I mean it's like a movie or . . . it's a kind of dream I have while I'm awake . . . in bed like this . . . walking along the street . . . I just think of how I have disappeared and nobody can find me and I can't see myself either, there's nothing to see, it's like my place at the table back home was empty but nobody could see that either, it was just empty without . . . without. . . .

But where do you go? Robert asks. What do *you* see?

I'm not there to see anything, Naomi says. That's the point.

Charlotte had a minor accident with the car, the pavement was slick with freezing rain, she'd skidded into the rear of a bus. Of course she was shaken but she wasn't injured. Thank God, Robert thought, she wasn't injured.

He moved out in late November, after Thanksgiving. It wouldn't be fair—in fact it wouldn't be possible—for him to endure another ceremonial holiday. Now he thinks of the Christmas tree in the living room, he thinks of the happy ritual of decorating the tree, year after year, the lovely quaint precious ornaments, Charlotte's mother's, his mother's, glass icicles, fragile rotating snowflakes the size of his fist, strips of golden tinsel, carved wooden animals from Germany, bright-feathered birds from Scandinavia. . . . (But the birds were discovered to have been manufactured in Hong Kong. What a cheat, Bobbie said.)

He moved out to an apartment in a high-rise building near the expressway. A location convenient for commuting to work, convenient for privacy. He was grateful for his wife's dignified restraint and for the tact of her questions. Why do you want to destroy everything? she asked calmly. I'm just trying to understand.

He couldn't speak coherently to her. He couldn't trust himself. What if he confessed that his secret sorrow has been gathered like phlegm at the back of his throat, and he wants only to spit it out in triumph . . . ?

I've been too happy all my life, he tells Naomi. My soul is so shallow, anything can placate it.

She has fallen asleep, she doesn't hear. He wonders if, in her heavy childlike sleep, his figure looms over her, his warm breath commingles with hers.

Naomi has begun collecting things on the beach. What sort of thing?—oh anything that strikes her eye, anything droll or strange or—for instance a piece of driftwood, surprisingly heavy, shaped like a human forearm; and a child's sneaker washed clean and white by the surf; and a pear-sized shell, of the faintest saffron hue, marked with hundreds of tiny stipples in rows like spines. She holds it in her hand, staring. A tense reverent moment. Would you like me to carry those things for you? Robert asks. I think we should be heading back to the car. . . .

It is after four-thirty and the sun is slanting toward the horizon. The Atlantic wind has become increasingly cold but Naomi doesn't seem to notice. She hands her worthless little treasures to Robert and turns away to find more. There is something antic, coltish, too willful about her behavior but Robert supposes it is genuine. She impersonates no one, she hasn't the skill.

They have hiked a mile or more beyond Congress Street and the old Washington Hotel. At this end the beach is rougher and shabbier, the sand is eroded into curious little ditches, there is broken glass underfoot, the mummified remains of dead fish. They are beyond the boardwalk but a flight of wooden steps leads to the crest of a weedy hill, about twelve feet high.

A wet pungent odor of rot, released underfoot, makes Robert think of the plankton field off Cape Cod. That frenzied feeding, the savagery of appetite, eel-like silvery flashes of fish, the water foaming, churning, children on board the ship shouting in excitement. Is it sharks?—is it sharks?

Naomi? he says. Shall we head back?

She doesn't hear. She is trotting off in search of new treasure, her breath steamy. Robert thinks ahead to the evening—to the night—a room in one of the handsome old Victorian inns—utter privacy, secrecy. Why do you want to destroy everything, Charlotte asked. Naomi's long nervous legs, her slender body, the thrust of her pelvic bones, her eyes rolling back in her head in passion or the mocking pretense of passion. . . . Once, irritated, impatient, he had grabbed her hard around the hips and she'd snorted with surprised laughter, tearing at his hair, clawing his cheeks, puppyish, playing rough, her gums bared. She'd been high then, flying high, her skin was dry and burning to the touch, an artery pulsed in her throat.

Robert tells Naomi not to climb those stairs: the wood looks rotted.

Naomi ignores him because she has glimpsed something in the weeds overhead—it looks like a broken doll.

She climbs monkey-quick up the precarious steps and grabs the doll in triumph. Robert stares at her, his heart pounding. If she should fall, if she should injure herself . . . The thought comes unbidden, piercing him to the heart: he must have exclaimed because Naomi turns look at him over her shoulder.

I got it, look, she cries, waving a bit of rubbish in the air. It appears to be a raggedy ann doll, badly worn.

She climbs clumsily down and the structure begins to wobble, and when she's three or four feet from the bottom a step gives way, and collapses beneath her booted foot. She falls, crashing heavily down, grunting, dropping the doll. She can't have hurt herself, Robert thinks, stooping to help her up. She is dead weight at first, whimpering, tears running down her cheeks. Has she twisted her ankle against the rocky sand, has she sprained something? She staggers and leans heavily against him. Why the hell didn't you listen to me, Robert says, suddenly furious.

In room 15 of the Cape Motor Inn Naomi is sleeping, her cheek pressed against the ridged chenille bedspread in such a way that there will be deep creases in her skin when she awakes. She didn't trouble to undress, only tugged off her boots. There are mauve half-circles beneath her eyes, a tiny thread of saliva runs from her mouth, Robert stands over her and observes, scarcely daring to breathe. She hadn't sprained her ankle but the pain had been considerable and she'd cried herself to sleep, in her slow stubborn uninflected way. I love you, Robert says softly, I'll protect you, I will never harm you. . . .

It is all very simple. Why hadn't he understood, all his life, that love was so simple? If only she wouldn't disobey him.

Naomi sleeps the exhausted, twitchy sleep of a young child. Her breath is wet and rasping and irregular. Robert finishes the drink he has brought back to the room from the motel lounge—it's a noisy, casual place, unpretentious, no eyebrows raised, no quirky stares—and stealthily removes his shoes, watching the sleeping girl all the while, thinking, If only, like this, forever, like this. Carefully, cautiously, in luxuriant fear of disturbing her, he stretches out on the bed beside her, eases an arm across her thin chest, presses his warm face against the nape of her neck. Like this. O yes. Only this. Forever.

IRREVOCABLE ACTS

(VOL. 42, NO. 1, 1989)

Rilla Askew

....

Selena Sikes Willaman had held all her life an abiding horror of irrevocable acts. This fear of taking any step in the world that could not be turned back upon had kept her a virgin until well past her twentieth birthday and unmarried until she'd almost reached thirty. It had kept her from ever finally making up her mind to have children (because what if you had one and it turned out to be horrid?) and prevented her from her one great dream of seeing Europe (because—oh, this was the stuff her nightmares were made of—what if you got over to Italy and a war started or something and you could never, ever get back?). Her fear kept her from moving away from the tiny town of Cedar and getting the education she wanted and doing the things in the world she knew she could do.

She, of course, was the only one who knew she was crippled because the people of Cedar (as she so often had to tell herself) had no ambitions of the mind or the heart. They thought Selena was perfectly successful because her team of eighth graders won second in the state-wide debate contest three years in a row. They thought that because she sang in the church choir and taught Sunday School and had managed to stay slim when every other woman in the town had gone to fat, she'd reached the pinnacle of achievement. But Selena knew the secrets of her own heart and knew how little, really, she'd ever done in her life because of fear that it could never be undone once it had got started. So when she ran off to New Orleans with the new young Baptist preacher, abandoning in the process his young wife and her old husband and six children between them, no one was more surprised than Selena herself.

Three of the six children, to tell the truth, were John Willaman's grown kids by his first wife (two of whom already had children themselves), but Selena had to include them when she was reading off her list of sins to herself. She did read that list, over and over, as she and the preacher drove south through East Texas in perfect silence. Oddly enough, adultery was way down at the bottom and seemed to her to be one of her lesser transgressions. The sex between them had been so inevitable, so involuntary and necessary, like breathing, that she couldn't somehow find the proper shame to attach to it. But lying to everyone and sneaking around, abandoning John

Willaman, who had always been good to her, and his three grown children, forcing the preacher to abandon his little dopehead of a wife and their three toddlers, all of these things she believed she could feel ashamed of. She added the bad example she was setting for her eighth graders to the list, and the fact she was shaming John in his own town. Sometimes she included for good measure—though she knew it had never been listed as a sin in the Bible—the shock she'd be delivering to all the ladies of her Sunday School class when they found out, and tacked onto that sin the dubious trespass of causing those same ladies to commit the sins of gossip and wrath and, quite possibly, envy.

Selena mulled over her list in the silence. She tried to acknowledge the depth of her iniquity. She felt she ought to own all the proper amounts of shame attached to it and her due portion of guilt like a dull sickness in her chest. But, though she did manage at times to conjure up shame, felt it fiery in her cheeks and along her breastbone so that she knew she was not without conscience, Selena could not seem to drag up repentance and, try as she might, she could not find remorse.

Outside the window, great stern trees stood draped and bearded in moss on either side of the road, their trunks black and separate, knee-deep in water, and their boughs tangled together in the gray blur overhead. A thin fog clouded the far end of the highway so that they seemed to be always driving into nothingness and yet never reaching there.

But when she looked over at Brother Stephen's pale face, fine-boned, slightly frowning, she remembered the reason for her to be there driving in a car hundreds of miles away from Cedar in a strange part of the country she'd never heard of before. He would turn toward her from time to time and smile or reach across the seat to touch her hand. Then Selena would take the heat of him in through the skin of her fingers, and the small flickers of shame in her chest would turn to wanting. It seemed, in those moments, that all perception of the world came to her only through the dry, slight touch of his fingertips. His hands were long, pale as glass, and soft, as a preacher's hands should be soft, not like any man's hands that had ever touched her before. The hands, she thought, it was always those hands. And she would sit for a long time breathing the world in through the skin of her fingers.

Then Brother Stephen would pull his hand away to put it back on the steering wheel, and Selena would be left with the open ache of wanting, helpless and unsatisfied, so that finally she'd turn toward the window again and begin her silent litany of sins. She gave herself up to the little hidden surprise, the concealed pleasure, that she had actually done such a thing, and sometimes she mused (though not very seriously, and these were the only times she came close to her usual habits of thought) on the possibility of there ever having been a moment when she could have turned away and not done what she had done.

She thought of the first time his eyes paused on her face (stopped, and stood still for just the space of a breath, looked long and deep and secret into her eyes) as he paced in the pulpit delivering his sermon on a Sunday morning. She wondered lightly if that might have been the moment when she could have turned aside. But she could not take her eyes away from him. It was never possible for her not to look back. She knew that. She thought of the moment, standing near him in the church office with the amber autumn light falling across the floor from the high window and the Sunday morning bulletins flap-flap-flapping on the mimeograph machine, when she first saw the softness of the skin on his neck, saw the small intricacies of his tiny, perfectly formed ears, and felt her lips, the tips of her fingers aching to touch him. She knew that by then, long before the cold evening in the car on the way home from prayer meeting when she reached up with her fingers to touch his cheek, it was already too late.

When was it? she thought, joking with herself, because she knew there had never been a moment of turning back. The first time I laid eyes on him, she said, and thought of him standing in front of the altar with his little blonde washed-out wife and their blonde fidgety toddlers to be introduced to the church, and Brother Stephen with his impossibly black hair and his eyes burning in that white face, so long-legged and gangly and awkwardly graceful in his perfect blue suit. And Selena, knowing that even in that moment, before she ever knew a thing about herself or how the touch of him or the look of him would come to force such hot, unanswerable yearning inside her, even then it was too late, smiled to herself and turned to look at him.

His face was outlined against the gray of the whirling-past countryside, high-bridged nose standing out strong and elegant in relief, slick strands of black hair dipping over his forehead. The white of his skin looked like wax in the wintry light. It had always amazed her, his skin, the way it could look so cool and dry and fine, and then turn to fire under her lips. No, it wasn't his hands, she thought, it was that skin. Nothing that white should have so much fire inside it. She reached up with the backs of her fingers to brush against his cheekbone. He smiled, his eyes on the road. Look at me, she thought, turn and look at me.

But the preacher kept his eyes on the highway, and Selena, retreating from the ache of unanswered wanting, turned once again inward. They drove for hours in silence that way, with Selena counting up her sins and the young preacher thinking whatever mute thoughts he was thinking and the misty East Texas winter rushing past them in judgment.

In the thickening gray that signaled the approach of evening, they stopped for dinner at the Pizza Hut outside Jasper, Texas. The young woman who waited on them there had recently had her left hand cut off—the stump was still swathed in bandages—and somehow the sight of that irrevocably removed hand (or, more accurately, the lack of the sight of it) brought all of Selena's old terrors thrashing to the fore.

She smiled a great deal, at the waitress, at Brother Stephen, and tried very hard not to look at the stump, but inside her chest, her heart seemed to have given up beating.

"Y'all want Thin'n'Crispy or Deep Dish on that?" the waitress said, and smiled down at Selena, whose own smile was frozen like a wasteland across her face. Selena turned her frozen smile on Brother Stephen and nodded for him to answer. It mattered not at all to her, she wasn't going to be able to swallow a bite in the first place.

The waitress marked the slot on her pad for Thin'n'Crispy. She was really very good. She balanced a tray upon the stump and kept it from wobbling by the judicious pressure of her breasts. Her order pad was on the tray and she used a little stub of a pencil to mark down the order. When she'd finished, she poked the pencil behind her ear, clapped the tray against her chest with the stump, and smiled down at them. "Y'all can help yourself to the salad bar," she said, and walked off.

Brother Stephen got up to attend to the salad bar, and Selena sat in the booth and stared at the waitress as she read the order off to the boy ladling sauce onto pizzas in the back. She's so young, Selena kept saying to herself, she's so young for that to have happened. But Selena knew it wasn't just the girl's age that wrenched her stomach and squeezed shut her heart; it was the fact it had happened recently. The bandages, so clean and white and gauzy, propped under the tray, sickened Selena in a way that a naked, healed, flesh-colored stump never could have. To think, Selena said to herself, that no more than a few weeks ago that girl had a hand. She had one, like anybody has one, and then, suddenly, she didn't. How was that possible? How could you have one, and then not have one? How could you wake up in the hospital without it and know in one horrifying heartbeat that you'd never, ever have one again?

A slight moan slipped through Selena's closed lips.

The waitress came toward her with two cups of coffee and two glasses of water balanced on the tray. When she reached the table, she held the tray steady with her breasts while she lifted the cups and glasses. Selena smiled at her again, and turned to look out the window at the parking lot.

The preacher came back and slid into the booth opposite her and ate his salad. After awhile their Thin'n'Crispy Super Supreme came and he ate that too while Selena stirred her black coffee and stared at the dull cement and faded white lines in the parking lot. Once, she looked up and found his dark depthless eyes burning into her, and Selena felt her mind go blank and cold in some kind of startled confusion, but then he flashed his eyes and his old boyish grin at her, taking her with him in the old helpless way, and said, "You feeling all right, Selena?" Selena nodded and said she was fine, just not very hungry, and pulled a slice of pizza onto her plate in order to please him.

They never mentioned the girl's missing hand, never acknowledged the fact of it with their eyes, not even when she came to remove their half-eaten pizza and the tray slipped off her stump and clattered onto the table scattering crusts and black olives all over. She filled up their coffee cups, shy and embarrassed, and smiled awkwardly when she slid the check onto the table. "Thanks a lot," she said, "y'all come back." She moved up to the front where Selena watched her talking softly with the boy behind the counter. How could you ever talk to anyone again? How could you ever do anything again except sit and stare at the walls in stark holy terror? A cold wash of revulsion and fear slid over Selena and she smiled over at the preacher and said, "You about ready?"

The preacher's young face seemed to be getting younger and more bewildered by the minute. He nodded and reached across the table for her hand, but Selena slid it from beneath his and reached for her purse.

As they drove east toward New Orleans, Selena felt herself wrapped around in darkness. The wipers smeared road film in a great oily streak over the windshield, blurred the oncoming headlights and distorted the blackness, so that only the inside of the car seemed to be moving through space.

"I should've thought to change yours and mine both," Brother Stephen said. Selena looked over. The glow from the green panel lights alternated with the slow sweep of headlights on his face.

"I don't know how come me not to think of that." His voice barely rose above the sound of the engine, the wet rush of tires.

Selena was silent. There seemed to be something she'd forgotten, but she couldn't focus her mind on what it was. She only felt the steady thrum of the motor driving them onward and the gaping sense of wet, empty night all around her.

"Them blades," the preacher said, "I should've thought to do that," and his voice was hurt, insistent.

"Yes," Selena said.

His fingers touched the back of her neck, brushed her skin softly, a slow gentle circle sliding up under her hair.

"Yes," she said again, and felt the warmth of him drawing her, pulling at her from out of the darkness. When she looked up, she believed she could see the city of New Orleans ahead of them, though she knew they were still hundreds of miles away. She thought she could see the soft, pulsing glow of it on the horizon, drawing her to itself. The pull of the city and the warm, secret pull of the preacher sitting next to her in the car seemed to be two halves of the same power, sweet and dark and compelling, drawing her down. She thought she could drown in it, melt into it, lose her soul and herself into it forever. She did not struggle.

When he turned off the highway onto a soft, marshy side road and switched off the motor, Selena only sat waiting. And when he reached over and pulled her towards him, she went to him with no bones in her body, nothing firm to resist him but only the soft yielding of her being, folding into him. She touched him, trembling, cherishing his skin, the touch of it on her lips, the taste of it on her tongue. She ran her tongue over his nipples, tiny and pink and hard, like a child's, and felt him shudder beneath her. This, she said, just this, just this, and her mind would not think.

But when, in the damp gray light of dawn, they pulled into the motel parking lot and she saw the whorish florescent lights flashing pink and green along the motel roof, and later, when they stood in the shabby yellow room and she saw the knife holes, hundreds of harsh, thin slits stabbed helter-skelter into the peeling yellow pasteboard over the bed, the surprise and the horror came on Selena, and she knew she had committed an irrevocable act.

The knife holes were, she thought, the element that broke her, broke into her and made her pull back and recognize her madness. It had all been madness, of course, extreme and insane and inescapable, like a spell laid upon her, and now there was never, not ever, any turning back. The narrow slits kept drawing her eyes, seemed to glare, slant-eyed, at her from over the bed. They looked as if someone had played mumblety-peg against the wall, and there was such a corruption about the thoughtless way they were stabbed there, such a total disregard for property or sense or order, that Selena thought they exactly stood for the tawdriness of the room and the corruption of the gray sleeping city all around her. She hated them. She could not look at them without thinking about that knife flying across the room, stabbing into the wall, vibrating there. And the same hand (whose hand had it been?—what bored or menacing or insane man had stabbed that wall so many times?) pulling the knife from the wall, over and over again, only to let it fly and stick and vibrate once more. The cold metal glint of the knife in her mind's eye was equal to the cold metal slicing machine that had taken the waitress's hand (and it did not matter that she didn't know in reality what had happened to the girl's hand: it surely had been robbed of her by something metallic and glistening and sharp).

Selena could not sit down in the room, could not bring herself to touch the sheets or the ancient bathroom fixtures. She felt Brother Stephen's eyes following her as she paced back and forth, into the bathroom, out of the bathroom, to the ugly door with its peeling list of rules and its dead-bolt, around the sagging bed to the far back wall and the high window blocked up with an air conditioner, back to the bathroom and out again. If she stopped for a moment, she felt the germs in the room—other people's germs, how many hundreds of other people's germs—would swarm her, crawl onto her skin and seep into her pores.

Selena's fears had caught up to her. She did not know what she was doing in a cheap motel room hundreds of miles from Cedar with a stranger, some strange unknown black-eyed stranger. Brother Stephen reached for her as she raced past him, caught her and pulled her to him, held her tight against his chest, and she felt his heart racing against her breastbone, pounding against her, an insane, quick, tormented rhythm. He took hold of her shoulders then and pushed her away from him, held her there. Selena looked up at him out of a blankness. The flashing lights outside the window gave the only color to the gray light in the room. They played over the preacher's face, lit up his pale skin in alternating pink and green washes, buried his eyes deep in shadow.

"Selena—" he said, and then let go of her shoulders and stepped back away from her. Selena saw him for a moment, almost a boy, confused and unsure, waiting for something from her. And then the veil fell again, and Selena thought only of the fact that she had never once called him by name.

Late in the night her husband came to her in a dream and stood around in the motel parking lot, waiting for her. Selena rose from the harsh damp sheets and went to the window. The parking lot was slick and black with rain, and

John Willaman was not there. But still she felt him, and she went into the bathroom and turned on the water in the shower stall and stood in it, smelling the rust and the mildew, wanting the water, desiring it, while it gushed from the ugly shower head, pouring down, pounding down, hot and furious on her neck.

The heat of the water could not burn the image of her husband from behind her eyes. She saw his clumsy work boots shuffling on the asphalt, his shaggy big head tipped forward, bewildered, asking. She pressed her fingers against her breastbone, whispered a furious, silent no into the pounding wetness. She turned her face north and west, and saw the long black empty miles between her and Cedar. Her house, low-slung brick ranch house, sprawled low on the earth outside of town. The highway unraveled backwards, blue-black and empty, and she saw herself and the preacher in the gray, sinking place at the end of the land mass. The end of the earth, sinking into the sea.

"And I did this," she said out loud in the shower stall. She saw every moment that could have been different, every look, every touch, that could have been left undone. She knew then how the girl at the Pizza Hut lived over in her mind, every morning, every evening, those minutes before the accident, the whole day before the accident, her whole life leading up to that irretrievable second, examined every action and said to herself if only, if only . . .

Selena stood in the water and watched herself sitting in her pew on a bright Sunday morning, saw herself staring back at the preacher as he paced in the pulpit. She watched her cold fingers in the dark car reaching up for his cheek. She saw her husband hunched against the rain outside the motel room, shuffling his work boots on the slick parking lot. She would not say if only. "Madness," she said. But the word was not good enough. Of course it was madness, crazed, hungry, insatiable madness, but she could have turned aside from it if only she'd wanted. "I never wanted," she said, and took the full grief and loathing into herself with the words.

The water in the shower turned lukewarm. And then bone-chilling, rushing, ice-water cold. Still, she stood there. Her limbs went numb and dead with the coldness. She thought of Salvation, and Redemption. She knew they were just words and had never been real, and she hated that she had ever been taught them. Because no step in the world could be turned back upon. No step and no non-step ever allowed for turning back. John Willaman sank away into the glistening asphalt, and Selena reached up with her deadened fingers to turn off the water.

Selena stepped out of the bathroom, naked and wet and shaking, her mouth shuddering, shoulders trembling, thighs and breasts and arms trembling. The preacher stood in the middle of the room. His narrow chest looked ghostly, sunken, in the streaming light from the bathroom. He balanced himself awkwardly, his long legs shy and dancing, as if he were ashamed of his nakedness. But when Selena looked at him she saw him wanting her, straining toward her.

She went to him, hating him, hungering after him, and let him wrap his long burning arms around her and pull her down into the warmth and the sweet darkness.

DROUGHT WEATHER

(VOL. 60, NO. 2, 2010)

Lucas Church

....

Back to repay a loan with some hard labor, Zeke rolled up to the dark house of his childhood, slightly hungover. His father was gone, chasing tail at an Indian sweat lodge near Myrtle Beach. But this was the place: key under the mat, brushes and paint under the carport, and definitely no hot coffee. Breakfast was a half-full pack of sunflower seeds fished out of the glove box. Removing the meat from the shell with a quick crunch and swish of the tongue, he glanced around at what was left of the old neighborhood. Trailers languished with loose shutters hanging like baby teeth and kiddie pools melted in the dirt. Broadway Lake was just past the thicket of old fishing cabins.

Zeke got out of the pickup and rubbed his eyes. He was long and brown like a cattail, his hair a dark rust color, kept short. "Nothing left to do but push paint," he said to himself. He'd spent the last few years on paint crews, which gave him some of the freedoms he'd always associated with college kids. After getting caught in the act with a sophomore while on the job— the job was just a touch-up and the girl a brunette who turned out to be the lieutenant governor's daughter—he'd learned to fly under the radar of any authority figure that might be paying attention. He was equally adept at the opening seduction: a smile, a well-timed joke, and a few judicious glances designed to pique a girl's interest.

Painting shitty apartment complexes in St. Pete, Gainesville, and Tallahassee gave him an appreciation for the uniform transformation of one thing to another. A beige or dull gray replaced bare wood and changed the character of a building; what was once naked and imperfect became solid and respectable. It was this simple act that gave him great satisfaction, if only for his belief that the same could hold true for men.

A few hours into the first coat of primer, the dog showed up. It walked in the open screen door, its hide of possum-colored salt and pepper, the muzzle white with patches of dark fur around half-closed eyes. Zeke stopped and stretched to free his shirt from clinging to his sweaty back.

"Dog, take it from me," Zeke said as he made his way down the ladder, "this ain't a place to get comfortable." The dog cocked its head and pricked its ears as he spoke. Zeke growled, bared his teeth and let out a few cartoonish barks. It craned its neck as if its hindquarters were rooted to the floor. Zeke gave up and, sighing, let the dog sniff his hand, touching its rough nose. Within a few seconds the dog lost interest and lay yawning on the cool kitchen floor. The dog was a girl. Her breath slowed at his feet. Her skin was stretched thin over her ribs, her chest rising and falling in the steady rhythm of deep and earned sleep.

"Now, I got work to do," he said.

He bent over to push her awake. He felt a lump and parted the short hairs and found ticks fat with blood, abdomens pearly gray and distended to nearly the size of fingernails, clinging to the belly, back and inside the ears. Lifting up her tail she whimpered when he saw a cluster of bloodsuckers around her backside. Jesus Christ, he thought, tossing his brush into a tray of half-dried paint. He scooped her up in his arms.

In the bathroom he nudged the bathtub faucet with his boot. Exhausted, she did not fight the water. Careful and exacting, he snared them, twisting their heads with tweezers like turning a key in a lock. When she was clean and out of the water, he watched the dozens of tiny swimmers clog the drain. He decided to call the dog Bug. He swaddled her in towels on the couch and let her sleep while he went to town to buy food.

Back from town with Bug's food in hand Zeke saw the neighbor for the first time, walking to fetch the mail. She seemed to push through the heavy and humid air with purpose. Their eyes met briefly and he couldn't tell if she smiled or not. The days were so hot that almost nobody came outside. Before he saw her the only hint of life was a car next door roaring to life at 6 a.m. It was as if people had turned to dust.

He hadn't seen Bug since the first meal of kibble. At night, while staring at the water-stained ceiling, he heard howling and something crashing through the dried leaves of the forest. Then, as the neighbor woman stepped inside her house, Bug showed up wagging her tail and pawing at his screen door.

The dog bowed her head and picked up something dark and leathery in her mouth. Dancing and bright-eyed, she seemed to grin as Zeke pulled at the thing, starting a tug-of-war, and it immediately broke in two. It was a toad, long dead and dried out. It smelled musty and rich, like the mud around the lake. Its body flattened, the eyes gone. Mildly disgusted, he flung it to the woods and watched her bolt for the corpse. He followed her zigzag between the trees and noticed a little blonde boy playing alone next door. The child seemed to know Bug and called to her as he jumped excitedly. He looked young, maybe eight or nine.

Later, when Zeke was finishing up the kitchen trim in the morning heat, he heard an excited crashing through the brush. He turned to see Bug tearing towards him, her head covered in trash: coffee grounds, sinewy plastic wrap and bits of eggshell. A stench like rotten fish made him gag from yards away.

"Dog, what the hell—"

He heard cursing. "Shit!" She came around the corner of the house in a baggy t-shirt and worn jeans with holes at the knees. Her face was red.

"Is Rick here?" she barked, hovering in the doorway and looking at the mess of tarps and paint trays.

"Gone on vacation."

"Your dog—"

"My dog?" he interrupted. "Wandered up here looking for a handout." Bug sat between them, tail wagging. Up close Zeke could see the woman was older, maybe late thirties. Her skin creased around her downturned mouth.

"If you're feeding him he's your dog. Keep him out of my garbage."

"She's a girl."

"I don't care if—"

"Is that your kid?" he asked. The child was half hidden behind her. "Saw him outside this morning. Seemed to be having a good time with the dog." She put her arm around the boy. "Keep it tied up," she said. "I don't want to clean up after two children." She left with the same determination he'd seen earlier, dragging the little boy back home.

The next day he was determined to talk to her. He took a bouquet of cheap carnations he'd picked up at Bi-Lo.

"Look," he said when she opened the door. "I came off terrible yesterday. The kid seems to like playing with the critter." He presented her with the flowers and she crossed her arms.

"Don't ruin that because of me. Besides, ain't any other kids around here. Place ain't changed since I was little." Sighing, she took the bouquet and invited him in for an iced tea with a cool expression of forced gentility.

They talked. Slow at first, but then they found common ground: family— her father was from Deland, his from East Palatka—and her recent move to the area. She mentioned her husband's construction job on the big jailhouse project past the city limits.

"Guess that's why he's always gone," Zeke said between sips of iced tea.

"You should see it," she said, fingering the gold cross around her neck. "It's going to be real big."

"Hope they got my room ready," he smiled and cocked his eyebrows, "I'm liable to miss a parole hearing talking to you." She rolled her eyes, but smiled.

"I think Eli needs a nap," she said, getting up. Outside the front picture window of the A-frame house Eli and Bug played.

"Looks pretty happy right now," he said. "Besides, you ain't told me how you ended up in this backwater." She gave a tired smile and rubbed her wrists.

He would have denied it, but every day Zeke waited for her husband to go to work like it was Christmas morning. By the following week, lunch in her kitchen had become a regular thing, and he quickly found pleasure in trying to shock her with his sordid past.

"There was this one who always said she'd do anything I wanted her to," he said. She leaned in to listen while finishing up the dishes. He spun his empty beer bottle on the counter like in the kissing game.

"She spent a lot of time on the beach. She was dark, greasy. Smelled like piña coladas. I think she had some Mexican in her, maybe Cuban. Kept her hair pulled back in a ponytail."

"What'd you make this poor girl do?"

"She drove me crazy," he continued. "I remember the way her ponytail would bob up and down when she'd—"

"Stop!" she said, playfully hitting his arm and letting her touch linger a second too long. She seemed to like his stories. He sat back and took a sip of iced tea, tasted the watered-down sweet, and felt more comfortable than he had in a long while. It was during the afternoons, during Eli's nap, that they began to explore the air between them. Their movements became one—studied, hushed calculations as if they both quietly knew of the experiment. He would say how pretty her hair was; she'd laugh and make him feel like a man.

Friday morning the winds picked up, violent with the promise of a summer storm. She was at the kitchen counter painting her nails a sickly purple, the color of day-old bruises.

"Paper said it's gonna rain," she said, not looking up from her outstretched fingers.

"Well, we need it," he said. "Bad." He grazed her leg with his foot and grinned. She looked at the clock, shaking her hands to dry the paint.

She took his hand. The unexpected darkness through the upstairs window stopped them. Back to the bedroom door they watched the sky's plum colors change to pencil lead gray. Zeke felt his calluses against her soft skin and heard the oak's branches brushing against the house.

She made him look away while she undressed, but, in spite of the dimmed light, he could see nearly all of her. She had been made soft from motherhood: belly scored by stretch marks, breasts resting against the fleshy crevices of her arms, full hips and pale thighs pebbled with skin that quivered when she lifted her legs. The folds and blotches spoke to him in a muddled language of something he didn't understand. She paused, as if savoring the sight of him taking her in. He felt the comic book outlaw, the scarred child, all the characters he'd played for her dissipating, blowing through the tract houses and bait shops that surrounded them. She took him in her arms and guided his body, slowly and quietly, so to not wake the sleeping boy downstairs. The air was faint with the scent of lake mud.

"Shit, shit," she said when they both heard the car door slam. She pulled off of him, and, as she struggled to pull her clothes, Zeke tried to memorize her, the darkness of her crotch, the scatter of freckles under her pubic hair, knowing that this would be the last time. She closed her eyes. They both heard the front door open.

"Hide," she whispered. She pushed him into the closet. By the time he realized what was happening she was running downstairs, undoubtedly with a smile on her face.

With nothing to do in the closet, he fantasized of moving in, replacing the man downstairs. Love and affection, sex and fresh sweet cornbread would be lavished upon him; he could taste it all until her voice pulled him out of the daydream, the husband's voice, hers again, the words made indistinct. The funk of cheap beer lingered in his mouth and he panicked. Alcohol mixed with her smell and sweat and her husband would know, surely he would piece it all together. Zeke crouched, covered in sweat, and wondered how to get out of this. He held his breath over and over again until his head swam and his eyes pounded. The smell of mud grew stronger. The heat in the closet was unbearable. What light he could see was being swallowed by the gathering storm, waiting to upend itself onto the parched earth below.

"Oh God," he whispered. His hands felt hot and burned as if over ashy coals, drying out the skin and deepening the text of his palms. His mother had taught him to divine his future the way some taught their children shoe-tying: the simian crease, the life line and the Girdle of Venus. The sky was buckling when Zeke felt a presence, heard the wet smack of lips and then a whisper, a dry sound like leaves skittering over asphalt. A small hand touched him, left fetid mud on his arm and rattled his sunburned heart awake. Zeke turned and saw Eli's blue eyes in the dim light.

As he pitched open the closet doors, the room filled with a burst of white and an immense clap shook the house. Grabbing his clothes he tore open the window, jumping raw into the air. He landed with the first wave of rain, two stories down without closing his eyes. He crashed into the bushes and slammed his forehead against the hard earth. Pain blossomed through his skull, noise of wind and thunder dimmed and he could, for the briefest of moments, feel each drop of rain splash against his bare back. He tried to get up, cradling his clothes like a newborn, but collapsed. His ankle had twisted and his breath came quicker and quicker as he started to panic, desperate to get out of sight.

Crawling through the backyard on his elbows and knees, the rain shuddered down splashing mud into his face and eyes. His body scraped over the broken branches that lay scattered in the yard like bones. The soft itch of unconsciousness began in his heels and moved through his blood and up to the back of his eyes. As he crawled onto the patio, he remembered the summer—was it the same summer his mother left? or when he dropped out senior year and ditched town, leaving nothing, not even a note?—he had helped his dad pour the concrete, leveling it out with a trowel and waiting for it to dry for hours until it had set, liquid rock made solid again. He passed out just as his hand touched the wet slab.

The next morning his body ached, but Zeke got up and perched at the window, waiting until he caught sight of the boy, the little boy who knew too much. An old cane he found in the closet made walking easier. It was his grandfather's, made of a caramel-colored wood that was embarrassingly ornate.

He'd memorized their routine: breakfast, clean up, cartoons, followed by soap operas, and finally "outside time." Zeke's absence made no break in the schedule, and Eli eventually came bounding out the door in corduroy overalls. Zeke made his way outside and crept up to the boy, who was crouched and lost in something Zeke could not see until he was standing over the boy. A toad covered in sand was struggling under the boy's thumb. Eli watched it squirm, putting more pressure until the guts balled up under the jawbone. Its fingers slowed their frantic clawing and soon stopped moving altogether. Before Eli could react, Zeke had him pinned to the ground with all his weight on his good side. He shifted and trapped the boy's kicking foot under his own.

"You can't tell nobody," Eli said. "You don't belong here."

"Listen to me," Zeke said. His stomach soured. What did I think this would do? What if she saw him attacking her own son? The leaves above them had curled from the long dry summer, and the sun peeked through between their movements.

"If my daddy finds out about you," Eli said, struggling to break free, "you're going to be sorry." His nose was running even though he was not crying and snot was caked in dust. Zeke was going to plead his case, beg the boy not to tell and promise ice cream, bicycles, whatever it took to let Zeke have her and then the snap of a twig, the shock of teeth sinking into his arm interrupted him. He lost his balance, tumbling over Eli onto the ground. Bug was dragging him off Eli with Zeke's whole elbow in her mouth.

"No, girl—" Zeke started, his face pressed into the dirt. The dog snapped her head violently back and forth, tearing at the ligaments and tendons in his elbow.

"Get him Patches!" Eli screamed with joy in his voice. "Get him good!"

"Patches?" Zeke struggled to focus. He could not find the cane with his good arm and was groping the earth while the dog chewed and growled. He found a fallen branch from the storm and swatted at the dog, driving her away. The yard was quiet except for the squirrels' high-pitched chatter from above. Zeke heard them dance from limb to limb in the trees. Bug bared her teeth and let out a low growl, hackles raised, and stood firm between them. Zeke saw his cane next to the dead toad and, without taking his eyes off of the dog or the boy, bent down and picked it up. Eli's face was covered in dirt. Cradling his elbow, Zeke backed away until he reached his father's yard and got inside as quickly as he could.

Sunday he awoke, found his father's robe and took stock of the paintjob he hadn't finished. Pots caught the drips and the smell of wet began to settle over the place, making carpet feel oily between his toes. Cane in right hand, left arm crooked like an arrowhead, he shuffled around the inside, pulling up tape from the walls, tossing old brushes and paint stirrers onto the drop cloth that covered the living room floor. While smoking a stale cigarette outside, he found one of the dead toads under a tarp and stuffed it in his pocket. He sat in the living room on the couch he'd slept on since he'd come back, sat with the dead toad in his hand, feeling its dried, rough texture, until the summer gloom was just overtaking the trees; the blue-gray shadows made the lake across from him a dark and unknowable mass.

His movements were stilted and painful, but, carefully, he crawled up the deck stairs of his neighbor's house next door to watch them. Standing hidden from view, peering into the big picture window, the warm glow of yellow light rested on his face. Inside the dog jumped and playfully nipped at the husband's outstretched hand. The woman he'd ruin himself for laughed, clutching her husband's arm in a casual but loving embrace. All her teeth showed in her smile. Eli and the dog ran around the living room in a loop Zeke would play over again in his mind.

He waited longer until the lights had gone out in the house. He crept and searched for the bodies of Eli's victims, all the little toads, in small piles of leaves and under stones. Some felt like paper, others still had an alarming freshness, as if he'd been only a few minutes too late. The thrushes in the dark woods around him chirruped as he moved. Unaware of the hours that passed while he collected the moldering dead, every so often he stopped to rub his neck, to massage a piece of the ache that pulsed through his whole body.

He stumbled back to his father's house and picked a clear spot of land near the storage shed, free of brush, a space hemmed in by the oaks, cypresses and caliper elms that stood with their backs to him. His eyes never left the ground and he didn't notice the sky brightening, growing watery pink across the horizon. The spade from his father's shed cut through the muddy soil. He dug a grave, nearly big enough for a man, letting the sweat drip into his eyes until everything was blurred. He buried them all as the sun rose over the trees, saying no prayer.

THE TEACHER

(VOL. 68, NO. 2, 2019)

Faith Merino

....

Toni had gotten out of having to help pack up Grandma Mendoza's trailer by saying she was going to a work retreat with Josh in Santa Barbara, but when they walked into the sprawling house that overlooked seven hundred acres of bright green vineyard swells, she saw the men in polo shirts and khaki shorts laughing loudly in the foyer and started to back away. Josh squeezed her hand to pull her back, and one of the men—a partner named Gary Thompson—spotted them in the doorway. Thompson grabbed Josh's hand and pulled him in, overpowering the anchor that Toni had made of herself in the doorway, as he said, "Fuhrman!"

"Thompson," Josh replied with a smile.

Gary Thompson looked at Toni. "Oh, you brought your wife. You know, I don't think any of the other guys brought their wives." He looked back at the men in the foyer, scanning around as if looking for other women. He laughed, flashing straight blue-white teeth.

"But you know, it's better this way. She'll keep it from being a sausage fest."

Josh laughed, and Toni smiled. The men's voices were loud, echoing in the marble foyer, and Toni was hungover. Her head was thick with an underwater pressure, and she had a vague memory of Josh coming in with two Advil and a glass of water the night before. "Drink the whole thing, so you don't wake up feeling like shit."

She remembered being at Grandma Mendoza's doublewide in Palmdale, draining the flat strings of her fifth or sixth beer in the shadiest corner of the carport while the sun blazed on the white rock groundcover, raising the temperature ten or fifteen degrees. She remembered Uncle Leen complaining about the census counting Mexicans as white while the other uncles groaned. The aunts had been inside, sitting around the table, telling stories about their mother, Ethel Belle Mendoza (born Ethel Belle Clark—she refused to go by *Abuela*), and her terrible cooking (her husband had tried to teach her how to make tamales, but her masa always came out bland and dry), and Josh had been inside with the women, sitting alone on the couch, collar ringed with sweat. He always hated going to Palmdale, and Toni tried not to meet his urgent stare when she went inside to get beers for the uncles, another lemonade for Uncle Leen because he didn't think the buzz was worth the beer bloats. When she brought them out, the uncles patted her hand lovingly. Uncle Leen was still ranting as she sat down and popped open her sixth or seventh beer. She nodded off somewhere around the Treaty of Guadalupe Hidalgo and how The Man wasn't going to whitewash him and Uncle Chepe saying, "Oh, Jesus, stop." She woke up to the sound of scudding chairs and Uncle Jimmy saying, "It's not possible—he can't actually lift it," as they walked around behind Toni's grimy white '96 Corolla.

"Wait—not my car—" she'd said drowsily.

But Uncle Leen was already squatting down with a creak of his jeans, reaching his hands under the car to grip the bumper. He let out a single, short grunt as he strained, jaw clenched, surprisingly still—the tilted yoke of his bullish shoulders, the hard brace of his elbows—unmoving. Face blistering red, one thick vein branching down his sunburned forehead. Sweat pocked the back of his denim button-down shirt where it had seeped through his undershirt, inches below the telltale crease of the wrap he used to bind and flatten his breasts. And then the back tires of the car lifted off the ground, just an inch or two, and Uncle Leen released the car with a groan. It bounced down heavily and wobbled as he rolled his shoulders and pulled his elbows back to stretch, did a few springy squats to shake out his thighs. No one would ever guess that he'd been born Lurleen Belle Mendoza.

When they closed the door to the bedroom, Toni said, "I'm going to drive home. You can get a ride with one of the others. I shouldn't be here."

"It'll look weird if you leave now. You're already here. Just go get a drink and hang out in the pool or something," Josh said with a shrug as he threw his suitcase on the bed and unzipped it, taking his carefully folded clothes out and putting them in the dresser drawers by the sliding glass door. Their room had its own private balcony that looked out over the rolling green hills of grapevines.

"I feel weird. I'm out of place—I'll just ruin the . . . vibe," Toni said, waving a hand in the air. "No one wants me here."

Josh looked at her wearily. "Don't be histrionic. These guys will love having a girl to show off for. Here." He tossed her bikini across the bed to her. "Go for a swim. It'll help your hangover and give them a thrill."

Toni left the bikini on the bed and went back downstairs to the kitchen to pour herself a drink. Thompson smiled at her from the bar.

"Come on and fix yourself a drink. We've got a thirty-two-year-old single malt that I think Bradshaw here pimped out his wife to get," he said, gesturing at Bradshaw—another partner, athletic, clear-eyed—and the other men laughed.

Toni smiled anemically as she poured a scotch and went outside.

By evening, all of the partners, principals, and associates of Warner and Jones Capital were drunk and loud. They were grilling steaks on the barbeque, and the blue smoke was thick in the evening ocean air. Toni sat alone at a table on the other side of the patio, sipping her scotch, but she jumped when someone yelled, "Hey, Ian made it!" A tall, thin kid stepped out onto the patio, smiling as the other men grabbed his hand and pulled him in for a half-hug.

"Did you just kick some poor girl out of your bed at noon so you could spend the weekend with a bunch of old married fuckers?" said Thompson, patting Ian on the back. He didn't wait for Ian to answer before yelling to Bradshaw and another man, "I'm telling you, if these hookup apps had been around when I was in college, I would've gotten so much pussy."

Someone pushed a drink in Ian's hand and pulled him into a circle of younger men—associates. In the taxonomy of venture capitalism, the associates were the lower rungs on the ladder, guys who had just finished their MBAs at Stanford and had done their time at one of the big banks. But as the office manager and a twenty-three-year-old college dropout, Ian was even lower on the ladder than they were. He'd never be promoted to associate. Toni had heard all about him a few months ago when Josh came home from work one day and said, "You won't believe this new kid who's working in the office."

Ian had only been working at Warner and Jones for a week when the other men started noticing that different women were coming by the office to bring him lunch. When his car was in the shop for repairs, a different woman picked him up after work each day. Whenever the associates went out after work for drinks, they always invited Ian along, but he always declined because he already had plans.

And then one day, one of the associates asked Ian about his plans for the weekend—and Ian told him. Word spread through the firm, among the associates, principals, and up to the partners.

"He has three hookups scheduled tonight," Josh had said as he made himself a martini that he would sip temperately for the next hour to nurture a respectable buzz. "One from six to eight, one from eight to ten, and one from ten to midnight. He said he doesn't know when he's going to find time to eat and hydrate because they're three of his favorites, and he wants to give each one the time and attention she deserves."

And he had rules.

"He never schedules hookups less than two days in advance, and he doesn't meet girls on his birthday or holidays because he wants that time for himself," said Josh.

And Toni, home all day and halfway through her third vodka cran, got out her phone. "What's his number?"

They'd laughed as she texted him. *Are you still coming over tonight?*

His response came within seconds: *Who is this?* They'd sipped their drinks and wheezed as she texted back, *Are you serious?*

Now, smoke burning her eyes, Toni breathed slowly, feeling the alcohol spreading down her arms and legs like a water ring on paper. She squeezed her eyes shut, and when she opened them, Ian was sitting across from her at the table. He had his glass of scotch in front of him, but he hadn't touched it. He had a feminine face—overly large eyes, flower petal scoop cheeks—and a neat side-part. He was too skinny for his height.

"Don't even try it, Ian. That's Josh's wife," someone yelled.

Toni looked around the patio, but couldn't locate Josh anywhere, hadn't seen him since leaving him in the bedroom with her bikini.

"I've never been to one of these before," Ian said to her, and Toni tried to focus on him, but her eyes were drifting from the scotch.

"These?" she asked.

"One of these retreats," Ian said, pointing his thumb—for some reason—over his shoulder at the hilly vineyard behind him. Toni nodded and sipped her drink.

"If I had known we were allowed to bring dates, I would've brought mine, and then maybe you wouldn't be the only girl here."

Toni threw back the rest of her drink and did what she always did when someone started talking to her at a bar or club: "Did you know I was kidnapped once?"

It was usually enough to throw off the game of the person trying to take her home. She did it to Josh when she met him at a bar—he one month away from graduating, she one month away from dropping out. But it backfired on her: Josh had found it exciting, dangerous, and she ended up having sex with him in the back of her Corolla—the first and last time she ever tried to have sex in a compact car.

Ian frowned.

"My tenth-grade English teacher," she added. "I'd had a crush on him since freshman year, and one day after school, I went to his classroom and ended up kissing him on the mouth."

She leaned forward and smiled as she said, "I went back to the classroom every day after school. Eventually, we had sex on the carpet—one of those old bungalow carpets that's all stiff and thin and scratchy. It hurt. I bled way more than I thought I would, and he cleaned up the mess with rags and carpet cleaner that he got from the janitor's closet." That was usually the part that made men smile sadly, sip their drinks, and walk away as if hearing someone calling their name.

But Ian's eyes flicked into focus. "They found you in Nevada," he said.

Toni stared at him.

"You'd been missing for . . . two weeks—"

"Two months," Toni corrected, coughing. She scooted in her seat, thigh muscles shifting like a deer in recoil, ready to spring. No one had ever recognized her before, not even Josh.

"Was it like—"

"It wasn't like *Lolita*," she cut him off.

Josh had asked her that. Was it like *Lolita*? The teacher hadn't drugged her, hadn't forced her. It wasn't even his idea to leave. She'd shrugged and said, "He wasn't a predator, and I wasn't prey."

And Josh had said, "But he was an adult, and you were a minor."

She'd laughed into her vodka tonic, because she was sixteen when she got into the passenger's seat of the teacher's blue '92 Volvo station wagon, and she was twenty-two when she sat there with Josh, telling him about it.

Ian was frowning at the tabletop, thinking, trying to conjure the details.

"He got life for kidnapping and rape," he said, and Toni wondered if she winced involuntarily at the word "rape."

The teacher had actually been sentenced to ten-years-to-life for kidnapping and taking a minor across state lines. Statutory rape was only added on opportunistically because she'd admitted that they'd had sex at least four times a week for the two months they were on the run.

She grabbed her glass and stood up to go pour herself another scotch, because she'd made a rule of not explaining why she left with the teacher—a fifty-six-year-old man who dyed his hair black but not his frost-white eyebrows, who'd been married for thirty-two years and ate the ham and cheese on potato bread that his wife packed for him every single day. A man who she'd had a crush on for two years for reasons that never made sense to anyone—the way he laughed with an open mouth, even though his teeth were too crowded and large, lending his face a long, equine look. The way he inhaled sharply through his nose before he laughed in his rushed, uneasy way. Things that most people—all of his students—hated about him.

And she knew that the next thing coming was the question, "Why?"

Toni took a step, but she was drunk, and the ground swung forward and spun out. In another moment, she was on her hands and knees, vomiting in a potted juniper.

When she woke up at five in the morning dried out and desperate for water, she was thinking of Uncle Leen's doublewide in Palmdale, in the same park where Grandma Mendoza lived, where the sweeping vistas of cracked clay and rocky cliffs held the heat and shimmered white in the sun as temperatures spiked to 120 degrees. The only air conditioning unit in the house was in the living room, so that was where she slept, on the rumpled carpet, mouth open and arms and legs thrown out in an expansive X. In the morning, Uncle Leen would vacuum around her, bumping her with the vacuum cleaner and occasionally sucking up her pajama shirt. Her parents would come get her after their night shifts, and her father would balance a cream puff on her nose while Uncle Leen took a picture. She always woke up thirsty, coughing for water, and her mother told her it was because she slept with her mouth open. How many spiders had she swallowed in her sleep that way?

She got up, leaving Josh snoring in the bed, and went into the bathroom to stick her head in the sink and drink from the faucet. The water tasted medicinally sweet and turned her stomach, which was why she always kept Gatorade at home for hangovers.

She remembered vomiting in the potted juniper. She had a watery memory of Ian waiting for her to finish before pulling her up by her arm—strong, despite his weedy frame—and guiding her inside with an arm around her waist. A memory of falling into bed and looking over her shoulder, thinking—just for a moment—that Ian would follow her inside, but seeing him close the door between them.

She put on her bikini, grabbed a towel, and padded quietly downstairs. Skin feverish and tight, she slipped outside into the cold morning air. The pool was dark and still, and she dived in—bracing cold. As she skimmed the bottom of the concrete bowl, she remembered the Green Mesa Resort, a rundown desert motel with a pool full of worms, splintering wooden picnic tables hung heavy with black widow webs, where she and the teacher spent those last two weeks.

She didn't tell Ian or Josh that it was Uncle Leen who saw her and the teacher together as he came out of Home Depot heaped with four huge coils of slotted drain pipe—whose eyes met hers in the blue Volvo as the teacher reached under her jaw to tuck a lock of hair behind her ear—and gave them the reason they needed to leave.

Uncle Leen, who once found a small iridescent green butterfly chrysalis dangling from the umbrella of a leaf, put it on a cinder block between them both, and used his pocketknife to cut it open. A viscous brownish soup oozed out, and Toni would later learn that that's what happens. The caterpillar digests itself—turns itself into slurry inside its own chrysalis, and then designated eye cells, leg cells, wing cells, and organ cells feed on the protein-rich soup to multiply and rebuild the entire body. The butterfly that emerges is a complete rewrite.

She slept off the hangover in a cushioned lounge chair by the pool. Josh came to her once to bring her some sunscreen and a vodka on ice. He didn't say anything but grazed a knuckle across her hot cheek. He rarely got drunk. He ran in the mornings, took a huge sloshing ninety-ounce water bottle to work with him. He'd never even paid a late fee on anything because he'd never missed a bill payment. His parents had paid his tuition and rent throughout college, so he could graduate debt-free; he paid off Toni's credit cards when they got married.

She could hear the men's voices and laughter throughout the day, could feel them watching her. By evening, Thompson and Bradshaw were talking loudly nearby, and when Toni rolled her head and opened her eyes, she found them staring back at her from the barbeque. Bradshaw went back to scraping the grill while Thompson winked. Toni got up and carried her towel inside. She poured herself a scotch in the kitchen and carried it upstairs, but when she stepped out onto the terrace and closed the sliding glass door behind her, she saw Ian at the table. She froze, said, "Sorry—I didn't think anyone was up here—" and tried to open the slider again, but Ian said, "There's plenty of room."

She sat down at the table with him. As the sunlight faded red to dusty purple, the men below started lighting cigars, and the smoke drifted up to the terrace, peppery sharp. She heard Josh saying something and laughing, but she couldn't locate him or make out his words.

"So. Preferences?" she asked Ian.

He looked at her and didn't hesitate, as if he'd anticipated the question. "Older," and took a sip of water. She, twenty-nine, said, "Why older?"

"Because they know what they want. They're not worried about hurting my feelings if they tell me what to do." Looking at her levelly, unconcerned, but waiting to see her reaction.

"Who's your favorite?" she asked. And as if he kept the answer in a pillbox in his pocket, he answered, "Sarah J."

"Who is Sarah J.?"

"I can't tell you that. She might be your best friend, and then she'll find out she's my favorite, and I can't have that. It'll ruin our thing."

The men burst out laughing below them, and someone turned up the music. The sun was gone, and the terrace was lit dimly by string lights—old-fashioned-looking clear glass bulbs that gave the scene a Christmassy feel. Ian was watching her in the dimness as Toni swallowed the rest of the scotch, lifted the glass in a "cheers" salute, and got up to leave.

"Did you think you were going to spend the rest of your lives together? You and the teacher?" he asked, and she stopped and looked at him.

"Why are you asking me that?" He stared back at her and didn't answer.

She sat back down and questioned him. "How many women have you slept with?"

"I have no idea."

"Do you always use a condom?"

"Not always."

"Have you been tested?"

"Four times. Always clean."

"Does your *mother* know what you're doing?" She didn't know why that was among her primary concerns.

"I think she knows more than I'd like her to." And then he asked her: "Why did you leave your family to run away with the teacher?"

"I don't know. I was sixteen."

"Did you think you both could stay hidden forever?" he asked.

Truthfully: she had. They'd both thrown their cell phones into a slough ditch behind the school the night they left, so they wouldn't be tracked. He'd stolen a license plate off an abandoned car and fixed it to the Volvo. She dyed her hair and eyebrows black in a gas station bathroom. He'd gotten them fake IDs—he was Robert Byers, she was Cami Byers. They'd lasted those two months, but towards the end, the teacher became anxious, always convinced someone had recognized him in a store or gas station, always fearful of a too-long glance. The day Toni found the gun under his pillow was the day she stepped out of the liminal hang of childhood and into adulthood.

Josh didn't come to bed that night. Toni woke up at four in the morning to find herself alone in bed, and for a brief moment, she wondered if he had run away, leaving her there at the house to find her own way home. She sat up, alert, and put some shorts on before slipping quietly out of the room and down the stairs. The lights were on in the kitchen, the dining room, the living room, even the home theater. The house was quiet, but the beams hummed with kinetic male energy—booming chesty laughter, far-reaching voices—no effort made at smallness. The memory of barbeque and cigar smoke hung in the air.

Toni took her phone out of her pocket. No messages from Josh. She moved quietly through the house, peering through open doors to find beds that were empty but made up perfectly. No wadded sheets or strewn clothes or tossed shoes. She slipped into one room—whose, she didn't know—and studied the toiletries lined up on the dresser. Shaving cream, aftershave, cologne, bronzer, an old-fashioned silver-handled straight razor. She uncapped the cologne and sniffed it, coughed, tasting it in the back of her throat. She opened up the straight razor, which glinted in the hall light.

She put everything back exactly as it was and moved into the next room. No toiletries left on the dresser, but she pulled open the drawers to find crisply folded white briefs and undershirts side-by-side in the top drawer, khaki shorts in the second drawer, salmon and teal polo shirts in the third. In one of the smaller drawers, she found a small pouch containing sculpting gel and tinted benzoyl peroxide.

What would happen if she rose before the men and then walked into their rooms as they were putting on their tinted acne cream or nasty cologne or salmon polo shirts? Would they cover themselves? Or would they stare back at her the way Uncle Leen did when she peered through his open door and saw him binding his old woman breasts? She was supposed to be watching cartoons. When he took off his shirt, she'd stared in awe at the crushed brown rosettes of his areolas. He'd seen her in the doorway and stared back at her, cotton wrap half-wound and hanging from one armpit. He stared back at her until she left.

In the next room, she went into the bathroom to find an exfoliating clay cleanser, a sea spray toner, and a stack of magazines on the back of the toilet— *Men's Health, Men's Fitness*—with dog-eared pages. "How to Get Ripped Abs in 21 Days." "The Steamy Fantasies She'll Never Tell You About." She used to steal magazines from the Longs drug store on Fort Tejon Road, where mothers pushed shopping carts through the aisles because it was air conditioned and stopped to talk as their babies, wearing nothing but diapers, tried to crawl out of the carts. She'd stuffed the magazines into the waistband of her shorts and pulled her shirt over them, then walked calmly out into the dry desert blaze, through the parking lot littered with crushed soda fountain cups, rolled up diapers, and plastic bags that breathed like lungs in the hot breeze. More than once, she'd walked along Fort Tejon Road and passed the carcass of a scarred-up pit bull.

When the front door opened at five and a cloud of bass male laughter blasted into the house, Toni put the magazines back and hurried out of the bedroom. The men were slurring, drunk. Thompson tried to walk sideways to talk to someone behind him and tripped over his own ankle, stumbling and ramming a shoulder into the wall. The others roared.

Josh was tripping along in the back, laughing with the others. His eyes were floating around in his head, and he stumbled past her without seeing her leaning against the hall corner. He was wearing the Rolex his parents gave him when he was promoted from associate to principal. He and another principal supported one another as they made their way up the stairs. Toni followed them, smelling the sharp, chemical exhale of their cologne, and something else. A vanilla smell. They both tripped into Toni and Josh's bedroom and fell into the bed. In another moment, both were asleep. Toni crouched down beside the bed to see Josh's face. It was smeared with glitter.

She left him there and went downstairs to the kitchen, where Thompson, Bradshaw, and three others were rooting through the pantry and cupboards. Toni got out the vodka and tomato juice and made herself a drink.

"Toni," Thompson said when he saw her in the kitchen. "Toni. Antonia? You must be the coolest wife ever. Josh doesn't have a clue how lucky he is to have you."

Toni capped the tomato juice, stirred her drink with a knife, and walked away, but Thompson grabbed her by the elbow, and her glass fumbled out of her hand, slopping tomato juice down her front. She heard the shatter of glass on the floor but didn't see it as Thompson pulled her back.

"Toni. Don't be mad, Toni," he said. His grip was strong, and Toni's heart was flapping. "I'm just going to give you a kiss for being such a great wife."

He threw her backwards into a dip, and Toni went ragdoll because if she tightened up, he'd drop her, and she'd smash her skull on the concrete floor. She could hear the other men laughing. He loomed over her, and she tucked her chin in time for his kiss to land on her nose instead of her mouth. She turned her face away and through her own hair, she saw Ian in the doorway in a t-shirt and boxers, hair disheveled with sleep, eyes alert.

"Gary," he said.

"There, see?" Thompson said, standing her back up again. "I just wanted to give you a little kiss on the nose."

Toni pushed past him and stumbled out of the kitchen, passing Ian as she ran into the bathroom and locked the door behind her to wait for the men to go to bed or pass out on the floor.

When she came out of the bathroom, the mess had been cleaned up. The broken glass was in the trash, the tomato juice had been mopped, and the floor showed nothing of the early-morning fracas. The other men had been too drunk to clean up after themselves, which meant Ian did it.

The house was silent, and the first risers came out of their rooms at four in the afternoon in their slept-on hair and boxers, eyes puffy, staggering into the kitchen to look for food. One of the men—the others called him Weimar—had been in the kitchen when Thompson kissed her. Weimar looked at her in a dry-eyed daze, frowning. He blinked quickly, squeezed his eyes shut and rubbed his forehead as he whispered, "fuck . . ." He went to the fridge and got out the vodka and tomato juice. He made himself a drink and looked at Toni again, as if trying to place her face. She grabbed her drink and went outside to sit by the pool, where Ian was swimming laps. There was no music today, no boisterous laughter. Just the briny wind, the looping gulls, and the distant tidal pull of the sea.

Toni sipped her drink and watched Ian's long, sea-cliff back in the water. When he got out of the pool, his streaming trunks clung to his bony boy knees. His legs were pale and apparently hairless, but when he moved into the low red sun, Toni could see the glint of tiny golden hairs on his shins. He rubbed his face dry with his towel but stopped when he saw her. He blinked. Surprised.

"Do you need a ride? Home?" he asked clumsily, droplets of water still clumping his eyelashes.

"I have a car."

"Right." Frowning at her.

He sat down in the lounge chair beside her, water soaking into the cushions as he leaned his head back against the headrest. He was looking out at the vineyards, at the verdant rows of grapevines rolling across the shallows and swells, glittering with twists of tinfoil to keep the birds away by tricking them into thinking the vines were on fire.

"Did your dad skip out on you when you were little or something?" Ian asked.

"Is that your pick-up line?" Toni asked, sipping her vodka cran.

"Did you go to Whitney High?"

Toni looked at him. "What?"

"That's it. That's my pick-up line. If I want to start talking to someone, I ask her if she went to my high school, even though I know she didn't."

"Oh," Toni said flatly, disappointed. She'd expected something more interesting. "What's your favorite position?" Because that was as interesting as she could pretend to be.

"Reverse cowgirl. Obviously."

"Do you do period sex?"

"All the time."

"What about anal?"

"If she suggests it."

Toni sat back. Ian's room was the only one she hadn't gone in, and she wondered now what she'd find. Deodorant, toothbrush, nail clippers. Neutrogena cleanser. Drug store lotion.

"Did you love the teacher?" he asked.

"No." She finished her drink and thought of leaving to go refill it, but she stayed, swirling the ice.

"Do you always put this much time into it?" she asked.

"If I think it's worth it."

She sighed. She'd never cheated on Josh, not even when he confessed to sleeping with a prostitute on a business trip a year into their marriage. She'd been hurt, but not surprised. They moved on more quickly than she thought married couples usually moved on from those things.

What would she find in Ian's dresser? Three cotton t-shirts, three pairs of shorts, three pairs of boxers. He'd been wearing blue-checked Hanes when he watched her from the kitchen entryway being dipped and kissed.

He stood up, water still drooling from his trunks, and she watched him walk back to the house.

She and the teacher had stayed in hotel rooms in and around Las Vegas in the beginning, when they had money, and it was neutral space. The same floral bedspreads, the stiff universal carpet, sample-sized soaps, shampoos, and lotions. Housekeepers cleaned up after them. Then, as money became tight, they started staying in cheaper motel rooms where furniture was missing handles and the ceiling was acoustic tile—always one or two missing above the bed or shower. They'd spent whole days together in the car, driving as far east as Amarillo, Texas, because the teacher had some vague idea about crossing the border into Mexico—an idea he later abandoned because he worried border patrol would catch them. They drove back to Nevada and lived out those last two weeks at the Green Mesa Resort in

Goodsprings, a desert town that was somehow smaller, flatter, and more arid than Palmdale.

Somewhere between Nevada and Texas, the neutral space dissipated, and then she was smelling his smells, watching him eat, hearing him pee and fart. When they stopped at gas stations for lunch, he got the same thing for every meal: a ham and cheese sandwich from the cooler, and she wanted to grab it out of his face and throw it out the car window.

In those last weeks, when the teacher became anxious and couldn't sleep at night, he went days without showering. He sat on the floor at the base of the bed and watched the news and old movies on TV all night, eyes dry and rooted red. His hair became greasy, ropy, and his skin smelled coppery, like a handful of dirty pennies. When she found the gun, she saw flashes of movie scenes—red spray on the walls, old black blood sticky on the carpet. He was getting a bottle of wine from the twenty-four-hour liquor store down the street when she called her mom at midnight: "I'm at the Green Mesa Resort in Goodsprings, Nevada." When the teacher finished off the bottle of wine and fell asleep around two in the morning, she slipped out of the room and started walking west, knowing that Uncle Leen would be the one to come get her. It was dawn on Highway 15 when she saw his pickup truck driving out of the storm-blue horizon toward her.

She showered and shaved her legs, scrubbed her face with the washcloth to brighten her skin. Her hair dryer didn't wake up Josh, who snored, draped across the bed on his belly. At some point in the day, the other principal had dragged himself to his own room. She rubbed lotion into her legs and left Josh there. She moved quietly down the hall to Ian's door, pausing in the hallway and wondering if it was too late to call Uncle Leen, who once told her that a tadpole will stop eating for a week once its legs come in because its body is digesting its tail. Who used to take her with him to the grocery store to buy a giant bag of cat food because he couldn't bear to see the skinny, suffering strays—who would go to the empty lot on the corner of Hayes and Garfield to dump out the bag in three big piles on the ground so all the cats could eat. Who'd said to her, as she sat silently in his pickup truck heading west, "He'll be okay. He'll be relieved that it's all over." When she said that the teacher didn't do anything wrong, that she'd ruined his life, Uncle Leen smiled sadly and said, "You'll see it differently when you're older." And as she passed Ian's door, went downstairs, out the front door, and started walking east on Vine Boulevard toward the veiny network of highways and thoroughfares that would take her home to Palmdale, she believed him.

ON CERTAINTY

(VOL. 70, NO. 3, 2021)

Kristen Case

....

If this be error and upon me prov'd;
I never writ, nor no man ever lov'd.

1.

Mornings I think about Rosemarie Waldrop's sentence *All resonance grows from consent to emptiness* and imagine a wordless being. The leaves move individually, slightly, and though their movement is independent of the light it changes the appearance of the light, which becomes watery. The leaves are lit, or half-lit, or shaded. These possibilities of leaf-light are layered into a picture of infinity.

I am reading Wittgenstein's *On Certainty*, his last work, posthumously assembled, in an old paperback edition that belonged to a now-dead poet who once lived in my town.

Consent to emptiness may be either the description of a progress or the description of a position. *This* suggests the near-to-hand. A hand is briefly near the word for it, then vanishes. In June, externally lit objects exceed their names and I begin various programs of self-regulation.

At dinner with an older couple who generally seem touchingly fond of each other I catch the man looking at the woman with contempt. It passes quickly, but it is all I remember about the evening.

In another book, Wittgenstein says this about pain: *Suppose everyone has a box with something in it: we call it a "beetle." No one can look into anyone else's box, and everyone says he knows what a beetle is only by looking at his beetle.*

I imagine the holder of the beetle box feeling a mixture of tenderness and revulsion toward the object inside. I wonder if the box is serving mainly to hide the beetle or to contain it. I wonder if Wittgenstein considered other possible names for the thing in the box, like "rock" or "mouse," and whether these variations would change my impression of Wittgenstein's theory of pain.

The thing in the box, he says, *has no place in the language-game at all.*

My initial, instinctive response to the man's contempt was to wonder why the woman has not learned, after so many years, how to avoid exposing herself to it.

Wittgenstein's *On Certainty* was translated by G. E. M. Anscome, whose own work addresses, among other subjects, the difference between cognitive and conative states. The main difference is that a conative state involves desire.

According to his biographer, Ray Monk, Wittgenstein was highly influenced by a book he read as an adolescent called *Sex and Character* by Otto Weinenger.

Weinenger: *Women have no existence and no essence; they are not, they are nothing. Mankind occurs as male or female, as something or nothing. Woman has no share in ontological reality, no relation to the thing-in-itself, which in the deepest interpretation is the absolute, is God.*

Weinenger: *Woman is neither high-minded or low-minded, strong-minded or weak-minded. She is the opposite of all of these. Mind cannot be predicated of her at all; she is mindless.*

Weinenger: *Man is form; woman is matter.*

Weinenger also believed in a strict separation between love (masculine) and desire (feminine). Monk ascribes Wittgenstein's *conviction that sexuality is incompatible with the honesty that genius demands* to Weinenger's influence.

On Certainty: For months I have lived at address A, I have read the name of the street and the number of the house countless times, have received countless letters here and given countless people the address. If I am wrong about it, the mistake is hardly less than if I were (wrongly) to believe I was writing Chinese and not German.

I "know" but do not summon to clarity the negative adjectives you would use, internally, to describe me. My feeling of knowing that you use these words to yourself is like my feeling of knowing that my body has never been far from the surface of the earth. I feel close to them. If I were to pronounce these words inwardly it would be difficult not to imagine that we were in some way communicating.

If my friend were to imagine one day that he had been living for a long time in such and such a place etc. etc. I should not call this a mistake, but rather a mental disturbance, perhaps a transient one.

Wittgenstein imagines a friend who imagines a life of some duration about which he (Wittgenstein) gives us no details but suggests that such details (*such and such a place etc. etc.*) exist within the frame of the *mental disturbance*. I am interested in whether Wittgenstein was thinking of a particular friend when he wrote these sentences, at the end of his life, in response to a book by the philosopher G. E. Moore, who was his friend.

I am interested in the fact that Wittgenstein's translator was a woman. I google "Wittgenstein and women." The results are predictably disheartening.

Not every false belief of this sort is a mistake.

Even imaginary or failed intimacy entails a good deal of empirical knowledge.

The world of your thinking and feeling that I have built is like a miniature glass house, with glass furniture and glass appliances and glass boxes of cereal. It is hard not to feel tenderness towards this world even as I suspect that I have been all wrong about it. Or, rather, that it has been all wrong.

Wittgenstein also designed a house. You can see pictures of it online.

But what is the difference between a mistake and a mental disturbance? Or what is the difference between my treating it as a mistake and my treating it as a mental disturbance?

Before he died, my father's particular delusions, which concerned the rules of baseball, the operations of clocks, and international terrorism, wove themselves together into a cohesive fabric, a *picture of the world.*

Can we say: a mistake *doesn't only have a cause, it also has a ground? i.e. roughly: when someone makes a mistake, this can be fitted into what he knows aright?*

I am wondering whether the ways I have been wrong about your thinking and feeling are more like being wrong about my address or being wrong about language. Or is it incorrect to say "wrong" in this context because the thinking and feeling of others is always a boxed beetle and not something it is possible to be right or wrong about? Was my mistake to believe in the possibility of mistakes (and therefore, of a ground of non-mistaking?)

Realizing that you have been wrong about another person's thinking or feeling is perhaps like realizing that you have made a mistake about your address, in spite of having received countless letters there. In this way it is also like a mental disturbance.

I am trying to write this *you* in a way that might point to any number of relations or lost relations but that is at the same time highly specific. I am trying to get at the specific way of being of this kind of mistake. I am not certain why I want to do this, what is at stake for me in this conative state.

I did not get my picture of the world by satisfying myself of its correctness; nor do I have it because I am satisfied of its correctness. No: it is the inherited background against which I distinguish between true and false.

My body resists paying attention to the knowledge I am trying to articulate and, in articulating, register: that the glass house I have been making is not *accurate.* Or perhaps, is not *habitable.* In the face of this knowledge I order new sheets and rearrange the objects of our actual house.

When a relation has moved into the inherited background, our wrongness about it becomes more consequential. The air is hot and full of dandelion seeds which drift like airy flakes across the deck and into the woods. The spiders' webs are full of them, dusty galaxies between the propane tanks, across the corners of flower boxes. It is difficult even to imagine a non-conative state. What size desert would I have to cross? how many days would it take?

I think what I want is not to be wrong in this particular way again.

2.

Time settles into everything. The hard seed is almost invisible, a grain between your fingers, the loose fibers make a cloud around it.

In the biography, Monk describes "personal remarks" that Wittgenstein left in code in his philosophical manuscripts.

The wet ends of the white towels I have hung on the clothesline fold on themselves in the grass, the towels' weight tugging the line groundward. Because they look so defeated, I consider repositioning the wooden clothespins at the ends of the line, shifting the towels away from the slack center where they are clustered, but am daunted by the energy this will require.

According to Monk, *these remarks were separated by Wittgenstein from his philosophical remarks by a simple code that he had learnt as a child (whereby a=z, b=y, c=x etc.).*

The grass is thick under the line: their contact with the ground is unlikely to make the towels dirty. On the other hand, to admit this poverty of motivation seems dangerous, a threat to the whole infrastructure of my life.

When we first begin to believe anything, what we believe is not a single proposition, it is a whole system of propositions. (Light dawns gradually over the whole.)

I am particularly interested in the fact that these coded remarks exist side-by-side with Wittgenstein's philosophical writings, not in a separate notebook.

The wet ends of the white towels meet the grass in oblong shadow shapes.

What the coded remarks also reveal is the extraordinary extent to which Wittgenstein's love life and his sexual life went on only in his imagination.

Picture two elaborate glass structures, in some places connected by many small points to our actual lives and so, indirectly, to each other; in other places, split off entirely from the actual, built precariously out over the air.

Wittgenstein's perception of a relationship would often bear no relation at all to the perception of it held by the other person.

Or: one elaborate glass structure, and one person not imagining anything at all.

Gradually over the hole.

3.

From the translator's introduction to *On Certainty*: *The material falls into four parts . . . What we believe to be the first part was written on twenty loose sheets of lined foolscap, undated. These Wittgenstein left in his room in G. E. M. Anscome's house in Oxford where he lived (apart from a visit to Norway in the Autumn) from April 1950 to February 1951.*

I try to picture G. E. M. Anscome's house, and Wittgenstein's room in it. I think about what it means to have a room in someone else's house.

Anscome: *I am under the impression that he wrote them in Vienna, where he had stayed from the previous Christmas until March, but I cannot recall now the basis of this impression.*

I try to picture the twenty loose sheets. When I zoom in to make it bigger, the text in front of my eyes blurs slightly for a half second and then refocuses as if to remind me that what I am writing is only an image of words, a photograph of words. A little string of ghosts.

I cannot recall the basis of my impression that certain men believe without articulating it to themselves that *mind cannot be predicated of me at all.*

The potted basil flourishes. I practice writing the word *beetle* using Wittgenstein's code.

The rest is in small notebooks, containing dates; toward the end, indeed, the date of writing is always given. The last entry is two days before his death on April 29 1951. We have left the dates exactly as they appear in the manuscripts.

I wonder whether Anscome wrote the words of the introduction in a cognitive or a conative state.

Sunlight streaks the deck, the lilac, my daughter's easel, the spiders' webs between objects. Waking early you can see the way the night hangs on, and the way light penetrates at the threshold of visibility. The *you* I was writing has vanished, leaving only the diffuse and impersonal world.

4.

May 4:

[Here there is still a big gap in my thinking. And I doubt whether it will be filled now.]

Here there are gaps between sounds and between branches, a receding and a yawning forward of a dark between. I had sunk myself so deep into the wordless interior that when you failed to register the reflecting surround the shadows came for their objects and my name fell right off my face.

Violence is a secret key. Emptiness and the terror that attends it.

I spend the morning reading all the pages of the biography that relate to Wittgenstein's lover, Francis Skinner.

Outside one of the hemlocks is bare as though stripped, except for a few sparse branches at the top, its skeletal branches orient toward me as though reaching out while trying not to appear not to be reaching out, or like the tributaries of rivers on a map.

Skinner's letters were kept by Wittgenstein, and were found among his possessions after his death, and from them we can reconstruct how the relationship developed. (Wittgenstein's letters to Skinner were retrieved by Wittgenstein after Skinner's death and were, presumably, burnt.)

In *On Certainty* Wittgenstein attempts, repeatedly, to illustrate that it is a false move in the language-game to say that you "know" or "believe" something that it is impossible for you to doubt. What we call "knowing" or "believing" bears a particular relationship to doubt-feeling.

(He is at pains, however, to remind us that our inability to doubt something does not necessarily make it true: *Certainty is as it were a tone of voice in which one declares how things are, but one does not infer from the tone of voice that one is justified.*)

I am interested in the untrue thing whose truth you can't doubt; in ways of being wrong that cannot be detached from the foundation of the language-game and thus suggest that you might be wrong about the fabric of being.

It is nonsensical to say that I might be *wrong* about the fabric of being, but that is what I mean.

Francis to Wittgenstein: *I think a lot about our relation. Are we going to act independently of each other, will I be able to act independently of you?*

Wittgenstein, in coded remarks: *Lay with [Francis] two or three times. Always with the feeling there was nothing wrong in it,* then *with shame. Have also been unjust, edgy and insincere with him, and also cruel.*

I am trying to get closer to the feeling of abjection in its relation to conative states. This has something to do with the question of what is possible between people. What is possible between people has to do with the fabric of being I may be right or wrong about and also has to do with politics. After the rain the darkest-shadowed green in the layers of shadowed and half-shadowed leaves out my studio window is nearly black and hurtles through the generalized months into my particular mouth.

I return to the repeated *also* in the coded remarks about Francis. *Have also been unjust. Also cruel.* Monk calls him *Francis* rather than Skinner, though he mostly uses last names to refer to Wittgenstein, his colleagues, and his students. Probably there is a non-conative explanation but I imagine this as a slip that suggests a feeling of tenderness on the part of the biographer to the object of Wittgenstein's simultaneous desire and aversion, an unregistered and, in any case, totally unrealizable wish to console.

Monk: *What is striking is the juxtaposition of his account of their lying together with observations of his lovelessness toward Francis. Or perhaps what he is expressing is his fear of becoming loveless.*

In 1938 Wittgenstein translated, with a student named Yorick Smythies, portions of the mystic play *Raja* (often titled in English *King of the Dark Chamber*) by Rabindranath Tagore. The king to whom the title refers is never seen by anyone. According to Monk, *the play concerns the awakening—or, one might say the humbling, the subjugation—of the King's wife.*

I make a sketch for a glass structure called Lovelessness enclosed in a second glass structure called Fear of Lovelessness. I look at photographs of Haus Wittgenstein online.

Coded remarks: *Thought: it would be good and right if he had died, and thereby taken my "folly" away.*

yvvgov yvvgov yvvgov
yvvgov yvvgov yvvgov

5.

Riding my bicycle back to my desk I notice the single meandering track in the dirt made by my bicycle earlier in the day. It is startling to be confronted with my past self in this way.

When I feel that another person's desire for me carries with it the secret wish that I were dead, is this a mistake or a mental disturbance? Whose?

In the glass house of Lovelessness there is a dark chamber.

I read art books, look at pictures of art, consider Francis.

The window in front of my desk is a glass grid of twenty-five squares, marked off by white wooden frames. Above this grid is half circle of glass divided into four sections, each divided again into three. Light penetrates the layers of leaves, then penetrates these surfaces. It is strange to remember that this occurs *sequentially*.

A numbness attends certain conative states. These are several occasions and the same occasion. A winnowing of shimmering difference into a single darkness, dispersion of sensation into the surround. The trunk and branches of the almost-dead hemlock are stark, lichen-marked. It has to do with the feeling of being wished dead.

Francis to Wittgenstein: *I feel very unhappy that I should have given you cause to write that you feel I'm away from you. It is a terrible thing that I have acted in a way that might loosen what is between us. It would be a catastrophe for me if anything happened to our relation. Please forgive me for what I have done.*

I know that it is likely a matter of translation but I am moved by the urgent simplicity of the phrase "I feel very unhappy." I can't imagine uttering this phrase. I can type it, however, with little feeling of self-consciousness: I am only depressing the small back squares on this mark-making machine. I feel very unhappy.

Mornings you feel the little winter inside of August. In the trees a single hermit thrush bodies the air in sound, which penetrates as if to loosen what is between. I consult the weather of the future and check to see what my device has collected while I slept. Through the canopy, the early sunlight finds the trunks of two maples which radiate accordingly though the comparative gloom.

Wittgenstein retracts the wish that Francis *had died* in subsequent sentences. Though of course it may only be an accident of translation, I am interested in this strange grammatical formulation, as though Wittgenstein were conjuring not a single imaginary event but a whole imaginary world in which Francis *had died*.

Francis did, in fact, die—of polio—in 1941. By this time, the biography notes, the relationship *had deteriorated*.

The wanting-dead with which I am concerned, if real at all, is of course the unconscious kind which has to do with one's being a woman and not with one's personal qualities, or the personal qualities of the person or persons who may or may not unconsciously and surely only momentarily wish me dead.

I consider which of the following, if any, Wittgenstein would allow:

No one really wishes me dead.

I do not believe that anyone really wishes me dead.

I know no one really wishes me dead.

I may be mistaken, but I do not believe that anyone really wishes me dead.

When I am feeling very unhappy I turn to the pages in my art books with reproductions of paintings by Agnes Martin. In one of these, alternating dark and light gray stripes are overlaid with a grid of small rectangles, drawn in pencil, which creates the feeling of infinite repetition in all directions. This painting is called "The Tree." After looking at it for some time the sensation of being wished dead disperses into image, the book, the table, and the screened-in porch in which I am sitting.

The argument "I may be dreaming" is senseless for this reason: if I am dreaming, this remark is being dreamed as well—and indeed it is also being dreamed that these words have any meaning.

I touch the tiny black squares of the mark-making machine, which makes a clicking sound as if to remind me of someone's home.

6.

I do not know how the sentence "I have a body" is to be used.

Saplings in the understory, mainly beech. Wide-leafed to the sun. Imagine a feeling like a grid. Like a canopy.

Francis, Monk writes, *is remembered by all who knew him as shy, unassuming, good-looking, and above all, extraordinarily gentle.*

The bicycle tracks multiply in the dirt. Unmoving, they mean *movement.* I move along them, tracking. The long coast downhill is a wordless impersonal pleasure, like a painting.

He was also *utterly, uncritically and almost obsessively devoted to Wittgenstein.*

In the sentence Wittgenstein doesn't know how to use, the *I* hovers above the syntax and its body, claiming possession. I want most to be dispossessed, released into a wordless and grid-like ether. I consider *The King in the Dark Chamber* and wonder if humbling and subjugation are necessary for this escape.

The feeling of being wished dead, like the feeling of being thought of as *matter*, is likely related to an event. The details of this event are so typical and uninteresting I am embarrassed to recount them. (He was twice my age; it seemed romantic and exciting at first; I froze but did not verbally refuse; he moved very quickly; afterwards I cried and walked home alone, etc.)

Light breaks and remakes itself in the almond-shaped beech leaves and the hand-shaped maple leaves and the tear-shaped birch leaves in the canopy, each with its gradually shifting portion of shadow and its gradually shifting portion of light. They make a reflection like water on the saplings beneath them. Even the striped-bare hemlock is beautiful.

All resonance grows from consent to emptiness.

Skinner to Wittgenstein, March 25, 1934: *I long to be with you in any open space.*

I repeat this sentence to myself in my mind, imagining any open space, imagining a desire so extraordinarily gentle. I wonder where Francis is buried. Last night's rain erased my bicycle tracks, so riding to the studio I have the sensation that time has started over.

I do not often think about the event but when I do I cannot shake my surprise that I have allowed something so banal to contort my interior life in this lasting way. I have no feelings at all about the person who lifted and handled my body as though it were a dead animal: why have I stored and reanimated, thousands of times, the view of myself and my body his treatment of me seemed to signal? In particular, why the feeling of valuelessness, of inert deadness, of being so much disposable matter?

I cannot be certain he knew anything at all about what I felt. The words we use for this kind of event depend on variables that are in this case, uncertain. It may have been a mistake.

I do not know how the sentence "I have a body" is to be used. Whose body? How it is to be used?

I long to be with you
                                    in any open space.

Notes

William Shakespeare, Sonnet 116; Rosemarie Waldrop, *Curves to the Apple*; Ludwig Wittgenstein, *Philosophical Investigations*; Ludwig Wittgenstein, *On Certainty*; Ray Monk, *Ludwig Wittgenstein: The Duty of Genius*.

PART IV

PLACE

There were Princes and Presidents in our family,
mother told me;
and I believed,
this being America
and all.

—GLORIA ODEN

WHAT must a person sacrifice in order to believe in a place? In the words of Terese Svoboda, "What in the wake is being planted?" For Gloria Oden, what's planted is an "appetite of roots"—a family tree against the odds of racism in America. And what if that place is surrounded by borders, real only to the extent that one is allowed entrance? As Ha Jin suggests, "a country is an imagined place"—a place for creating, for expanding, for embracing. Before it claims an army, "issue[s] a visa or a passport," a country exists in the mind. The following twelve poems explore the concepts of home, country, community, and property through contingencies: sometimes, home is where we are loved "categorically" and sometimes it is where we are surveilled. Michael McFee remembers being swallowed by the "rotten mouth of Georgia"; Ron Rash catches his breath in "an Appalachian igloo," finding rest in the smallest space. Alicia Mountain questions the conditions of surviving in public: "in capitol, in seminary ... in sundown town," who is tasked with the "Fight" to stay alive? From "private things" and "private thoughts" to "vast public halls," these authors choose their place and take their stand.

I PLEDGE ALLEGIANCE

(VOL. 12, NO. 3, 1960)

Gloria Oden

....

There were Princes and Presidents in our family,
                    mother told me;
and I believed,
                  this being America
                            and all.
Solemn bunny bright eyed at her knee,
burning in baptism of ancestry,
I pictured "south,"
                    her seedland,
an immediately out of reach box of goodies,
fancy free of the fact that
she had left it.
I never thought about them
                      much.
The Prince, I mean.
Northbound to democracy,
                      fraternity, equality,
his blue-blood (mine) I dismissed for Grimm
                      wherein, anyway,
such silver-salt of birth
                    flashed forth
                              more real than
all the talk
          —no showing—
                  of how
on her father's side
my great grandpa was prince.
Oppositely,
          Mr. President
                      was on her mother's side.
She said it; but it
was not true.
In appetite of roots

I checked;
              learning
how in the human need for kin
             hand-me-down talk
had ladder-rung fish with fowl
to approach identity.
        Yet,
           this scholarship which downed
an old wives' tale
        raised up her true forbear;
and his;
blood stems of me.
All windmills in my mind.
In these tight times when
           some of us
have as feed the sour grapes
of citizenship;
while others report themselves "American"
only after (*country of your choice*)
I turn
      in the basement of my loyalty
search lighting these great grand men who
in the natural history of America
equalized themselves upon
my family tree.
One
   —that black, un-
common man
was a late arrival in our fields,
               and
I feel sure
none too happy with his royal loss of right
and privilege.
        Yet, his labor
made cotton darkly king;
no small accomplishment
considering how

                    in our day
                              we have seen
kingships broken down more
than raised.
The other
              the pink fruit
                              of an old inhabitancy
which
              since his grandpa stood General under
                    Ol Hickory
at the battle of New Orleans
makes me
              I think
                    pioneer. Or,
certainly
close to it since several cities
                              by their name
celebrate
my English-German-Scotch-Irish
Jewish integrity.
One, immigrant;
                    one native-born;
I, too, could second class this land. Except
                    I don't.
For
       in hyperbole of truth
                    I am America:
its golden Rule made visible;
its manifest of justice and liberty.
Self-consciously,
              I say who sees himself my foe
looks most upon
my country's enemy.

WAR & WAR PROTEST WAR

(VOL. 22, NO. 3, 1970)

Albert Goldbarth

....

April–May, 1970

I

Carbondale: burns the bituminous night.
Madison how deeply under
martial law?   Unreal
                                nation.
Maps become real: thick purple lines, dividing
a difference of states; above the head,
you can't see through. A hundred different
directions: pull. How to live
here, or leave it? When the garish light
of flaming cities dies and we can't see
anyway, we save our plans for leaving this map
until the ashen morrow. The country is folded
and shut in the drawer. We need a new one
with legible scales.

II

Carbondale burning. Madison sunk
with the dead weight of citizenry. My dreams
are more valid: I am tracing this day
back to its source. The red smoke of holocaust
vacuumed into its shiny containers; corpses
leap backwards onto gym shoes, and bullets
exit flesh pulling the warm plugs of suntan safely
closed behind them—I am at the source.
Morning. The swollen mother of this sad day.
        I staunch her cunt
          like any ugly wound.

FATHER FISHEYE

(VOL. 30, NO. 2, 1978)

Peter Balakian

....

The sun is gray and without a rim,
what light there is the water catches and keeps.
Fishmongers bear the crossed keys of the saint
on their arms. St. Christopher lived on the gulf
and sang for the kingfish when the winds left,
let his arms out from their joints when the old men
left in the dark with their trawl.

Father Fisheye, I come here to the rocks where the fires
are all ash, where the dockmen have disappeared
for the day of Genaro, where the boys with straw hats
have left with their fathers' empty creels and sandworms
in their pockets, where old men still sit staring
at the short ripples that go white at their feet.

I come to this inlet for eels and crabs,
for gangs of minnows that move like a long tail
and turn silver in the gray sun.
Father Fisheye, the air is still, trees motionless,
the sky touches my chest.
The sun is lost in the gray dusk water, gone into the gullets
of fishes that wander slowly out to the far waves.

HISTORY

(VOL. 45, NO. 1, 1992)

Jane Satterfield

....

Always I live for the sudden
shift—boundaries lifted,
well-wrought walls giving way, whole

kingdoms dissolved into dust, and even more
than annihilation I love
what lies under a tonnage of dirt—the little

that can be recovered—pipe pieces, petrified
grain, whole hoards of treasure
tossed down to the Thames . . . O river, O mud-

driven stream
for weeks I've walked
these crumbling banks to get a glimpse of the true,
the only current,
land in the act of loosening,
like flesh learning to let go. So this is history, then—

that smallest act of rescue,
the whole tale gleaned
from the rubbish, wrecked body
brought back to this side,
sands peeling back unheard of ruins.

PEARLY GATES

(VOL. 46, NO. 3, 1994)

Michael McFee

....

Sweet Aunt Thelma, coaxing me
to eat spoonfuls of mushy food,
sings her little off-key song:
Open up those pearly gates!

I watch the fishy silver dance
of spoon in air, the golden flash
of molars in her model mouth,
then laugh, and open up, and eat.

Years later, bored together
in the lugubrious backseat
on a family drive to Florida,
I say to her, *Let's play dentist!*

and reach to tug on her front teeth
and find myself holding the slick
pink roof of my Aunt Thelma's mouth,
kernels of teeth in a perfect arc.

I gasp as if bitten, then I gag,
dropping her half-smile on the floor,
terrified by her altered laugh
filling the cavity of the car

and the rotten mouth of Georgia
swallowing us as we head south
and the hungry sky behind the sky
with its unreachable pearly clouds.

AMERICAN LAKE

(VOL. 48, NO. 1, 1995)

Terese Svoboda

....

Return to the closed bowl,
kept taut by sand and jetty,
where waves lap in a lake way,
mum about the moon. Face the emptiness:
brown thumbs of ridges with names
no one knows anymore, so few animals
to eat at their curves. Maybe aboriginal
Arthurs played the original here—
chipped rocks that were once weapons
pattern the bottom. The veined vegetation
repeating under the cottonwoods say
history happens, say the Indians came,
no more native than sparrows, than you.
The canoe, the geese drag their hulls
and what in the wake is being planted?
Lie down where the old words grind
at victory, each stone at the other,
in no tide. Or keep out of it,
for the monster we bear between us
will not swim off, will breathe.

ONLY LOVE

(VOL. 48, NO. 3, 1996)

Heather McHugh

....

Some days in dazes I was Sinai'd: that's
incited, and required, requited,
vaulted, volted, jolted out
of all mere means.
But the days I intend
to attest to today
are the ones I was
carried on, ferried around,
borne across, held above, tided over,
afforded—routinely rewarded, by
undersung hosts. I was saved by the

busdriver, shoemaker, bank-teller,
x-ray technician, and highway patrol. I was moved
by a friendship, by worship, by warship,
by B-train and quatrain, by train of event;
served by Farm Aid, by barmaid,
by chance and by contract, by mercy, by curtsey,
by swagger and sway; I've been carried
by creditors, married by editors, followed by haulers
away of disposables (reams rumpled up, all those
meanings manqué)—I say

thank you ad hominem, thank you ad nominem, (thank you ad nauseam),
thank you to all. To the squadrons unseen
who put out magazines
for my girlhood to gloss through, my hopes to employ.
To the panoplies manifold, boys with amenities
(meant for hosanna, hooray and amen).
And to keepers of kitchens,
and fillers of urns;
and to cool liberality, giving us leave

to find private provision in vast public halls: all the
comforts of styrofoam, future of pyrodome, meaning
of hire-a-home, semblance of mall. We're at ease nowhere more

than in such a decor, in domains institutional, chambers of cool,
with their harbors of food machines, boxes of xeroxes, hundreds of
thousands of lockers and stalls, where there's tearable paper
and chrome-levered flush, where the clockhand's omniscient,
the anteroom plush. I adore public property, surely it stands

for the love democratical, love categorical, love
of so many it's love of no one. When I enter the rest stop,
or airport, or library, that's
when I know I am

not here to stay.
I am blessed automatically, unprepossessed. It's the
modernest model of

mere agape.

HOMEWORK

(VOL. 52, NO. 1, 1999)

Ha Jin

....

Under his pencil an island appears.
He says This is my country.

In no time it burgeons into colors.
A blue bay opens a horseshoe on
the shoulder of a glacier.
Below them a chain of mountains
zigzags, greened by rain forests.
Farther down he plants mines of metals:
aluminum, silver, copper, titanium,
iron, gold, uranium, tungsten, zinc.
Two oil fields beside branching rivers
are kept apart by Mount Fanfrane.
In the south a plain stretches
into vast fertile land, where
he crayons farms that yield oranges
potatoes, apples, strawberries,
wheat, broccoli, cherries, zucchini,
poultry, beef, mutton, cheese.
There is no fishery
because he can't eat seafood.
Volcanos are put to cool on Lulu Lake.

On the same map he draws a chart
railroads crisscross the landscape;
highways, pipelines, canals
are entwined; sea lanes curve
into the Pacific while airports
raise a web of skyways.
He imposes five time zones.

For a child a country is an imagined place
that doesn't keep a navy
or issue a visa or a passport.
His map hasn't been marred by a people.

JUNK CAR IN SNOW

(VOL. 52, NO. 3, 2000)

Ron Rash

....

No shade tree surgery could
revive its engine, so rolled
into the pasture, left stalled
among cattle, scabs of rust
breaking through blue paint, the tires
sagging like leaky balloons,
yet when snow came, magical,
an Appalachian igloo
I huddled inside, windshield
my window as I watched snow
smooth pasture as though a quilt
for winter to rest upon,
and how quiet it all was—the creek
muffled by ice, fox squirrels
curled in leaf beds, the crows mute
among stark lifts of branches,
only the sound of my own
white breath dimming the window.

WINGING THE FLOOD

(VOL. 52, NO. 3, 2000)

James Applewhite

....

The TV reported biblical floods
           drowning cities, villages and piney woods.
Now through our propeller's sheen
               tin roofs gleam an estuarine

horizon. Fields and forests drift,
           entangled in the currents flowing east.
A river surrounds a cemetery and steeple,
               islanding pigs with their people

at the cut-off farmhouse. Refuse
           mats against cars with logs, as the Neuse
refuses limits, deluge-delirious.
               Barns diminish in a victorious

brown sheet, that the clouds plate. Our shape
           flickers a submerged road where cars creep,
trailing wakes like boats. Windows and porches
               look on lawns that sun scorches

through three feet of live creek.
           Second stories drift off to sleep as sleek
ripples coil them. Tractors in sloughs
               plow quickly vanishing rows.

As if after the pastor's deluge, when a deep
           overflowed those towns of my sleep,
I founder in a threatened judgment
               brought finally to fulfillment.

Near metal sheds, a hog farm's effluent
           fans Pepto-Bismol pink into the current
unfurling its nasty plume downstream.
               Pigs rosy as in a dream

ride a metal roof, sunburned bathers.
      I imagine grandfathers and great grandfathers,
unable to swim from capsized skiffs those years ago,
         below the marble rows

that hold out still on a fenced knoll
      beside one brick church, as torrents roll
historically seaward. Two tobacco rows
         cast their parallel glows

as if yellow-green soldiers standing at attention.
      An attack and retreat exceeds dimension.
But the land is not swept clean, men
         who farmed hogs will again

brim lagoons with liquid waste, the past
      will insist on houses and lives cast
in the old molds: blacks in downhill shacks
         near creeks and railroad tracks

their faces held skyward while hope flashes
      as quickly over as our plane's image passes
where a bridge is submerged, then vanishes
         coastward. All I imagine

is in vain, though I suffer this inarticulate
      East again in language. Its sites originate
new recognition and failure as I see land
         emerge and a river wind

like the serpent returned, through New Bern,
      in this long-ruined place where I learn
by error if at all. Boat-furrow tills
         an alluvial drift of ills.

A highway-bridge rises like thought
      over the muddy mix and our flight
turns back from apocalypse. Hurricane Floyd
         seems history, flood to avoid

or endure, stained by hog manure. We'll raise
       more tombstones above it in continuing days
as this seaward streaming reflects us
             winged—runs brown and mysterious.

HAYMAKER BARNBURNER

(VOL. 67, NO. 2, 2018)

Alicia Mountain

....

And so the spotlit Fight of the Century
starts slowly—
   timid tapping airborne hands

like featherweight bees
bobbing between
apricot tree and apple.

All this, the work of a singular bounty,
the out-of-reach hound crowd,
their howling sound.

Surveil and surveil and survive,

keep alive by footwork
   that writes   l u n g e—   and retreat
                     l u n g e—   and retreat

In capitol, in seminary, in extant sundown town
whose fist is raised?
Whose liver-spotted hand smears ointment in the corner?

COLONY COLLAPSE

(VOL. 69, NO. 1, 2019)

Oliver Baez Bendorf

. . . .

begins without shelter in a storm, what
I have to do next. I sleep best
at anyone else's house. I like the ones that bees
like. I think madness is colonization. I know
grace is how I'm still alive, shock
of bluejay on an oxidized fence. I try
to make a religious exception, don't die
of perfection, heave along the goldenrod—begin
to live more together. I try to unravel Spanish

ways of knowing, for example, crown on my head

in an empty field . . . we plant
lavender and let it grow
bushy for the bees, sexy how they feed on blooms.

pleasure, time, money, faith, yucca, evil, each
one multiplies—we never eat alone, come
over, I will be a confidential lover
to each
one of you. private things, private thoughts, we bake
bread crumbs into royal
jelly. I love with every hand, horse, water, wind, if you wonder
where to rear the young, if you too fall
feverish after that communal feeling, swear to god
when I'm
dead I'll spend years waiting for the living
to call, offer wine and dance. I need
everyone I love. I'm too tired

time to feed our missing before they come
gone. third eye is a gloryhole. door's open. soup's on.

PART V

MEMORIAM

How does memory
serve, serve the earth?
—DENISE LEVERTOV

DEATH, Jill McCorkle writes, can "happen in numerous ways, to the world at large or to the world of an individual." These authors remind us that acts of writing, drawing, and memorializing help us contend with death, and strengthen our collective memory. In Raymond Carver's story, death happens "just like that," and those in its periphery are forced to confront their own mortality. When death happens in the "far fields of . . . life"—slowly and without company—as it does in James Salter's story, the honor of the fight (to keep on living) is overshadowed by the question of who will remember the solitary fight of a lonely man. In Linda Bierds's poem, life and death collapse into a single gruesome lesson: proof of what *cannot* be endured. And what cannot, and *must* not, be endured, Camille Dungy shows us, must not get the final word. There is always time for refusal, recollection, reparation—one person "keep[s] still" even when the "chant of the tedious season" sweeps history and its injustices along. And sometimes, memory is lodged simply in the shape of a letter. Ross White traces those shapes, traveling along the "rounded sides of words" to arrive at the past.

THE NIGHT THE MILL BOSS DIED

(VOL. 63, NO. 1, 1963)

Raymond Carver

....

A wind came up that afternoon bringing gusts of rain and sending the ducks up off the lake in black clusters looking for the quiet potholes out in the timber. Jay was at the back of the house splitting firewood and saw them cutting over the highway and dropping into the marsh behind the trees. He watched them for a few minutes. Groups of five or six, but mostly doubles, one bunch behind the other. Out over the lake it was already dark and misty and he couldn't see the other side, where the mill was. He worked faster, driving the iron wedge down harder into the big dry chunks, splitting them so far down that sometimes the rotten ones fell apart between his hands. On his wife's clothesline, strung up between the two sugarpines, the sheets and blankets popped shot-like in the wind. He made two trips and carried all the wood onto the porch before it started to rain.

"Supper's ready," Anne called from the kitchen.

He went inside and washed up. They talked a little while they ate, mostly about the trip to Reno. Three more days of work, then payday, then the weekend in Reno.

After supper he went out onto the porch and began sacking up his decoys. He stopped when she came out. She stood there in the doorway watching him.

"You going hunting again in the morning?"

He looked away from her and out toward the lake. "Look at the weather. I think it's going to be good in the morning." Her sheets were popping and blowing in the wind and there was a blanket down on the ground. He nodded at it. "Your things are going to get wet."

"They weren't dry anyway. They've been out there two days, and they're not dry yet."

"What's the matter, hon, don't you feel good?"

"I feel all right." She went back into the kitchen and shut the door and looked at him through the glass. "I just hate to have you gone all the time. It seems like you're gone all the time."

Her breath came on the glass then went away.

He put the decoys in the corner and went back into the kitchen for his lunchpail. She was leaning against the cupboard with her hands on the edge of the draining board.

"I'm not gone all the time," he said.

She shook her head. "I know it. But it seems like it sometimes."

He touched her hip with his hand, pinched at her dress.

"You wait'll we get to Reno. We're going to have some fun, huh!"

She nodded. It was hot in the kitchen and there were little drops of sweat over her eyes. "I'll get up when you come in and fix you some breakfast."

"You sleep. I'd rather have you sleep." He reached around behind her for his lunch pail.

"Kiss me bye," she said.

He hugged her. She fastened her arms around his neck and held him for a minute. "I love you. Be careful driving!"

She went to the kitchen window and watched him, running, jumping over the puddles until he got to his pickup. She waved when he looked back from inside the cab. It was almost dark and it was raining hard.

Two hours later she was sitting in a chair by the living room window listening to the radio, watching the few cars and trucks go by on the highway when she saw the pickup lights turn into the drive. She got up quickly and hurried to the back door.

"Honey. What is it?" He stood there in the doorway, and she touched his wet, rubbery coat with her fingers.

"They told everybody to go home. The mill boss had a heart attack. He fell right down on the floor up in the mill and died."

"You scared me." She took his lunch pail and shut the door. "Who was it? Was it that foreman named Mel?"

"No, his name was Jack Granger. He was about fifty years old, I guess." He walked over close to the oil stove and stood there warming his hands. "Jesus, it's so funny! He just came through where I work and asked me how I was doing and probably wasn't gone five minutes when Bill Bessie came in and told me Jack Granger had just died right up in the mill." He shook his head. "Just like that."

"Don't think about it, honey." She took his hand between hers and rubbed his fingers. "I'm not. Just one of them things, I guess. You never know."

The rain belted the house and slashed across the windows. Each time the house shook the oil stove puffed and brightened. Jay looked at the stove, at the way the shadows glowed and faded on the wall behind, then wiped his hand across his face. "God, it's hot in here! There any beer?"

"I think there's some left. In the bottom of the icebox."

Anne followed him out to the kitchen. His hair was still wet and she ran her fingers through it after he sat down. She opened a beer for him and poured some into a cup for herself. He sat drinking it in little sips, looking out the window toward the dark woods.

"One of the guys said he had a wife and two grown kids."

"That's a shame! It's nice to have you home but I hate for something like that to have happened."

"That's what I told some of the guys. I said, it's nice to have a holiday, but Christ, I hate to have it like this." He edged a little in the chair. It was kind of silly saying that, especially that about the holiday. "You know, I think they would've gone ahead and worked, but it took the ambulance so long to get there. Some of the guys up in the mill said they wouldn't work. Him laying there like that. They knew him better than I did." He finished off the beer and got up. "I'll tell you—I'm glad they didn't work."

"I'm glad you didn't either! I had a funny feeling when you left tonight. I was thinking about you when I saw the lights."

"He was just in the lunch room last night telling jokes. He was a good guy. Always laughing."

She nodded. "I'm sorry. I'll fix us a snack if you'll eat something?"

"I'm not very hungry, but I'll eat something."

Afterwards they sat in the living room together and held hands and watched television.

"I've never seen any of these programs before," he said.

"I don't much care about watching it anymore. You can hardly get anything worth watching up here. Saturday and Sunday it's all right, but there's nothing during the week nights."

He stretched his legs and leaned back. "I'm kind of tired. I think I'll go to bed."

"I think I'll take a bath and go to bed too." She moved her fingers through his hair then dropped her hand and began smoothing his neck. "Maybe we'll have a little tonight. We never hardly get a chance anymore to go to bed together this time of night." She laid her other hand on his thigh, leaned over and kissed him. "What do you think about that?"

"That sounds all right." He got up and walked over to the window. Against the trees outside he could see her reflection standing behind him and a little to the side. "Hon, why don't you go ahead and take your bath and we'll turn in." He stood there for a while longer watching the rain spatter against the window. He wasn't really sleepy but he felt kind of tired. He looked at his watch. If he were working they'd be on their lunch hour now. He went into the bedroom and began getting undressed.

In his shorts he walked back into the living room and picked up a book off the endtable. *Best-Loved Poems of the American People.* The book had come in the mail from that club his wife belonged to. He went through the house and turned off the lights before going back into the bedroom. He got under the covers, put her pillow on top of his, and twisted the gooseneck lamp around so that the light fell right on the pages. He opened the book to the middle and began to look at some of the shortest poems. In a few minutes he laid the book on the bed stand and twisted the lamp away toward the wall. He lit a cigarette, then put his arms behind his head and lay there smoking, looking straight ahead at the wall. The lamp light picked up all of the tiny cracks and swells in the plaster. In a corner up near the ceiling, there was a cobweb. He could hear the rain running down off the roof and guessed the wind had stopped because the house was still and the rain was a steady drizzle. He was glad the shade was pulled.

She stood up in the tub and began drying herself. When she noticed him watching she smiled and draped the towel over her shoulder and made a little step in the tub, and posed, like she was about to dance.

"How does it look?"

"Fine," he said.

"You don't sound very encouraging."

"I thought you were still on your period."

"I am." She finished drying and dropped the towel on the floor beside the tub. She stepped out onto it. The mirror beside her was steamy and a faint, sweet odor of her body carried into the bedroom. She turned around and reached up to a shelf for the Modess box. Then she slipped into her belt and adjusted the white pad. Several times she looked through to the bedroom and smiled.

He turned over and crushed out the cigaret then picked up the book again.

"What are you reading?"

"I don't know . . . crap," He turned to the back of the book and began looking through the biographies. "Most of the guys in here are dead, anyway."

She turned off the light and came out of the bathroom brushing her hair. He watched her giant shadow up on the wall behind her.

"You still going in the morning?"

"Ah, I don't think so."

"I'm glad. We'll sleep in late, then get up and have a big breakfast."

"Sounds good to me." He reached over and got another cigarette.

She put the brush in a drawer then opened another drawer and took out a nightgown. "Do you remember when you got me this?"

He nodded.

She raised the shade, came around to his side of the bed and slipped in beside him. They lay quietly for a minute smoking his cigarette until he nodded he was finished, and she put it out. He reached over her, kissed her on the shoulder and switched off the light.

"You know," he said, lying back down, "I think I want to get out of here. Go someplace else."

"What's wrong, honey?" She moved over to him and put her leg between his. They lay on their sides facing each other, lips almost touching. He wondered if his own breath smelled as clean as hers .

"I just want to leave. We been here a long time. I'd kind of like to go back home and see my folks. Or maybe go up to Oregon. That's nice country."

"If that's what you want."

"I think so," he said. "There's a lot of places to go."

She moved a little then and took his hand and put it on her breast. Then she opened her mouth and kissed him, pulling his head down with her other hand. Slowly she inched up in the bed, gently moving his head down to her breast. He rubbed his lips over the smooth, warm breast then took the nipple and began working it in his mouth. He tried to think how much he loved her. He could hear her breathing, and outside the steady rain. They lay like this for a while and he traced his fingers up and down her leg.

In a while she said, "If you don't want to, honey that's all right."

"It's not that," he said, not knowing exactly what he meant.

"Cuddle me," she said, turning over with her back to him.

He moved over closer and put his arm around her. She began to cry, holding her face against the pillow.

"Please don't cry," he said. "What's the matter, Anne?"

"Nothing."

He pressed his hand on her stomach and moved as close to her as he could, until her back flattened against his chest and his legs lay tight against hers, slightly bent. She relaxed and in about half an hour he could tell she was asleep. He let go then and turned over to his own side. He listened to the clock ticking on the dresser. Every five ticks or so, it skipped. Then it was regular again, then it skipped. He wiggled his toes against the sheet. He shouldn't have said what he said about the holiday. The guys looked funny. He would be glad when they got to Reno. He tried to remember all of the light and noise on the second floor of Harold's Club. The thunk of the slots and the way the dice clicked and how shiny they looked turning over under the lights. The sound the roulette ball made as it rattled around the bright wheel. He tried to concentrate and move up closer to the wheel where he could follow the white ball with his eyes but just when he had it almost down to a pattern, red, black, black, red, someone reached out and stopped the wheel. Try as he might, it all began to fade. Now there was only a group of men left standing around a man lying face down on a board floor with his arms gripped round his sides. He looked away from the man up toward the glaring, white lights overhead. All over the mill the saws and machinery were slowing up, coming to a stop.

He got out of bed and walked over to the window. It was black outside and he could see nothing, not even the rain. But he could hear it, running thickly off the roof and into a puddle under the window. He could hear it pelting all over the house. He ran his finger across the wet drool on the glass and then pulled the shade.

When he got back into bed the one o'clock mill whistle began to blow. It shrilled out across the lake and the timber and over the little town and pierced his ears. Then it would stop, then start again. It kept piercing. He moved closer to her warmth and put his hand on her hip. "Hon, wake up," he whispered. But she only shuddered and moved over a little farther to her own side. She kept on sleeping. "Wake up," he whispered, "I hear something outside."

COWBOYS

(VOL. 23, NO. 2, 1971)

James Salter

....

Death was coming for Harry Mies. He would lie emptied, his cheeks rouged, the fine old man's ears set close to his head. There was no telling the things he knew. He was alone in the far fields of his life. The rain fell on him, he did not move.

There are animals that finally, when the time comes, will not lie down. He was like that. When he kneeled he got up again slowly. He rose to one knee, paused, and finally swayed to his feet like an old horse.

His helper, Billy, was under the house. It was cool there, it smelled of the unturned earth of fifty years. He was on his back inching along a little at a time. A kind of rancid dust mixed with bits of wood and dirt sifted down through the floorboards and fell on his face like a light rain. He spit it out. He turned his head and, reaching carefully up, wiped around his eyes with the sleeve of his shirt. He looked back towards the strip of daylight at the edge of the house. Harry's legs were in the sun—every so often, with a groan, he would kneel down to see how it was going.

They were leveling the floor of the old Bude house. Like all of them it had no foundation, it was built on pieces of wood.

"Feller could start right there," Harry called.

"This one?"

"That's it."

Billy slowly wiped the dirt from his eyes again and began to set up the jack. The joists were a few inches above his face. They ate lunch sitting outside. It was hot, mountain weather. The sun was dry, the air thin as paper. Harry ate slowly. He had a wrinkled neck and white stubble along his jowl line.

"Feller in town with all the hair . . ." he said.

Billy's fingers were making black marks on the bread.

"The hair."

"What's he supposed to be?"

"Yeah, I think a drummer," Billy said.

"A drummer."

"He's with a band."

"Must be with something," Harry said.

He unscrewed the cap from a battered thermos and poured what looked like tea. They sat in the quiet of the tall cottonwoods, not even the highest leaves were moving.

They drove to the dump, the sun in the windshield was burning their knees. There was an old cattle gate salvaged from somewhere, some bankrupt ranch. It was open, Harry drove in. They were in a field of junk and garbage on the edge of the creek, a bare field forever smouldering. A man in overalls appeared from a shack surrounded by bedsprings. He was round-shouldered, heavy as a bull. There was an old green Chrysler parked on the far side.

"Looking for some pipe, Al," Harry said.

The man said nothing. He gave a sort of half-hearted signal.

Harry had already gone past and turned down an alley of old furniture, stoves, aluminum chairs. There was a sour smell in the air. A few refrigerators, indestructible, had fallen down the bank and were lying, half-buried in the stream.

The pipe was all in one place. It was mostly rusted, Billy kicked aimlessly at some sections.

"We can use it," Harry said.

They began carrying pieces back to the car and put them on the roof. They drove slowly, the old man's head tilted back a little, pale stubble on his cheeks. The car swayed in and out of holes. The pipe rolled in the rack.

"Pretty good feller, Al," Harry said. They were coming to the shack. He lifted his hand as they passed. The man was not there. Billy's mind was wandering. The ride to town seemed long.

"They give him a lot of trouble," Harry said. He was watching the road, the empty road which connects all these towns.

"There's none of that stuff much good out there," he said. "Sometimes he tries to charge a little for it. People feel like they ought to be able to carry it off for nothing."

"He didn't charge you."

"Me? No, I bring him a little something now and then," Harry said. "Old Al and me are friends."

After a while he added, "Claims to be a free country, I dunno ..." he said.

The cowboys at Gerhart's called him the Swede, he never went in there. They would see him go by, long nose, dangling arms, the slowness of age as he walked. He may have looked a little Swedish, pale-eyed from those mornings of invincible white, mornings of the great southwest, black coffee in his cup, the day ahead. The ashtrays on the bar were plastic, the clock had the name of a whiskey printed on its face.

It was five-thirty. Billy came in.

"There he is."

He ignored them.

"What'll it be, then?" Gerhart said.

"Beer."

On the wall was the stuffed head of a bear with a pair of glasses propped on its nose, a red plaster tongue. Above it hung an American flag and a sign: No Dogs Allowed. About the middle of the day there were a few people like Wayne Garrich who had the insurance agency, they wore straw rancher's hats rolled at the sides. Later there were construction workers in T-shirts and sunglasses, gas company men. It was always crowded after five. The ranch hands sat together at the tables with their legs stretched out. They had belt buckles with a gold-plated steerhead on them.

"Be thirty cents," Gerhart said. "What're you up to? Still working for old Harry?"

"Yeah, well ..." Billy's voice wandered.

"What's he paying you?"

He was too embarrassed to tell the truth.

"Two fifty an hour," Billy said.

"Jesus Christ," Gerhart said. "I pay that for sweeping floors."

Billy nodded. He had no reply.

Harry took three dollars an hour himself. There were probably people in town would take more, he said, but that was his rate. He'd pour a foundation for that, he said, take three weeks. There was not one day of rain. The sun laid on their backs like boards.

Harry got the shovel and hoe from the trunk of his car. He was tall, he carried them in one hand. He turned the wheelbarrow right side up, the bags of cement were piled beneath on a piece of plywood. He flushed out the wheelbarrow with the hose. Then he began mixing the first load of concrete: five shovels of gravel, three of sand, one of cement. Occasionally he'd stop to pick out a twig or piece of grass. The sun beat down like flats of tin. Ten thousand days of it down in Texas and all around. He turned the dry mixture over upon itself again and again, finally he began adding water. He added more water, working it in. The color became a rich river-grey, the smooth face broken by gravel. Billy stood watching.

"Don't want it too runny," the old man said. There was always a feeling he might be talking to himself. He laid down the hoe. "Okey-dokey," he said.

His shoulders were stooped, they had the set of labor in them. He took the handles of the barrow without straightening up.

"I'll get it," Billy said, reaching.

"That's all right," Harry muttered. His teeth whistled on the "s."

He wheeled it himself, the surface now smooth and shifting a little from side to side, and set it down with a jolt near the wooden forms he'd built—Billy had dug the trench. Checking them one last time, he tilted the wheelbarrow and the heavy, slamming liquid poured from its lip. He scraped it empty and then moved along the trench with his shovel, jabbing to fill the voids. On the second trip he let Billy push the barrow, naked to the waist, the sun roaring down on his shoulders and back, his muscles jumping as he lifted. The next day he let him shovel.

He lived near the Catholic church, Billy, in a room on the ground floor. It had a metal shower. He slept without sheets, in the morning he drank milk from the carton. He was going out with a waitress at Daly's. Her name was Alma, she had legs with hard calves. She didn't say much, her complaisance drove him crazy, sometimes she was at Gerhart's with someone else in a haze of voices, the bark of laughter, famous heavyweights behind her tacked on the wall. There were water stains near the ceiling. The door to the men's room slammed.

They talked about her. They stood at the bar so they could see her by turning a little. She was a girl in a small town. The television had exhibition football coming from Grand Junction. She was at their mercy. They were thinking of her legs as they watched the game, she was like an animal they wanted. She smoked a lot, Alma, but her teeth were white. She was flat-faced, like a fighter. She would be living in the trailer park, Billy told her. Her kids would eat white bread in big, soft packages from the Woody Creek Store.

"Oh, yeah?"

She didn't deny it. She looked away. Like an animal, he thought. It didn't matter how pure they were, how beautiful. They went down the highway in clattering steel trucks, wisps of straw blowing clear as they passed. They were watched by the cold eyes of cowboys. They entered the house of blood, its sudden bone-cleaving blows, its mulled cries. He didn't spend much money on her. He was saving up. She never mentioned it.

They poured the side of the house that faced Third Street and started along the front. He thought of her in the sunlight that was browning his arms. He lifted the heavy barrow and became strong everywhere, like a tightened cable. When they finished in the evening, Harry washed off everything with the hose, he put the shovel and hoe in the trunk of his car. He sat on the front seat with the door open. He smiled to himself. He lifted his cap and smoothed his hair.

"Say," he said. There was something he wanted to tell. He looked at the ground. "Ever been west?"

It was a story of California in the thirties. There was a whole bunch of them going from town to town, looking for work. One day they came to a place, he forgot the name, and went into some little restaurant. You could get a whole meal for thirty cents in those days, but when they came to pay the check, the owner told them it was a dollar fifty each. If they didn't like it, he said, there was the state police just down the street. Harry walked over to the barber shop, he looked like that musician, he had so much hair. The barber put the sheet around him. Haircut, Harry told him. Hey, wait a minute, how much will it be? The barber had the scissors in his hand. See you been eating over to the Greek's, he said.

He laughed a little, almost shyly. He glanced at Billy, his long teeth showed. They were his own. Billy was buttoning his shirt.

It was hot in the evening. The hottest summer in years, everyone said, the hottest ever. At Gerhart's they stood around in big, dusty shoes.

"Shit, it's hot," they told each other.

"Can't get much hotter."

"What'll it be, then?" Gerhart would ask. His idiot son was rinsing glasses. "Beer."

"Hot enough for you?" Gerhart said as he served it.

They stood at the bar, their arms covered with dust. Across the street was the movie house. Up towards the pass, the sand and gravel pit. There was ranching all around, a macadam plant, men like Wayne Garrich who hardly spoke at all, the bitterness had penetrated to the bone. They were deliberate, their habits were polished smooth. They looked out through the big, store windows.

"Hey . . ."

"She's something, isn't she?"

They laid out the phrases in low voices, like bets. Their arms were big as firewood on the bar.

"Sure wants someone to do her, don't she?"

"Bet she does."

The foundation was finished at the beginning of September. There was a little sand where the pile had been, a few specks of gravel. The nights were already cold, the first emptiness of winter, not a light on in town. The trees seemed silent, subdued. They would begin to turn suddenly, the big ones going last.

Harry died about three in the morning. He had been leaning on the cart in the supermarket, behind the stacks, struggling for breath. He tried to drink some tea. He sat in his chair. He was between sleep and waking, the kitchen light was on. Suddenly he felt a terrible, a bursting pain. His mouth fell open, his lips were dry.

He left very little, a few clothes, the Chevrolet filled with tools. Everything seemed lifeless and worn. The handle of his hammer was smooth. He had worked all over, built ships in Galveston during the war. There were photographs when he was twenty, the same hooked nose, the hard, country face. He looked like a pharaoh there in the funeral home. They had folded his hands. His cheeks were sunken, his eyelids like paper.

Billy Amstel went to Mexico in a car he and Alma bought for a hundred dollars. They agreed to share expenses. The sun polished the windshield in which they sat going southward. They told each other stories of their life.

LIFE CLASS

(VOL. 24, NO. 2, 1972)

Annie Dillard

....

Death class. At least a kind of death for Elizabeth, probably even the kind of death that set Philbo driving her convertible like a Jehu, scattering her ashes, torn bits of paper, over London, the Midi, the Villa Sciara. In Naples, posing as her brother to get past the desk, I saw she was just a mess of wires, all hollow, ragged outlines like a map. The nurse brought her tray and she sat in a way that couldn't possibly have supported her torso. Her buttocks beneath her flannel gown had no curve nor shadow, no sign of the weight of her meeting with the mattress. Philbo never could draw, and now she was a lifeless sketch, a hard-pencil doodle on a paper bag, executed without humor or grace, while he was worrying, not about her, but about his car (he whispered to me in the corridor outside her room where we'd left her to sleep): "Some idiot backed into the pumpkin Porsche and they have to send away for parts." Poor Elizabeth. Her arms and legs were hollow tubes, her hands and feet were too small, if her feet were there at all, and she had no neck.

But these are common enough failings in beginners. Philbo didn't even know how to sharpen a pencil, how to hold a crayon; his embarrassment contributed to hers the first couple of classes until he settled into the pattern he stuck with all spring, even after I had graduated to color: filling sheet after sheet of newsprint with lines, ragged charcoal lines, as if the intricate, receding horizons of the form, of Elizabeth herself seated primly on the mattress, an awkward hand on her hip—as if those horizons were delineated in black tape marking the boundaries between what could be seen and what could not, black-tape boundaries which coursed around her form like an ant trailing ink, oblivious to weight distribution, the subtle pull and counterpull of muscle, organ, bone.

But Elizabeth got used to it. Although even in May, when our sheets of newsprint sweated together and our fingers stuck to the chalk, even in May when Philbo presumably knew every inch of her by touch if not by sight, even then she still kept her skirt well down on her knees, and half the time she wore long-sleeved blouses. It was a sad little gesture: when she'd taken the pose Philbo wanted, she'd pat her skirt down, a ritual check on the security of hidden valuables that seemed to assure her, merely by its repetition, that what she was trying to conceal was indeed valuable—though she was already getting lined and ragged at the edges, with pale circles at her knees and elbows, the trademark of Philbo's style, if he could be said to have such a thing.

That she was beautiful goes without saying. Only the beautiful girls ever modeled. In the past, according to rumor, there had been some very beautiful girls, who consented to model nude. Only the beautiful girls, past or present, naked or clothed, could be comforted enough by their own vain imaginations to suffer being twisted like wires, treated like posts, for a few cigarettes and the minimum wage. Oh Elizabeth was lovely when she first modeled, pink lungs, white buttocks, and lovelier still as I learned from her, even as she turned awkward and smeared before my eyes. At first I used to draw her entire reproductive system, the delicacy and detail of her Fallopian tubes focusing interest on the otherwise flat, bare abdomen—not to mention the ugly, inorganic lines of her skirt—but Philbo shamed me out of it, and it upset Elizabeth.

She didn't talk much. Philbo maintained a steady patter, an exhaustive, hollow monologue, spotted with bright, current phrases like pebbles of fool's gold in desert sand. Some of it, especially the gossip, would interest me in spite of myself, and I would look up from my nude to see Elizabeth swathed in heavy clothing, mesmerized by the steady waves of innuendo and irony, even the apparent wit, that spewed from Philbo's face while his hand marked lazy circles on the page. I called her once from the underground station; her accent seemed harsh on the phone. I tried to imitate the sudden glissandos, the diminuendos of her speech in the hope that she would find me less strange; but she would not meet me. Was Philbo listening, his ear against her cheek? When she saw me in the courtyard, she cried and said she was unhappy. She was uncomfortable in her beauty, but when it left she began to disappear, began to be lost in the mob scene, the Hieronymus Bosch landscape of the clumsy, weightless dead. Elizabeth! It's not that Philbo didn't love you, for he did. He starched your clothes and brushed sizing in your hair till it looked like streaked cement; he gave you a clown's nose and ankles mangled past hope of repair; but he loved you as God and the serpent loved Eve newly-made and for the asking in the garden. But there's no talking to Elizabeth. Now she's lost her ears altogether, her ears which her hair always covered to Philbo, rounded, intricate ears, more stately mansions which I drew lovingly, which I still draw now, though the innermost detail of hammer, anvil, stapes' curves eludes my hand.

For Easter I went with my family to the seashore. There Elizabeth rode the waves on a scallop shell, in color for the first time. There I boxed up my conté crayons, my smooth sticks of charcoal, and laid her out in crimson and delicate creams on canvasses big as beds while mother made stews in the kitchen and Jerry my brother crouched by the wall in the garden, watching the lizards sun. I still have most of those canvases now and am adding to them; I gave Philbo one, the virgin of the herring gulls, to save for Dolores when she's older.

Acquired traits, in this case, were not inherited; Dolores stood solid and sturdy as a Michelangelo at the side of the hospital bed, fingering the two-dimensional, unmodelled square of newsprint that was Elizabeth's hand. In class that hand loved me. It would make turgid gestures to me as I worked, or it would aspire limply, with a fluttering motion, to the portraits Elizabeth saw on the page when she walked behind my easel, backstage as it were, during her break. Much later, when I was in my liver period, which lasted two weeks while I was reading Li Po, Elizabeth's liver, in some ways her loveliest most classical feature, made a tremendous conscious effort to match the warm and vibrant earth-tones on my canvas, and failed. I am not bragging when I say that she loved me, that she still loves me if she is alive, as the saints love Christ. But the *via negativa* was her way; it became her only truth; it sucked her life into its vacuum. The other she would not dare. She was dimly aware that I knew; at the wedding the arch of her spine revealed itself in shadows warm and rounded when she saw me, her face came into focus and her hair loosened and swayed.

For so often Philbo forgot the face, or ignored it, laying a careless ellipse directly on the horizontal bar that was all he knew of her shoulders. The instructor, for there was an instructor, would stand unseeing at Philbo's side, or take a chalk and draw on Philbo's paper the lines that he knew were there: the ecstatic arch of the neck and the curve of the latissimus dorsi filling her blouse in back. M. Arnaud: who could not bear what he, and he alone, called "the studio," who left us for days and weeks at a time to pursue our fraternal twin visions of Elizabeth three stories up in the warm tones of dusk through the skylight. M. Arnaud, who, according to legend, woke one day to find art in his life like a flock of doves in the garden, and woke another morning to find it just as thoughtlessly gone.

Only rarely did he judge or advise us. On one occasion he watched Philbo trying to sort out the relationships of Elizabeth's arm and legs and skirt as she sat with her hands clasped over her knees, watched as Philbo drew bold graceless lines across the page at apparent random, and remarked merely, "Watch your inner spaces." Philbo seized on the expression and made it his own, until from sheer repetition it grew as hollow as the space between Elizabeth's arm and her waist when she stood relaxed, that space shaped like a blown-glass ornament, receding to infinite depths without form. Philbo would look at my drawings, my hundreds and hundreds of figure drawings, portraits, cartoons, anatomical studies, essays in the dance, orthodonty, architecture, later giant canvases, walls of color in oils, gesso, Judith and Holofernes, the destruction of Sennacherib—and say, "Watch your inner spaces"; and laugh.

But there was no malice in him; only innocence. After the class had disbanded he would confide in me, leaning forward in his chair on the patio of the café on the Rue Rosette to which he had grandly invited me to be his guest at breakfast, that Elizabeth was afraid of the baby ("Please stop, oh please don't cry"), that she had lately been troubled by dreams that neither of them understood, that the doctors were worried and baffled. Flocks of rock doves wheeled overhead, keening for Elizabeth. But they were wrong, short-sighted and afraid as natural creatures are. Whenever I pass that café now, at whatever time of day, Elizabeth sits in the empty chair at our old table, swathed and proud in her nakedness as though it were cloth-of-gold. If I pause to admire her kidneys, smooth and snug in their jackets as babies, she greets me as a lover, and bids me sit and eat. Winged bowls of fruit appear at our places, ripened pears and opulent grapes. In the forest sweet nutmeats fall at our feet, and for her sake I dig up some truffles. I am painting her portrait now, a *mater dolorosa* in the courtyard where she once stood head bowed and grieving; it is going well. Through the prism of her clear, transfigured form, sunlight shatters into shafts and circles of pure color, scattered over the canvas, the courtyard, the hospital, the room in which we drew to the edge of the earth. That day in Naples, underneath it all, Philbo was desperate, knowing she would die and he would be bereft and tied to the child. I looked into the room where she lay folded and crumpled in sleep. All her internal organs were gone, all of her tendons and most of her muscles and bones. "Goodbye," spelled the ragged, charcoal lines of her arms which had held fat Dolores and insolent Philbo so lightly, without understanding, "So long." She languishes now on the desk as I write, rounded and full as a fruit, Susanna bathing in a pool of light. On a marble slab in the sink my colors are rising to meet her, to claim what is mine.

NURSERY RHYME 1916

(VOL. 35, NO. 2, 1983)

Alice Fulton

....

(in memoriam: James Callahan)

> On fine days he lay outside, juggling
> the sun with toes, hands, tongue.
> Then neighbors came with angel food
> cakes. They kept nightwatch
> by his white plush case.
> Heaven was a greedy place.
>
> Mornings, he'd turn the porridge bowl
> over his head and cry "Done!"
> The crape hung, pink as divinity:
> air, sugar, eggs, whipped to a shape
> that dissolves before its taste.
> Heaven was a greedy place.

THE TERMS OF ENDURANCE

(VOL. 38, NO. 1, 1985)

Linda Bierds

....

The last bell has not yet left your ears
as your friends crowd in around you:
girls in reversible skirts—green plaid
to red—in powdered, white buck shoes.
And now the boys, ringing in
with their cleated wing-tips, autumn
sweaters still tight at the neck.

It is that time of endurance.

Together you watch an oval dish, boiling
with water. Beneath it, a bunsen burner flame
flattens to an amber coin. Now observe,
the teacher tells you, dropping the body
of a pond frog to the jumping water.
In one motion it lands, senses, leaps,
its pale underside extending to an arrow,

a filament of light. The flame
is turned down, the dish replaced
Within it, the reptilian body
languishes in luke-warm water—gradually
heated, heated, until the small
boil bubbles churn at the rim of the dish
and the frog turns its lifeless belly
to your face, to each face, presents
it slowly, like a sigh: *Here.*

And what does this tell us? the teacher
asks. You are stunned, unable
to speak, unable to comprehend yet
the terms of endurance. You think only
of that motion, the scorched belly
turning up like a sigh, and wonder
why the animal did not leap as before,
why it did not understand its own
tolerance, and why it would stay there,

in that water too long its element.
Heavy and troubled, you walk
back to your seat, past the blackboards
and the long mural of Civilization
and its Great Wars. On this cold autumn morning,
you cannot understand your own grief,
how it swells and recedes. Already
the instruments for Music
are arriving, bold and familiar;
the sleigh bells and castanets, and
for you the shining triangle, its one note
so perfect in your hand.

ANAMNESIS AT THE FAULTLINE

(VOL. 45, NO. 3, 1993)

Denise Levertov

....

> For Barbara Thomas, after
> experiencing her installation,
> "What Is Found, What Is Lost, What
> Is Remembered," 1992

I

In each house, imprinted,
a journey.   Partings, tearings
         apart: storm, loss, hands
         upraised for rescue,
         onrush of wave,
         exile.
Long-hidden, the time
of arrival, plumb-line,
first foundation.

How does memory
serve, serve the earth?
         Columns
         of turned wood placed
         among broken stones,
         perches for companion
         ravens. A way
         of witness.

II

House, hill-field, open
shell of stillness:
         passage

                                    through
                                    from doorless
                                    doorway
                                    to doorway
                                    to sky.
The wind
                    where it listeth.

                            III

In each bird,
storm-voyage.

In each tilted
cross, human
dreams,
clouds,
the shifting
seasons.

And in each grave.

                                    In each stasis,
                                    impetus. Dark
                                    edifice, backlit, bigger
                                    than house or grave. White
                                    gold of its aura.

FROM CAROLINA MOON

(VOL. 49, NO. 1, 1996)

Jill McCorkle

....

These days, Tommy does a lot of work for Ms. Purdy (she has recently changed the pronunciation to Pur DAY). She dresses the same way exactly and her hair, though gray, is still yanked back in a bushy ponytail that reaches the middle of her back. Tommy does carpentry and brick work, furniture refinishing and repair. He recently finished building a huge deck to surround the hot tub he installed for her new business (a quit-smoking clinic), and now he's building a closet in the small apartment she has over her garage. He once tried to tell Mrs. Purdy (she insists he call her Quee, though it doesn't come off his tongue easily) what an impact she made on him with that trip, but she wouldn't allow it. He was hoping to work his way up to thanking her for that other time she had helped him as well, that time when he was in high school with nowhere else to turn.

Now he kneels in the firm, damp sand that belongs to him. He pays forty-one cents a year in county taxes and eleven cents to the city. Every day he takes a break from work and comes here, sometimes just to sit, sometimes to wade in and pace off the lot, seventy feet deep and fifty feet wide. He sits back, jeans and sneakers wet and sandy, and scoops his hands into the sand. One of the few times he actually talked to his father, they were here, at the beach. Tom was ten and interested in the stories his father had to tell about the pirates who once inhabited these very waters. Cecil told him that their name, Lowe, was derived from George Lowther's, a pirate from England who killed himself. "It makes sense that he would," Tom's father had said that day, the hem of his khakis damp, the sleeves of his white dress shirt rolled up to just below the elbow. Then they drove back into town where his father took him to the new bank building to ride the elevator up the third floor. It was the highest building in town.

Tom tried that day to absorb all he could about his father. It had been six years since he had seen him and might be another six before he saw him again. He realized he had his father's coloring, the straight, almost black hair and hazel eyes; he had the sharp facial bones and full lips. But his father was a lanky six feet and two inches, and Tommy was one of the shorter boys in his class.

In the car, his father talked about Atlantis, how maybe somewhere out in the depths of the ocean there existed a whole world that had been swallowed, bottled. Tommy had tried to imagine it, his own town submerged, wavy and dark in the deepest depths. He imagined their house, a small brick ranch washed through: windows black, drapes undulating like sea anemones, sparse furniture held in place by the weight of the water. Cecil talked about how easily the world could come to an end—it could happen in numerous ways, to the world at large or to the world of an individual. "For instance, the world your mother and I created," he said and paused, the car idling at the intersection. "It ended." He stared straight ahead, jaw clenched, and in that moment Tommy understood why his mother hadn't wanted him to go on this outing. This was what she was scared about. This is what she must have meant all of those times she told Tommy that his father was a dark-hearted man. "It was sad that it ended," he continued. "I love your mother. That wasn't what it was all about." Tommy wanted to ask then—as he has many times since—what was it all about, then? Was it him? Had his being born ruined that world, because his father had certainly never said anything to take that burden away from him.

His mother, on the other hand, told him many things, maybe too many things. She told him how she waited to hear from his father during Hazel, how Tommy was just an infant but Cecil had thought nothing of heading down to the beach with his buddies. He sat there, shit-faced (Tommy's mother had used the word *inebriated*), and watched the storm, which he later described to Tommy's mother with such clarity—the slate gray of the sky darkening still, while ferocious winds swept porches and piers into the sea like so many matchsticks. The rush of the blinding rain and the crazy kick of adrenaline as he braced himself for death.

Tom's mother had told him that when his father returned home two days later, it was like she was seeing a ghost. He hadn't shaved, and he stood all hunch-shouldered out on the stoop where the rain still dripped from the aluminum awning that had fallen to one side. She told Tommy that she greeted him with a shush and pointed to the corner of the room where Tommy was sleeping in the playpen. Cecil went straight to the corner and knelt there, addressed his child as if he were an adult, informed him that it was a great shame but due to forces of nature beyond his control he had just lost Tommy's inheritance, a lovely piece of oceanfront property that should have been worth thousands. Whenever Tommy's mother told that story, he tried to imagine his father out on the stoop, looking like a ghost. He wanted to believe that his father was like Gray Man, the famous apparition who arrives as a warning, a safety sign to those lucky enough to glimpse his shadowed form. It was in a book Tommy had read at school along with other ghost stories like "The Maco Light," in which a headless man wanders the train tracks in search of his head, and the one where a Confederate general appears at dusk on the very spot he died at Fort Fisher.

SMOKE-OUT SIGNALS
Put your butt out and bring your butt in:
Today's the day—you're guaranteed to win!

Quee has run her ad in the local paper for two weeks now and she already has folks booked on a waiting list. The word is spreading around Fulton and in neighboring towns. "If smoking is an addiction like they say," she said on a local radio show, "then a smoker deserves to be treated like an addict. A smoker ought to be able to go somewhere like the Betty Ford Clinic and get loved and pampered right out of the addiction."

"And just how do you do this?" the interviewer asked. He was a round, red-faced fella, originally from Raleigh, who smoked like a locomotive. "I mean, I'm an addict. What can you do for me?"

That was the beginning. Quee promised to take him and reshape him. She promised him good food and long hot baths, foot rubs and back massages, scented oils and fine wine, endless videos on her brand-new widescreen TV. He would have his own room for two weeks; he would have her undivided attention.

"My wife might not like it," he said and laughed a laugh that turned into a dry hack, a choking cough, a need to rush over to the watercooler while Quee completed her wonderful free advertising.

"What? Your wife wouldn't like for you to stop choking and spitting all over creation? Your wife wouldn't like for you to have white teeth as opposed to brown?" Quee leaned in close to the mike and cooed to her waiting public. "You will have round-the-clock therapy, be it physical massage or talk therapy. Put your butt out and bring your butt in, honey. I can cure you."

Now the guinea pig deejay is in his last phase of the smoke-out. He's as lazy as a coonhound—oiled and loosened, with pores that are clean and clear. Quee has knocked herself out on him because this success could cinch the business. The final phase of his treatment will include a little talk therapy from Denny, who ought to be arriving any second now, if she didn't have to pull off the interstate to remove her clothing. The child temporarily lost her mind—totally, it sounds like—but at least she did have the good sense to get herself out of a bad situation.

Now Quee is seated on the big velvet ottoman with her client's plump foot in her lap. She has greased the foot with bag balm, and now she's massaging while he listens to his substitute newsperson on the radio. His arches melt under the firm pressure of her thumbs. "I may never go back to work," he tells her, his eyes closed, terry cloth robe (furnished by Smoke-Out Signals) pulled loosely around his body.

"Marry me, Quee."

"Honey, you're not old enough for me," she says. "I like my men old enough to have gone around the block a couple of hundred times." She watches him jerk and then relax when she twists his ankle around with a loud pop. "I've buried so many men that they call me the Hospice Lover in these parts. Besides, you're married."

"Oh, yeah."

"Besides, we got to get you back on the radio and get this guy that murders the Queen's English back selling ads where he ought to be."

"He's running overtime, too." He shifts, giving Quee a glimpse of his hairy thigh. No thrill there. Lord, lord, you can't always be loving a man for his looks and parts. You gotta love the whole man, gotta find the heart and soul. She preaches this very lecture all the time to her assistant, Alicia, who should already be here by now, steaming towels and getting ready for the future arrival of the Spandex Poet and several others chomping at the bit to get in.

Quee's house is a ranch-style that has been added on to twice and will continue to be added on to if business is good. Her dream is to have a big extension out into the backyard, kind of like those barracks on *Gomer Pyle, USMC*, which was a show she hated but watched faithfully way back because Lonnie thought it was hilarious. Lonnie used to always tell Quee that she resembled Lou Ann Poovey, Gomer's girl, which of course was nowhere near true but was a sweet thought to be sure.

Alicia has kept a low profile with the radio man here, because her husband is also a deejay. Her husband, Jones Jameson, is known around the county as the local Howard Stern. He says horrible things on the radio, sex things, racist things. But he's real handsome, and comes from money (at least what might be considered money in this neck of the woods), so people try very hard to overlook him. Alicia is his complete opposite and certainly deserves better.

"The Big Man Jones isn't here yet," the substitute deejay is saying. "So we're going to go ahead and have the Swap Shop show. If you've got something you're itching to sell, something you mighta never woulda bought no way, then give us a call. . . ."

"Turn it off, turn it off." Quee's client opens his eyes for the first time in an hour. "That idiot's going to cause me to have to smoke again."

"There, there, sweetie," Quee presses into his arch, rubs up and down with her knuckles until he relaxes again. She kneads his squatty calves. When he's almost asleep she leads him back to his little room, which is kept dark and cool, turns on the ocean wave tape and the lava lamp and leaves him to the first of several naps of the day. Sleep is very important to the person kicking a habit. Forget that he's now as fat as a little toad. The only mirror in this house is a skinny mirror that she borrowed on time from a department store over in Clemmonsville; of course she had to go out with the manager a couple of times to get it, but that's what sacrifice is all about. She doesn't dare let the fat little deejay anywhere near his clothes, yet. She keeps him in her loose terry cloth robes that she bought in bulk from one of the local textile mills; she has now ironed SOS onto all the pockets. Fat. That will be her next project; move over, Duke University, with your old rice diet, here comes Quee Purdy, healer of man, fully licensed driver on the byways of life who knows a little medicine, psychiatry, chiropractic whatever, and therapeutic massage. If Elvis were alive he'd book himself at Quee's house.

For Myra Carter there is nothing quite like a big load of topsoil from down near the river where the moss and ferns have been growing and shooting their spores into that thick musty air. The only thing better is a nice big load of manure, practically steaming from some old cow's bottom. She likes to think of that, the steamy plop that she had watched as a girl on her grandparents' farm. Those cows would stand there and stare you right in the eye without a single change in expression as they raised their tails and delivered a fine dollop of fertilizer. It is so exciting to think of fertilizer; she feels embraced by life and filled with energy. It makes her think words like "fecund." Now what would a therapist make of that? Well, she won't ever know because there's not a therapist on this earth who can understand Myra Carter. Howard couldn't, and he might as well have been a psychiatrist, he was every other kind of doctor in town. It is the curse of Myra's life that her husband knew what everybody—man and woman, boy and girl—looked like without their clothes on. Ruthie sure can't understand her; Ruthie can't even understand herself these days, she's so man-crazy.

from *Carolina Moon*

Myra breathes deeply over the new topsoil that Mr. Digby left first thing this morning. If Mr. Digby wasn't forced to live such a lower-class life, she would envy him his property there near the river bottom. If they were of the same kind of people, she might even invite him in for some tea some afternoon just so she could sit there near him and breathe in the dirt and manure and river rot from his clothing.

Fecund, fecund, fecund. She sings in her head while she digs in with her shovel and tosses loam to the wheelbarrow. She tried to get Ruthie to use "fecund" in a poem, and Ruthie chewed on her pen, which is her main food source, and then said after about two hours that she couldn't think of a single thing that rhymed with "fecund."

"Well, does everything *have* to rhyme?" Myra asked, to which Ruthie shook her head and laughed, said, *Who is the poetess in this room?*

Fecund, fecund. The shovel strikes a rhythm; dig and toss, dig and toss. Fecund. Fecund. Dig and toss. Deacon. Beacon. Dig and toss. Myra stops and rests, takes a deep breath. "Rhymes," she mutters, and Sharpy runs over to her. "Miss Crow will say that my words don't have a *d* on the end and therefore can't work." It makes her mad and she grips the shovel harder and gets ready to set into some serious damn digging. She dares anybody to match what she can do with a shovel. Howard couldn't. Ruthie can't. Dig and toss. Dig and toss. I'm the boss. I'm the boss. Take that Connie; take this shovel in your big wide grinning mouth. Tell us how like Jesus you are now. Myra is just getting up to a full- fledged rage when her shovel strikes something solid. If that Mr. Digby has camouflaged some trash and brought it to her yard, she will have his poverty level reduced to subpoverty. Probably if he worked harder he wouldn't be at poverty level to begin with, this is America after all. She keeps pushing in with the shovel, striking like a snake and every time hitting something solid. She is red in the face and getting winded, so she throws the shovel to the side and gets on her hands and knees to start digging. Sharpy thinks she's playing a game, like when she sniffed around the yard and taught him to lift his leg like a man dog ought to, and he runs over to help. And Sharpy is the one to get there first. Sharpy is the first one to find skin, pale and pulpy, bluish gray. Sharpy's natural instincts make him back off and growl deep in his throat.

"What is this?" Myra is demanding. "What in the hell, pardon my French. . . ." She reaches in and grabs with both hands, pushing against that pile with all the strength she has. She rips off her gloves so she can get to whatever it is, dog corpse or chicken or old rotten fish. The smell is there now hitting her like a two-by-four in the face. She would probably vomit and pass out if she wasn't so furious that her wonderful fecund dig-and-toss afternoon has been ruined. Now she's reached something hard and solid, and she locks her fingers around the edge and pulls and pulls. There's resistance. It's big. Whatever is in there is big and she feels like the top of her head is about to fall off when all of a sudden the pressure gives and she falls back flat on her back, a soggy weight clutched to her chest, the noonday sun burning black spots into the world, and in one of those spots she would swear she saw Howard, and he was grinning; he was looking just like he did that day that she came up on him talking to that old Mary Stutts. *Medical matters, dear,* he said to Myra later when she questioned him, *medical matters, confidential.* He's saying it right now, plain as day, his face blinking and twitching in the sun, like it might be covered in ants or termites, and she has to close her eyes against such ugliness, *It's confidential information.*

THE UNCLE'S GIRLFRIEND

(VOL. 52, NO. 2, 2000)

Daniel Wallace

....

The day Ray's family moved, Bones ran away. His father dropped a lamp on his toe and both of them broke. Ray's mother almost cried walking from room to room, the echo of her heels making a sad sound, like nails dropping into a can. Then Eloise couldn't find the money she'd buried in the back yard a year ago, and she *did* cry, sobbing in the dirt with a plastic yellow shovel in her hands, surrounded by shallow holes. Uncle Eddie discovered a bed of snakes in a pile of old rags in the basement, Aunt Lurleen made a big plate of tuna fish sandwiches, and Ray found an old piece of paper with his secret name written on it. All this happened and it wasn't even dark yet, though you could see the moon, a pale sliver, in a corner of the sky.

After Ray's mother left with his dad for the hospital, Uncle Eddie brought one of the snakes up from the basement and set it on Aunt Lurleen's neck—a harmless little green snake, he said. He held its head while it wriggled across her nape, and Aunt Lurleen screamed. Ray had never heard anybody scream as loud as Aunt Lurleen did when she figured out it wasn't her husband's fingers but a snake that was on her. Turning, she lashed out with one of her arms and he dropped it, and Ray watched the snake glide off into the cabinet beneath the sink.

Aunt Lurleen ran out of the house and sat on the porch, in the porch swing, where she remained for some time. Uncle Eddie and Ray went out to look at her, but she ignored them. Her face was set icy tight. She didn't even blink. She wouldn't talk to Uncle Eddie when he apologized to her. She wouldn't talk to Ray, either, because he had been there and known what was going to happen and accidentally laughed about it. She just sat on the porch swing and trembled, and stared across the street at the Seibals' azaleas.

"Lurleen," Uncle Eddie said to Ray in the kitchen, winking. "Lurleen, now, she has sure got a nerve problem." He picked a tuna fish sandwich and bit at it. Then he looked at it. He looked at it as though it had bitten him.

"How about seeing if there's a beer in the fridge for me, Ray."

Ray found a beer, and he gave it to him. Uncle Eddie took another bite of the sandwich, chewed some and washed the rest down with the beer. He looked thoughtless as he glanced out toward the porch. He looked like a man who really liked to eat.

Eddie was Ray's second uncle, having only just married Lurleen, his mother's sister, two months before. Ray hardly knew him, but he could tell by the way Aunt Lurleen acted when she introduced him that Ray was supposed to feel the same about Eddie as he had about his first uncle, Spencer, who died in a car accident a couple of years before, when Ray was eleven. But it wasn't working out for Ray. It wasn't the same. Eddie was a small man without a hair on his face, his face was as soft and pink as a baby's, his eyes a deep sky blue. Sometimes it looked like there was nothing behind them, just that color. The hair on his head was thick and black, and he must have put something in it, because it was always shining. He was in the Navy for a couple of years, and got a tattoo while he was there, an eagle holding a bomb in its talons, wings spread across the top of his arm. Ray tried to imagine Uncle Spencer with an eagle on his shoulder and he couldn't. Uncle Spencer had to shave every day, his chin so prickly when he rubbed it across Ray's belly that Ray almost died laughing.

"Your mom that way too, Ray?" Uncle Eddie asked him.

"What way?"

"Nervous," he said, wiping a bit of mayo off his chin with the back of his hand. "Jittery. On edge. Your dad sure gets on her nerves, doesn't he?"

"No," Ray said, trying to think. What was his mother like? He couldn't say in words. "Not really."

"What?"

"She's not nervous, really."

"Is that so?"

"Well, maybe a little."

He smiled, liking that answer better than the other one. He had quite a smile. When he smiled his lips stayed together at first, until, parting slowly, he showed every tooth he had.

"I thought so," he said.

Uncle Eddie was a salesman until recently. He sold reproductions of the world's great art—and not on poster paper, but on hard, solid cardboard. He sold the frames, too. He'd carried it all in a briefcase that was four feet long, three feet high, and two inches wide. But he no longer did that. Ray was listening to him talking to Dad last night in the living room, packing, and heard him say that the company he was working for had become unreliable, unable to ship the great quantity of art he sold on time, or they were out of stock—just generally unreliable. He couldn't work for a company like that, so he quit, and he was between jobs now. But he had kept the briefcase full of samples, which was always in the back seat of his car, a lime green Dodge

Dart, just in case, Ray thought, he was suddenly possessed by the need to sell something.

"Why did your grandaddy name her Lurleen?" Uncle Eddie asked him, out of nowhere. "Where did that name come from?"

"I don't know," Ray said.

"Lur-leen," he said, drawing it out. "*Lur-leen.* Is it a family name? Is that the explanation?" He laughed. Then he winked at Ray. "I got pet names for her anyway," he said, almost whispering. "Don't use the Lurleen word much at all, actually."

She was still out on the porch. Her back was to them, but they could tell she hadn't changed a bit, that she was still staring across the stress at the Seibals' azaleas. Ray could hear Eloise packing her last-minute stuff. Nothing was the way it was before. Even his dog was gone.

"I've got to find Bones," Ray said.

Uncle Eddie looked at him. "Bones'll be back," he said.

"I think we spooked him," Ray said. "All the moving and packing. I've got to find him."

Still Uncle Eddie stared at him. It was like he didn't trust Ray, like he knew that one of the things Ray was trying to get away from was him. Then his lips spread open to a wide-mouthed smile.

"You mean *we've* got to find him." He jingled his car keys like little bells in his pocket. "Let's go, sailor!" he said.

"But what about Eloise?" Ray said, following him out the front door.

"She'll be fine," Uncle Eddie said. "Lurleen can take care of her. Take care of Eloise, Lurleen," he said to her as they passed. But he might as well have been talking to himself, because Aunt Lurleen didn't move a muscle. Even as they drove away Ray could see her, her eyes like cold little marbles sitting heavy in her head.

"She's trying to remember why she married me," Uncle Eddie said, catching a glimpse of her through the rear-view mirror. "Sometimes it takes her a while. She'll be okay."

In the car, Uncle Eddie told Ray how much he liked to drive. He said he just loved it. He'd been about everywhere, too, driving. Working. He used his thumb to point to the briefcase in the back. This old Dart had been places! he told him. Oh yes! Driven to the edge of America, where the waves slap against the two-lane black-top as it bends into the sea. Once he drove too close to the sun as it set, he said, burning the end of his nose. And he touched it like it still hurt a little. In the Navy he drove a fork lift, and he got good at it,

Daniel Wallace

angling those rusty tusks into places nobody'd believe they go. A little more horsepower and he'd be driving one today.

"I wish your Aunt Lurleen liked to drive," he said. "But she just about breaks down crying every time she gets into a car."

"Because of what happened to Uncle Spencer," Ray said.

He nodded. "That's right," he said. They were traveling about fifteen miles an hour down an empty street. "I think she'd rather ride on an elephant's back than get into a car. I swear. But that comes from her nerves, not having the best life in the world."

That was true. Ray's parents often talked about Aunt Lurleen and her awful life. Even before her first husband was killed in a car accident, she had been involved in a number of situations which, they said, always seemed to turn out badly for her. She had been robbed, her car had been vandalized. She had to sell her house to pay back taxes Uncle Spencer left behind. Bad luck and natural disasters seemed to follow her around. The day Ray's mother and dad found out she was marrying Eddie Del Vecchio, they just looked at each other and shook their heads, the way they did when another bad thing happened to Aunt Lurleen.

"Eddie Del Vecchio," Ray's father said.

Ray and his Uncle Eddie drove around the block, looking. They passed the house, where nothing had changed. Aunt Lurleen was still on the porch. Uncle Eddie waved and Aunt Lurleen raised her hand slightly. That was a good sign, he said.

They kept driving. Uncle Eddie's car smelled like old rubber. "I don't see him," he said.

They drove around the block again, then around the next block, on a back street near the high school, and there was no Bones. Ray called to him from the window, but there was still no Bones.

"He'll be back," Uncle Eddie told him. "Don't you worry about that dog. Today, tomorrow, the next day. He'll be back."

"But we won't be there," Ray said.

"Oh," he said. "That's right. We should get back and be finishing up while your dad gets that foot fixed, shouldn't we?"

Ray said yes, he guessed they should.

But they didn't go back. Uncle Eddie said that as long as they were in this neighborhood they should go visit an old friend of his. More than an old friend, he said. She was family.

"And family's not like—" Uncle Eddie crinkled his eyes, "—like a can of soup," he told him. "A family don't have an expiration date on it. Family is family forever whether you like it or not." And he gave Ray a wink. He gave those winks out with regularity, Ray thought.

They drove to the end of the good part of town or the beginning of the bad, it was hard to tell which. There was a chain link fence around a small brown yard, running alongside a pale blue wooden house. The fence, Ray thought, was the nicest thing about the whole place. It looked strong and shiny where everything else looked scraped and torn. The little walkway leading up to the screen door was broken with grass shoots growing through it, and beyond the screen door it was so dark Ray thought there may have been nothing at all in there.

As soon as the car stopped out front a woman walked out of the house and stood on the porch. It was as if they were a surprise and she was expecting them, all at the same time. She was a big woman with brown hair hanging down to her shoulders, barefoot.

"She's nice," Uncle Eddie said, waving to her through his window. "She might not look nice from here but she is. Don't worry. You'll like her."

He grabbed Ray's knee and squeezed it, and with his other hand pushed his hair back so his forehead shined in the sun.

Uncle Eddie was halfway up the walk before Ray got out of the car. Ray wanted to stay there, but the farther away Uncle Eddie got the harder it was for him to stay. The woman on the porch watched Ray come forward, and Uncle Eddie turned to grin, and then Ray felt a strong urge not to be there at all.

"This here is Ray, my nephew," Uncle Eddie said to the woman, holding Ray by the shoulders in front of him. "Ray, say hello to Sally."

"Hi Ray," she said.

Ray said hello.

"Sally and I were married once," Uncle Eddie said. But it was like he was telling her that, and not Ray. Like she might remember too well. "Before Lurleen, of course. Before Lurleen it was me and Sally. Three matrimonial years together. But then one thing led to another, right Sally?"

"I guess that's right, Ed."

She seemed to be speaking against her will, as though the words were being taken from her, or barely escaping through a crack in her mouth. But Uncle Eddie was a salesman, and he kept trying to sell her. He kept talking. He gave her that smile of his, Ray bet.

"'Till death do us part,' I vowed," he said. "But we couldn't quite do it."

"Not for lack of trying," she said.

Uncle Eddie's grip on Ray's shoulder tightened. Ray could have been a piece of wood, a fence, or a tree.

"Now, Sally," he said, trying to keep it friendly. "That's all in the past, isn't it?"

"Feels like the present now."

Uncle Eddie laughed. "I can't believe this," he said. "I come over to say hello and introduce you to my nephew and here I am put through it all over again. Can't we just be like normal people and have a regular conversation?"

"I am a normal person," she said.

Sally had on a t-shirt with the name of a bakery on it, and white shorts that clung tight to her big legs. There was a bruise the color of dark water on one of her legs. She didn't look like anybody's aunt to Ray.

"Who's not normal?" he said and laughed. Then he was quiet. Then he said, "I guess you heard about me getting married, huh?"

"I think I might have," she said, sighing. "Maybe I read about it in the papers."

"It was in the paper?" he said, seeming genuinely excited.

"In the obituary section," she said.

"The obituary—what do you—"

Ray could tell that things weren't going well for Uncle Eddie. His fingers dug into Ray's neck, and Ray thought: I have to go. But he continued to stand there, a human shield, between them.

"You know, I've got some art out in the car," he said. "Got some pretty pictures that might look good in your living room, hallway or foyer. One by Renoir I've got looks a lot like you, Sally. Care to have it? Gonna get rid of them one way or another."

Sally didn't even answer him. She just shook her head like she couldn't believe he would think of offering her some art. They stood there a while longer, not talking, but not going anywhere. Sally hadn't moved since she came out of the screen door, and Uncle Eddie just held Ray out in front of him, hands on his shoulders, as though they were about to get their picture taken.

"What is it you want, Ed?" she said, finally.

"Want?"

"You didn't forget anything, did you? Pair of socks or anything? Something you need to come in and look around for? A book?" she said, and laughed.

"No," Uncle Eddie said, dropping his arms to his side now. "Me and Ray are here, we're looking for a dog. We're looking for a dog, aren't we Ray? Ray's dog run away. You hadn't seen it, Sally, have you?"

"Nope," she said quickly.

"But we haven't even told you what it looks like!" he said.

"That's all right, Ed."

"He's dirty white," Ray said. "Medium-sized. With pointy ears. Named Bones."

"Sorry," she said, looking at Ray for half a second, then back at Uncle Eddie.

"Come on, Ray," he said. "Let's go. She's no help. She's no help at all, is she?"

Ray knew he wasn't supposed to answer that question. He waved to her, a flip of his arm, and turned and walked with Uncle Eddie back to the car. She watched them go, not moving from her porch until they lost sight of her around the next corner.

The sky was dim and orange. The road was dark beneath the trees. Some cars had their lights on already. Ray wished they were going home, but Uncle Eddie didn't want to go home just yet. Uncle Eddie wanted to drive. They weren't looking for Bones anymore. Bones wasn't a part of anything they were doing. Uncle Eddie was doing what he wanted to do.

"She wasn't very nice," Uncle Eddie said after a while.

"She seemed like she could be nice," Ray said.

"But she wasn't," he said. "She could have been but she wasn't. I'm sorry, Ray, sorry you had to see that."

They turned off the main road then and hit gravel. Uncle Eddie lost control of the car for a second, but then it rightened itself. The wind was cooler here, and moist. Ray's hand clung to the door handle the way it did at the dentist. They were in a strange place now. The trees bent low over the road, and kudzu grew thick around the branches. Ray couldn't say how Uncle Eddie saw ahead.

Uncle Eddie stopped in front of a big tree at the edge of the forest, its thick and gnarly branches spiraling out into the sky. He turned off the engine and said to Ray, "This is where I come to think." Then he reached into the back seat for his big thin briefcase full of art, and got out. Ray didn't move until Eddie stuck his head back in his window. "You coming?" he said.

There was a dirt trail winding through the forest, the trees covered with vines, and Ray followed Eddie down it. Eddie was walking fast, the briefcase banging against his leg as he went. Ray could hear a sound ahead of them—it was like static, he thought, and he imagined there was a television out there somewhere, in the middle of these woods, shining blue and gray. But it wasn't a television: it was a river, and the sound he heard was water falling over rocks and between logs. He could see it plainly by the light that fell through the opening in the trees above it—a river, not too many miles from his home, and he had never seen it. He had not even known it was here. Nobody had ever told Ray about it or brought him to it, not until Uncle Eddie did that night, and now Ray was moving away. They were moving. Not too far away, but too far to come back here. It was like it had been planned this way, like the river had been saved for very last, when there was nothing he could do with it but remember.

Uncle Eddie was quiet as they sat there on the bank, the briefcase on the ground beside him. His face caught the sky light and drank it up. After a long time he spoke.

"Ever wonder where the stars go in the daytime, Ray?" he asked.

Ray shook his head.

He laughed softly. "If they was light bulbs," he said, "somebody would have to go around and shut off every last one of them."

"They're not light bulbs," Ray said.

"No they're not, Mr. Smart Guy. So where do they go?" he asked again.

"They don't go anywhere," he said. "The sun's just brighter."

"Correct," he said. "They don't go anywhere. The sun drowns 'em out." He looked up at them. "Hey, you're not going to tell Lurleen where we went today, are you?"

"I hadn't thought about it," Ray said. He gazed toward the opposite bank.

"Well?" Uncle Eddie said.

"I won't tell her."

Uncle Eddie gave Ray his smile and nodded.

"You're okay, Ray," he said.

They sat there for a few minutes longer, until Eddie stood up with a groan and stretched.

"Watch this," he said. He opened his briefcase and pulled out one of the cardboard pictures. He took a look at it, squinting in the moonlight.

"Van Gogh," he said. "Van Goghs can really fly."

And with a flick of his wrist he sent the picture flying over the river, disappearing into the trees on the other side. Ray could tell he'd done it before. He could tell this wasn't the first picture Uncle Eddie had sent flying. He reached for another.

"Picasso," Uncle Eddie said. "Better than a frisbee."

It wasn't really better than a frisbee, Ray thought. It didn't fly straight, but it could go high and far, like a boomerang, only not quite coming back.

"Give it a try," Uncle Eddie said.

He handed Ray the cardboard art.

"Who is it?" he said.

"Let's see," Uncle Eddie said. "I think—I think that's Caravaggio. You probably never heard of him. Note the use of chiaroscuro—how the light and dark come together. Great for the bath or hallway. Toss it."

Ray did, but it didn't make it to the other bank. The picture went almost straight up into the air and disappeared into the darkness of the sky. For a second Uncle Eddie and Ray both were looking straight up, star gazing, and couldn't see a thing. It had disappeared. It was like some hand had come down and snatched the picture up. But then it came, cutting the air like hummingbird's wings, straight down out of the darkness, whirling and turning corner to corner so fast that it didn't seem to be turning at all. He could see the dark picture of the lady at the old oak table, a candle shining on one part of the small canvas, her deep white shoulder illuminated, her face lost in the shadows. Out of the sky it came, turning and turning and finally landing right in Uncle Eddie's forehead. It kind of stuck there for a second, and the sharp sudden pain of it knocked him down. He fell on the bank of the river and began to moan, holding his head with his hand, bringing it back stained with blood.

"God damn it!" he said. "God damn it! I hate art. *Hate* it!"

He stood up and kicked his big briefcase into the river, where it floated for a couple of yards until it snagged on a fallen branch. He stood there, enraged, breathing deeply.

After a while, he seemed to be okay.

"Reckon we ought to be getting back," he said.

Uncle Eddie drove slowly now. A little stream of blood, like a river on a map, had dried up on one side of his head. Looking at it made Ray feel a little bit sick. But Uncle Eddie didn't say a word. He was like a different man, but different from what, Ray couldn't say. He was like a stranger. Ray looked across the seat at him driving—the way his small hands clutched the steering wheel, the way his stomach fell over his belt just slightly—and wondered who he was. Nobody really knew, he thought—not even Aunt Lurleen. Or maybe she did, but Ray didn't think so. I might as well be with a man I never met, Ray thought. And now here they were on their way home. It was okay now.

"My goodness," Uncle Eddie said, as they turned the corner to the street Ray lived on. "Look at that, Ray."

The lights from the car panned the house, sweeping across it like it was a prison yard. But the house was dark. The electricity must have been turned off already. Aunt Lurleen wasn't on the porch anymore, and Elouise wasn't there, and Ray's mom and dad weren't there either. The moving van was gone, too. Beyond the windows of all the rooms there was just black space, nothing there at all now. And no Bones.

Uncle Eddie laughed as he pulled into the driveway, but it wasn't a good laugh. It was the laugh of a man who didn't have a better sound to make. The engine rumbled even after he turned it off. Then, leaving the lights on, he got out of the car and walked to the front door, where there was a note tacked, and he came back with it, waving it in the air like a little white flag. He got in the car and sighed, looking back and forth, from Ray to the note.

"They'll be back," he said. "Says they'll be back real soon." He stuffed the note in a pocket. "Says to wait right here."

"Wait?" Ray said. "We're supposed to wait for them here?"

"Sure," he said. "You don't believe me?"

"I believe you," Ray said. "I was just asking."

"Okay," he said. He moved around in his seat, trying to make himself comfortable, and he yawned.

"Does it say anything about Bones?" Ray asked him.

Eddie had to think about it for a minute, staring through the windshield at the house, still glowing in his head lights.

"It sure does," he said. "Now that you mention it. Says they found him. Says they have him there with 'em and everything's okay." He looked over at Ray, to see if he bought it. "Good news, huh?"

"Good news," he said.

"Yes, sir. Everything's just grand," he said. "Everything's fine and dandy. Not a thing in the world to worry about. This is happy ending time."

Uncle Eddie laughed, and winked, and hit the lights, and it was all darkness then, except for the stars. He turned the radio on low, almost too low to hear at all, and the dial glowed a sweet pale green. For a while he just sat there, staring out into the night. Then he closed his eyes, and his head fell back against the seat, his mouth just barely open, breathing deep and regular. Soon he was snoring, sound asleep. Ray watched him. Ray thought he looked like somebody who would sleep in his car. He looked like somebody this had happened to before.

ASPIRE

(VOL. 56, NO. 2-3, 2004)

Camille Dungy

....

August, and a lash of gnats is certain, prophesied.
Corn and wheat realize their ambition, and hands
twist, harvesting, through fields. Gnats
and heat and work songs engorge the clotted air.

Horses wear straw hats and join tree-shaded whipmen.
Everything they do is done with the sanctioned ease
of the master's favorite pup. The horses are absurd
with laughter as they watch the harvest's progress.

One summer dawning he will not rise. The vermin
and heat will light around him, the chant
of the tedious season will mark time, but he will hold still
in the cool clay of his cabin. He will keep still.

REVISITING

(VOL. 56, NO. 2–3, 2004)

Evie Shockley

....

for l.b.s.s.

> i was waiting on a poem when
>   my grandfather pushed through
> the screen door, the wire-webbed
>
>   rectangle left slapping the wooden
> jamb behind him. i hadn't seen pop
>   too often since he died, hadn't let
> my mind zap the gray distance
>
>   from my cool bright here-and-now
> apartment back to the porch where,
>   a girl, i waited out tennessee evening
> heat in the cradle of the suspended
>   swing. down the dingy white cement
>
> stairs, across the dirt yard along
>   a track of rusting sheets of scrap
> metal and embedded flat-top stones,
>
>   pop goes, turns left at the road,
> then makes his way to the pasture
>   gate and through to call the cows.
> *sook, cows, sook, sook.* their lowing
>
>   answers him. they flick their ears,
> push themselves up from their knees,
>   come like dignified dogs to begin
> their procession to the barn. pop
>   shambles along in front, while

the cows, with their fist-sized onyx
    eyes and their patternless black
and white markings, pick their way

    over the uneven turf on precise
hooves. he pens them, tossing straw
    over the rails with a free hand—
golden, good. he comes back to me

    at 70—the youngest i ever knew
him—wearing an old man's baggy
    pants and wattled triceps, but still
able to saddle up and ride out
    to the cornfields each morning.

now, p.m. chores at the barnyard
    done, he mounts, swings his leg out
and over like the slow arm of a rusted

    compass. *gee up*. the mule trods
the gravel road up from the barn,
    past the house, to the stable. his
momma got a mule after the war,

    along with a life-sized portion of land.
one of the lucky ones. pop turned her
    forty into hundreds and hundreds.
black man with a few years of school
    and a head for figures surprised

everyone but himself. back from
    the stable, pop's boots molt mud
onto the porch. it'll stay there unless
    my grandmother comes back to me,

too, this evening, to whisk it away
    when it dries. i straddle the two
worlds: in the one, my seven-year

old legs motoring the swing, fat toes
callusing against the dusty floor
    planks they barely reach, the tired
beam that holds me aloft creaking
    loud enough to fill the half-easy

silence that always fell between me
    and my farmer-hero, and in the other
my thirty-three-year-old eyes able

    to spot the contentment in pop's.
he's pleased to perform his evening
    ritual in the company of his youngest
daughter's girl. the bowl of his pipe

    in the bowl of his palm, pop pries
open the red prince albert tobacco
    tin, tips out a tiny ration of the brown
ground and tamps it into the pipe's
    hollow, his work-thick finger just

the right size to fit. quick hiss of sulfur-
    scented flame and he's drawing peace
from poison, blowing the sweet

    aroma towards me like a misty kiss,
rocking in the thin, paint-bare arms
    of his old throne, watching the late sun
melt into the black branches of his trees.

Revisiting

HIS DEMENTIA

(VOL. 58, NO. 2, 2007)

Adam Day

....

While I slept with my face to the wall,
hands clapped flat between my knees,
my grandfather shuffled through the French doors
and put his hand on my shoulder—

I rolled over slowly, and I grasped him—crisp
hand-skin like black cabbage, the skin
of one badly burnt. He leaned close—

cataracts made his eyes
green marbles under ice,
and I could see beside the long darkness
of his ear's tunnel, a blue sore
like a decomposing berry,

and he said, that he wanted Houdini
alive in the Hippodrome with Jennie
the elephant, and his black stack
of scratchy Red Seal albums
for the crank up Victrola, and the dunes
and cut & pressed glass ruins of a coastal town.

I let him into bed, and we listened
a long time to the furnace—I sang Caruso
into his good ear, until he began nodding
and I escaped from my skin
leaving it beside an old, deaf,
nearly-blind man, a palsied
pile of nylons, a world of snow.

A LETTER TO YOU FROM A TIME WHEN I PREFERRED A DIFFERENT FONT

(VOL. 58, NO. 2, 2007)

Ross White

....

There is something romantic in the bold lines
of this font, so I am typing some of Richard Wilbur's
poems for you.
                    Notice how cleanly the words
break from each other. The quaint hook of j.
The plaintive cry of s. The sadness of a g,
looking into itself with a painful eye. The firmness
of capital letters. The stark dual edge of x.

I could let my fingers stray on a keyboard for
days and play with the words until they breathed
in synch with the spaces,
                          parading black across
impatient streets of white. Nothing extraneous,
just the rounded sides of words as they pile
onto each other.

SEASONS SAID

(VOL. 63, NO. 3, 2013)

Lisa Lewis

....

I bore away the old boards, boat battery, garter snake
beheaded by shovel. I bled rust for the chain link fence.
I suited up to strip poison ivy, pigweed, amaranth tall

and broad as an ordinary man, sameness of crabgrass
splashes like summer sparklers, widening, bleaching
twine-tight roots. I loaded my wheelbarrow

with the anguished skull of the lost cat no one spayed
and the stop sign bereaved of its ice cream truck, still
whistling pipes under the breath of Capricornus.

I took the screwdriver's one buck tooth to a barrel of oil
worth nothing but the iron filings of the lean old motors
it greased. I rolled it away, spilling a panful to stain

the asphalt no one on my street would forgive.
I double-bagged the trash, the trouble, luckless growth
of native flora uncultivated for beauty because their sisal

clasping the throats of the blessed clematis kills.
I steamed the gristle of hate away. I dug it up. I severed
worms, hell surrendered its dew below their naked reach.

The bare earth's readiness declared *bring me roots*,
in clay, in moistened hands—a poplar tree, dwarfed,
in a bucket. Sage, cress, bristling bluets, thyme

in vulgar flavors. I planted taxonomies I knew not
and named them for saints and ponies. I pried
a place for a clump of mallow striped like a jungle hybrid

and it smothered itself in shadow. Everything beneath
knelt down. I offered the spilt remainders of my kitchen's toil,
jigsaw morsels it couldn't swallow, and it swore obeisance

to the spirit of loam. A chorus hummed from grains
and grass. And it all came back, the tangle, the mass,
the weight of my labors like a jacket hooked on a fence:

the days dripped sweat, and the earth hurried to save itself,
shade from sugar, millet, eyespot, honeybees' soft spines.
Whatever I'd done changed. *This is no office*

for cubicles, it might've said or sung, but I had found
some kind of room for rakes and spades and a water hose
I coiled snake-shape behind my house. No killing left

in any of us, not much—just to keep a clearing,
beds for the comings and goings of a few spare blooms
I preferred, the rest whatever the clay would hold.

PART VI

MYTH

How huge seems mere event. Mere
Naked event that time heaves back from,
A white rock mastering the whole sea.

—FRED CHAPPELL

AR from claiming cosmological order, these eight poems reach toward multiplicity, daring to find in "shattered . . . voids" an infinite repetition of worlds made whole by ongoing acts of poiesis. In each poem there is a yearning to do what myth does: repeat across time and space to create the continuity of history—or, in the words of Fred Chappell, to "[plow] to another future, and another," and to find, in the words of Lee Upton, that "again and again / the world is lit, extinguished and lit." Though the world seems to tilt toward an impossibly fractured future—a fracture that begins in the past, as G. C. Waldrep and Matthew Moore well know—it's possible still for a whole and single raindrop to fall upon the hand, to touch skin and hold the present in place a while longer. In other words, it's possible still to be "startle[d] . . . into life," as Upton observes. Life collects in the clouds, years are "expressed . . . as leaves," and as each leaf turns gold, the canopy fills with wings, taking flight to the next season. The cosmos passes through and among poets who pause, just for a moment, as in James Applewhite's vision of autumn.

THE NAKED ARK

(VOL. 19, NO. 2, 1967)

Fred Chappell

....

1.

All tides, all marges.

He feels the land slide down its balance,
The world teeters wearily,
Wearily toward him. His instruments
Won't fix a latitude.

How huge seems mere event. Mere
Naked event that time heaves back from,
A white rock mastering the whole sea.

Yet the feeble yacht of his attempt
Plows to another future, and another.
If his vision narrows to a pinpoint
Possibilities jam it, volumeless angels
Dancing. And none
Among them jostles another.

If his journey were worst maimed,
The very sea ripped up, the guiding sky
Snatched off like a soiled tablecloth,
His senses fallen like five gold apples,
Beginning would remain.
Commencement itself abides,
Grand chance throws its shadow forward
Along the shadow of his voyage, the hungering
Future ravens toward the present.

Happening exists, obelisk-solid,
Protean, ductile as cloud.
Its amorphous figure sprawls his thinking.

2.

Each day he sees the lumpy continent
Burgeoning on the long limb of ocean,
Haze spilled about it like a bridal train;
And, rising, it dumps the curled sea toward him.

Now the white birds ride his wake.
He touches land, he clamps it
Fast with the keel.

He stalks on the reeling beach, dizzy
In the green halitosis of generation
The land spews on him from its life;
Harshly aswim in the opulent
Ordure of metamorphosis.

He fights to keep his knowledge clear,
But desperate sleep drops him to the matrix.
Dreams.

3.

Dawn, like the shock of cold water.

He rises.
The land opens like an eye, the face
Of it trembles, leans out to threaten.

   Unsteadier than the sea.

He arms his pure bones with desire and arms
His skin with touch. On his eyes
He claps deceptive sight, on his face
The vizard of identity. In every orifice
He stuffs discovery.

Senses advanced, he strikes the jungle
Which laps him over, and its roaring
Bites his thinking to a whimper.

This green and spermy sky he cannot breathe,
Its fervid unremitting change
Buoys him over like drunkenness.

He strives, he strives to break the habit
Of his mind. An ugly dog; it sniffs
And snuffles at his senses, that reeking armory.
His knowing is cut to the quick.

Two sizes he sees. A vivid cell
Clenches him about, imprisoning as blood;
But shine through the green walls
The huger walls: the old big life, boundless
As smoke, insistent
As the chains of his singular form.

4.

History like molecules, shock touching shock
And the whole is shattered in the voids.

What will the guts of being receive?

5.

A temple flounders in the woods.
A yellow temple leaps in the leaves,
Ripe with scurrying. Priests; virgins.
Music burns along the blooming,
A seething yellow liquor poured on his taste.

Light seen is light divine, but
Reflected light is knobbly shadow.
The blind hymn surges, swathes him in praise
He cannot recognize, a singing lame
And substanceless. No blood
In everduring adoration.

What's worshiped is what's left behind,
The fizz that escapes the noisy carcass.

He will not enter. These green altars
Cannot support his immanence, his eyes
Would smash the chalices.

He will not enter, he turns away. His thought
Lies wide across the palpitant land.

6.

On the stony mountain. He watches the country.
The cities, foul platters of streets and squares.
The women drop their fruit like other fruit.
The cities bear his name, nameless
To him. No vanity.

The country between.
The woods. The lakes winking
Like spilt pennies in the sun.
This water bites its fetters, it aches
Toward a freedom like the broad and fluid sky,
Fair pattern.

He has come far, he has come too far.
The land stirs vaguely, a spattered flag;
Its shape drifts up like steam.
Rend this gossamer!

With a word he could tweak its life.

He's come too far to go to sea again,
But he'll crush the earth to water.
He'll set tides in stone.

7.

All tides, all marges:
                    awash in bitter idea.

THE RIDDLE OF HATS

(VOL. 36, NO. 1, 1983)

Lee Upton

....

Walking that steep path to the car
you felt a heavy drop of rain
light on your hand,
a little bald star.
It startles you into life
the way your daughter must.
Running, she has found and left
a bird, all yellow beak and violet.
The day is violet. You imagine her

bending over that mechanism, more
new than she is. And now
you will go for a ride to see
the ill cousin
who bores your daughter very much.
Your worry box, your rattle contraption,
your daughter sits with strawberries
on her lap. This gift tightens
in its skin. A riddle:

the blind man,
the one-eyed man,
the sighted man,
two red hats.
You don't know.
The same answer two of the men give.
Your eyes travel
to the bad part in her hair, the
dark hair her father gave her. A bird

suddenly shoots into the air.
At the last instant the bird gives you
its white belly. Again and again
the world is lit, extinguished and lit.
The eyelid too is a gift.
A hat dear it is a sort of hat dear
that even the blind
    may see with.

ON YOUR WALL

(VOL. 41, NO. 3, 1989)

Martha Collins

....

The mountains are clouds
in the Chinese painting.

The houses are flowers, the color
of flowers, the flowers grow

at my feet. A temple rises
into the mountains, but so

do the houses, releasing
the flowers. Between the flowers

and houses, between the mountains
and higher clouds is nothing

but space which opens
the doors of the houses,

inviting me, the tiny figure
crossing the bridge, to come in.

ANGEL AND AUTUMN

(VOL. 55, NO. 2, 2003)

James Applewhite

....

All night in a house like a witch's hat
in a bed up the stairs
I dreamed on a mountain among the stars.
I expressed my years as leaves, a maple
by a lake. Weeping, an angel
sphered his tears with the fall,
refracting each leaf as a yellow-orange wing—
my canopy veined, a weightless stained glass.
It broke in the breezes, shuddering,
as I stretched my glitter on water,
an autumn idea beyond color,
purest October, descending—
from my mind to his, *before*.

A dog's bark, caught in the stairs
twisted into syllables, oaks printed
the faint dawn with age, flat
on its white, like the little line-sticks that depict.
Round in the dream, I soared on each wing
while the angel wept at autumn and uttering.

ON THE MISCIBILITY OF PLANES

(VOL. 61, NO. 3, 2011)

G. C. Waldrep

....

chronic page-break   supple verity
of choice's lone confession   examine

this disunity   spartan work ethic
the phone rings, someone guesses math's

gone too far this time   Smithson's
spiral jetty bleeds further into

Mormonism's tapped spine   cetaceous
it complicates, we say, & we mean it

crystallizes violets left in the hollow
base of the military   Wyoming / snow

marks out a gentler algorithm   trains,
for instance   it's not as if bundling

preserves the follicle, the impact weave,
craters detected miles beneath the

earth's surface   geophysical anomalies
support some hesitation in the fossil

record   the Tunguska Event, most likely
a meteor airburst, though who can say

what faith is like   in a vacuum
under the proper scientific conditions

asteroid detection strategies, like
Madonna keep genuflecting in the wrong

direction, salt cadavers assigned
to active duty in the Fifth Arrondissement

Look up, she said   and pointed
somewhere the sun goes to sleep but

off the record   microscopic magnetite
spheres embedded in the conspiracy

theory   the Lost Dutchman Mine
cue the Nephites in their phosphorescent

observatory   three-dimensional
modeling makes water baptism possible

what would it take   for you
to sever, say, a finger from a hand

if you knew its owner had committed
a terrible crime   if you knew

it could be sewn back   *on*, I mean
or replaced   as warning, as a cartouche

containing the desiccated corpses
of swallows   sure, you can experiment

inside the experiment   the democracy
hovering in the background,

slightly upwind of the horizon
the fragment of, say, a colliding body

accords with the voice of this righteous
depopulation   is choice anything

the fossil record supports, when you
really get down to all the civil air crimes

perpetrated upon the city of Florence
all that gilt   all that tunneling

glow inside the furnace equations
the petrophobia   behind their light

bearing occlusions isn't it safe to say
the harbor is still there   the little shops

marine encrustations   absurd
prophecies of miscast shepherd children

thrown back against the oil spectrum
mainframe   skylight   blue army

faction   the welts on her body
painted in old-fashioned merthiolate

bear the tattoo away   the central,
chemical story   adrift in the effluent

you draw a picture of it, then
light aircraft in the desert washes

milked of their dark honey   leaving
no obvious traces   no sea of glass

It looked like the sun came down
& gyrated for the people, someone said

only in some other, perfect language

MADAME NHU'S ÁO DÀI, 1946

(VOL. 69, NO. 3, 2020)

Jessica Q. Stark

....

for Trần Lệ Xuân

Before the fit trim and the clapping
    of hands: a face bent in

violent repose. Still, the photograph
    of a captured figure with a

blanket for a shield and a baby
    on a battlefield.

This is not where we die and later,
    she would deny an interview

after the age of fifty-two. The projected image
    is no match for time's continuous

undoings: crossroad cruelties
    etched under lash. A

student of the Lycée Albert Sarraut, Madame
    Nhu was fluent in protection,

utility, and beauty's arsenal, but the civilizing
    mission had one message:

to burn the piano that held no secrets,
    to cast the face away like stone. In

her prime, she spoke French at home
    and could not write in

her native tongue—sharp thorns
    catching fabric, aflame.

There is a tradition of noble and heroic
    mothers here. After all,

Lê Lợi hid from the Chinese under
    his mother's skirts. Buffalo

Girls know how to tie a permanent
    knot around incidence, how to

mine mythology's antidotes for the
    fate of carrying and burying.

Madame Nhu was many things
    including a dancer, once a

soloist at the Hanoi National
    Theatre. She

dragged hems

    across the knife edge

between death and retreat. It is here
    where we depart (still alive)

    while inside, the Viet Minh are
steadying the flame, forgetting about

    the baby who—covered by
her mother's jacket—is turning

    away from the tidy story.

Is taking heaps of cloth in laughter,

    undoing each perfect edge.

Madame Nhu's Áo Dài, 1946

SONG OF THE ANDOUMBOULOU: 245

(VOL. 69, NO. 3, 2020)

Nathaniel Mackey

....

>   *for Robert Duncan & Peter O'Leary*

>   Greed's faux goodness lorded over us, the
>   one-third had thrown us to the dogs. In-
>   to the recesses of love we now went, a new

>   word

>   we made up, "steepage," led the way, the
>   arrival Itamar's muse intimated loomed un-
>   reachable, there less there than in thought . . .

>   The

>   abandoned boy and the abandoned girl fell
>   into strife our non-arrival announced, fought as
>   to who stood abandoned more, each in a real

>   and

>   imagined way left out. Might the Golden Ones
>   be among us again we begged, intervening, be
>   them or be with them, the abandoned girl, the

>   aban-

>   doned boy. The fight's blue connotation wore
>   thin the more strongly we begged, prayer's out-
>   line or limit come upon as upon a magic wand, a
>   burial mound. Crux and curvature were oddly one

>   we

>   noted, new to their masonic drive . . . The Golden
>   Ones roamed occluded but for a glimpse not given
>   to linger, cloud enough to blot out the sun, cloud all

>   over

>   us. None other than the Greed, Brother B avowed
>   and Anuncia amen'd him, the Greed great beyond
>   words' ability to say, numbers' to tell. "Seep" ran
>   one with "steepage," a strange brew everything

>   more

than our means conjured up. *And there we wept*
   torn a new one, sand poured out of our cried-out
eyes. We were all but or about to be dead, density

                                       our
   witness, out into the appurtenances of night . . . That
the Golden Ones, next to never seen, might be glimpsed,
   redolent of coin absconded with, we stepped in . . . We

                                      told
   them, the abandoned girl, the abandoned boy, they
were not—the Greed, Brother B ranted, beyond belief—
   we told them, the abandoned girl, the abandoned boy,

                                         we
  told them they were not the on-
ly ones

            •

We slept inside myth but were stirred by ythm, fur-
   tive gold we the bereft ran with. Not that the Golden
Ones, next to never seen, be seen, Anjali, new to our

                                     crew,
   pronounced. It was that the haptic take hold of us,
a sense of being run with, auspice we more stayed
   inside than saw, stood inside, run though we would

                                      and
   though we did . . . The Golden Ones were gone but
for the beseeching, themselves the beseeching our
   best hope. Anjali said as much, raw recruit, new to

                                     our
   dismay's reconnoiter, churchical armful Bouadjé
put his arm around while she spoke . . . She was hope's
   main squeeze, hope as hope would have it, hope's
mere mention, the abandoned ones the Golden Ones, at

                                     each
   other's throats though they
were

Spitless, tongueless mouthing what passed for
　　love in the place we were in, bite what had been
kisses, grab took embrace's place, deep into lip-
　　lessness we now went. The life whose residue the

　　　　　　　　　　　　　　　　　　words

　　were surrounded us, Nub's new phase too horrid
to be ignored, reminisce the Golden Ones though
　　we did . . . No redemptive narrative paved our way,

　　　　　　　　　　　　　　　　no

　　matter we had somewhere to go, no matter no
way we'd have said we were lost. It was the every-
　　thing everything was, the keeping on kept keeping on.
It would do that until it stopped, as would we. No need

　　　　　　　　　　　　　　　was

　　there for summing up . . . Were the Golden Ones an al-
　　chemical conceit Huff's drift of late had us wondering.
A shyster conceit the more skeptical had it, the Huther-
ing Ones, Nub's new reality show. Kleptocratic switch

　　　　　　　　　　　　　　gave

　　gold a bad name . . . It wasn't gold we were after, we'd
been there and gone. Nor was it home, we'd been there
as well. Bits of bread marked our way, black bread and

　　　　　　　　　　　　　　　ru-

　　bles. "Salt sandwiches" awaited us we'd heard, salt
sanguinity. Neither were we lost nor would they be eaten,
　　such the sort of dream we were having, residual steep-
age more than we could know. "Please, please, Dr. D,"

　　　　　　　　　　　　　　　we

found ourselves begging, "bring them back," skeptical
or not, inured to not knowing, gnostic agnostics in a
pinch . . . We'd begun eking out the minutes, the hours, the

　　　　　　　　　　　　　　　　days,

　　our day soon come. We let ourselves linger in the space
between *a*- and *gn*-, the cut we called it, counting out where

　　　　　　　　　　　　　　　　　no

　　numbers
　　were

          ———————————

I stood witnessing it from afar, bodily breakdown
a language or a lexicon it seemed, hamstring tight
  as a fist, bone gone, the Golden Ones but a body of
                                       lore.
    I stood angry on all fronts, no churchical armful
  beside me, bodily breakdown's prophecy the future
    bore in, Brother B, so grim it got, went biblical,
  "The Greed giveth not," he proclaimed ... The life the
                                     words
  were the residue of receded ... It was ... It wanted all
    of itself ... It awaited ... It would begin its redoing,
  could it ... It went ... It wanted ... It was all accents and
                                  flats ...

  It waited ... It was
only

Out of the gold bell of many a horn, our Golden Ones
   the Crackling Blue Ones, of late between yes and
maybe, no and maybe, maybe and perhaps, a dotted
                                                    rest
        among microtones . . . Gold gave itself over into
   the palms of our hands, not that we renounced it, not
      that we thought it was ours, not that we'd ever not
                                                    call
it hard to tell, none of it never be known to be in vain, a
                                                    blue,
        shading late-
ness

——————————

(slogan)

The Golden Ones, the Crackling Blue Ones,
   wore birds' heads, cracked seeds thrown into
bells around their necks, the poverty of time
                                 gone
   again into the coin purse, lifted bells we rang
                                      free-

dom from

ANABASIS

(VOL. 70, NO. 2, 2021)

Matthew Moore

....

Counting is the epistemology of war.
—JAMES DAWES

In a sleepless number, the Ego conceives
In the still of the night. In the grain house each degradation time milks
    from its copper mouth
Begins to drip with a clarity caught that begins to look uncertain caught
    next to eventual next,
In clear glass brands, on the rack,
In the shade of that same grain's rainbow. Outside this stalled parable,
    National Guard
Motors start and run our voices together. I mean what I have done to
    you begins to list
In me and once more
I do not hear you, I enlist you—to extract exactness even fumes
    withstand,
Each concession to that self, I allow to breathe, what fortune's rude
    nimbus already wreathes.

That choice in fortune was daft about me.
Shit-stirrer to beach-comber, operatives flare, by dint of windfall,
    a symmetry on fire suffers.
Metallurgy extols the air to dress everyone's looks in their war dead,
    known by their swoons.
Love a shiver, shivers like a coda.
Georgia has Mars, Uncle Billy a cow: war sublimation chastens;
    a bigoted sufficiency;
Peroration gives shape their bailiwick; dysentery hearts swell a bubble
    on a sea of shit.
The eye has a nation,
Hit upon viewfinder: little measure, little ease. Framers precinct
    wingspan,
Swanned uniforms: another country on the installment plan; another
    country a golden means.

You move proof, I wait for parapet's flash.

No health, no wisdom, no love, evening ought weary and treasure, old enthusiasms fucked in

Apostrophe. By jove to sustain, on a caves fantasy, a starry starry night dispossesses vacancy.

Territory, comrades at extenuated.

Gathers buttress your forehead a fort of doubt; in the new terror, it's: heed one's friend

Illegally; somewhat deaf to fate, honorific, naked with title; fish tastes how it's packed.

The dyer has a glove

Difference in prescience, empty bath, and marronage, in fruit from blood.

Ease the gore out of the birth of Josephine, a pigment instructs a wave, it gulls into open boat.

The spits of waste spoked oblution wheeled
March en plein war, wet fire, lathe animals.
Sewages annotated with sumptuary instress.
Sherman segregated soul, use, and property,
No parts touched at Savannah colloquy and
Yawed one, that roved, amid many gehenna.

NOTES

....

Introduction

1. "Editorial," *Carolina Quarterly* 1, no. 1 (Fall 1948): n.p.; Hardin Craig, "A Literary Revival at the University of North Carolina," *Carolina Quarterly* 1, no. 1 (Fall 1948): 7–10, 8.

2. "Editorial," *Carolina Quarterly* 2, no. 1 (Fall 1949): n.p.

3. Archives for the *Carolina Quarterly* at Wilson Library contain subscription solicitation letters addressed to prominent local individuals and their spouses, including C. H. Shipp (of Consolidated Construction Company, based in Durham, NC), Justice J. Wallace Winborne (of the North Carolina Supreme Court), T. J. Lassiter (of the North Carolina Press Association), S. T. Peace (of *Gold Leaf*, a newspaper in Henderson, NC), Todd Caldwell (of the *Independent*, a newspaper in Fuquay-Varina, NC), Julius W. Cone (of Cone Mills in Greensboro, NC), and Clarence Poe (of the *Progressive Farmer*, a magazine based in Raleigh), among others. In early December 1950, letters advertising the *Quarterly* were sent to bookshops in Flint, Michigan; New London, Connecticut; Lexington, Kentucky; and Toronto, among several other locations. Box 1, folder 2 in the *Carolina Quarterly* Records, no. 40145, University Archives, Wilson Library, University of North Carolina at Chapel Hill.

4. "Editorial," *Carolina Quarterly* 3, no. 2 (Winter 1951): n.p.

5. "Editorial," *Carolina Quarterly* 2, no. 1 (Fall 1949): n.p.

6. Craig, "A Literary Revival," 9.

7. Glenn Altschuler and Stuart Blumin, *The GI Bill: The New Deal for Veterans* (Oxford: Oxford University Press, 2009), 89.

8. "Editorial," *Carolina Quarterly* 1, no. 2 (Winter 1949): n.p.

9. "Editorial," *Carolina Quarterly* 1, no. 2.

10. Frank Murphy, "New Southern Fiction: Urban or Agrarian?," *Carolina Quarterly* 13, no. 2 (Spring 1961): 18–26.

11. Murphy, "New Southern Fiction," 18.

12. Ralph Waldo Emerson, *Essays & Lectures* (New York: Library of America, 1983), 10.

CONTRIBUTORS

....

James Applewhite is the author of many poetry collections, most recently *Time Beginnings* (Louisiana State University Press, 2017). His other collections include *Cosmos: A Poem* (Louisiana State University Press, 2014), *Selected Poems* (Duke University Press, 2005), *Daytime and Starlight* (Louisiana State University Press, 1997), and *River Writing: An Eno Journal* (Princeton University Press, 1988). He is the recipient of a Guggenheim Fellowship for poetry and the Jean Stein Award in Poetry from the American Academy and Institute of Arts and Letters. He is a professor emeritus in creative writing at Duke University.

Rilla Askew is the author of five novels, a book of stories, and a collection of creative nonfiction. She is a PEN/Faulkner finalist and recipient of the Arts and Letters Award from the American Academy of Arts and Letters. Her novel about the 1921 Tulsa Race Massacre, *Fire in Beulah* (Viking Penguin, 2001), received the American Book Award in 2002.

Peter Balakian is the author of many books, including *Ozone Journal* (University of Chicago Press, 2015), winner of the Pulitzer Prize for Poetry, *Black Dog of Fate* (Basic Books, 1997), winner of the PEN/Albrand Award for memoir, and the *New York Times* best-selling *The Burning Tigris: The Armenian Genocide and America's Response* (HarperCollins, 2003). The poem "Father Fisheye" is the title poem of his first book of poems, published in 1979. His newest book of poems is *No Sign* (University of Chicago Press, 2022).

Oliver Baez Bendorf is the author of *Consider the Rooster* (forthcoming from Nightboat Books in September 2024) and two previous collections of poems: *Advantages of Being Evergreen* (Cleveland State University Poetry Center, 2019) and *The Spectral Wilderness* (Kent State University Press, 2015). He has received fellowships and awards from the National Endowment for the Arts, the Publishing Triangle, CantoMundo, Vermont Studio Center, and the Wisconsin Institute for Creative Writing. Born and raised in Iowa, he now lives in Colorado.

Wendell Berry is a native of Henry County, Kentucky, where he has lived most of his life. He is writing the history of Port William, Kentucky, which he began with "The Brothers."

Doris Betts, award-winning author of three collections of short fiction and six novels, was a beloved North Carolina writer and teacher. Her *Beasts of the Southern Wild and Other Stories* (Harper and Row, 1973) was a finalist for the National Book Award, and *Souls Raised from the Dead* (Touchstone, 1994) won the Southern Book

Award. She taught in the English Department at UNC–Chapel Hill for thirty years, advancing to the title of Alumni Distinguished Professor of English. Betts passed away in 2012 in Pittsboro, North Carolina. Her papers are held by the Southern Historical Collection at UNC–Chapel Hill's Wilson Library.

Linda Bierds has published ten books of poetry, most recently *The Hardy Tree* (Copper Canyon Press, 2019). Her work has appeared in many magazines including the *New Yorker*, the *Atlantic*, and *Poetry*. She teaches at the University of Washington in Seattle.

Rosellen Brown has published eleven books, one of which, *Street Games* (Doubleday, 1974) contains "Mustard Seed." Among her six novels are *Civil Wars* (Knopf, 1984), *Before and After* (Farrar, Straus and Giroux, 1993), and, most recently, *The Lake on Fire* (Sarabande, 2018). Her books of poetry include *Cora Fry's Pillow Book* (Farrar, Straus and Giroux, 1994). She teaches at the School of the Art Institute of Chicago.

Raymond Carver was born in Clatskanie, Oregon, in 1938. His first collection of stories, *Will You Please Be Quiet, Please?* (McGraw-Hill, 1976; a National Book Award nominee in 1977), was followed by *What We Talk about When We Talk about Love* (Knopf, 1981), *Cathedral* (Knopf, 1983; nominated for the Pulitzer Prize in 1984), and *Where I'm Calling From* (Atlantic Monthly Press) in 1988, when he was inducted into the American Academy of Arts and Letters. He died on August 2, 1988, shortly after completing the poems of *A New Path to the Waterfall* (Atlantic Monthly Press, 1989). He lived with his wife, the poet Tess Gallagher, in Port Angeles, Washington.

Kristen Case is the author of two volumes of poetry: *Little Arias* (New Issues, 2015) and *Principles of Economics* (Switchback, 2018). She lives and teaches in Farmington, Maine.

Fred Chappell is the author of more than thirty volumes of poetry and prose. He has received the Bollingen Prize, the T. S. Eliot Award, and the Thomas Wolfe Prize. His fiction has been translated into more than a dozen languages and received the Best Foreign Book Award from the Académie Française. He was the poet laureate of North Carolina from 1997 to 2002.

Michael Chitwood has published eleven books. His most recent book, *Search & Rescue* (Louisiana State University Press, 2018), received the L. E. Phillabaum Award from Louisiana State University Press and the Library of Virginia Literary Award in Poetry.

Lucas Church is the author of the forthcoming short story collection *A Little Gunpowder, a Little Boat, and Boom* (Press 53). His writing has appeared or is forthcoming in *Pleiades*, *Hotel Amerika*, and the *Nashville Review*, among other journals. He holds an MFA from North Carolina State University.

Martha Collins's eleven books of poems include *Because What Else Could I Do* (University of Pittsburgh, 2019), which won the William Carlos Williams Award, and *Casualty Reports* (University of Pittsburgh Press, 2019). Her fifth volume of cotranslated Vietnamese poetry was published by Milkweed in 2023.

Adam Day is the author of *Left-Handed Wolf* (Louisiana State University Press, 2020) and *Model of a City in Civil War* (Sarabande, 2015). He is the recipient of a Poetry Society of America Chapbook Fellowship for *Badger, Apocrypha* (2011) and of a PEN America Literary Award.

Annie Dillard is the author of many works of nonfiction, including *Pilgrim at Tinker Creek* (Harper's Magazine Press, 1974) and *Teaching a Stone to Talk* (Harper and Row, 1982), as well as the novels *The Living* (HarperCollins, 1992) and *The Maytrees* (HarperCollins, 2007).

Camille Dungy is the author of the essay collection *Guidebook to Relative Strangers: Journeys into Race, Motherhood, and History* (W. W. Norton, 2017) and four collections of poetry, most recently *Trophic Cascade* (Wesleyan University Press, 2018). A finalist for the National Book Critics Circle Award, she has edited three anthologies, including *Black Nature: Four Centuries of African American Nature Poetry* (University of Georgia Press, 2000). Dungy's work has appeared in *Best American Poetry*, *100 Best African American Poems*, *Best American Essays*, *Best American Travel Essays*, *All We Can Save: Truth, Courage, and Solutions for the Climate Crisis*, *The 1619 Project* of the *New York Times Magazine*, more than 30 other anthologies and over 100 journals. Her honors include the 2021 Academy of American Poets Fellowship, a Guggenheim Fellowship, an American Book Award, a Colorado Book Award, two Northern California Book Awards, two NAACP Image Award Nominations, and fellowships from the National Endowment for the Arts in both prose and poetry. She is a University Distinguished Professor at Colorado State University. Her website is www.camilledungy.com.

Charles Eaton (1916–2006), poet and professor, was born in Winston-Salem, North Carolina. Eaton received his BA from the University of North Carolina in 1936, studied at Princeton, and earned his MA from Harvard, where he worked with Robert Frost, who later recommended him to the Bread Loaf Writers' Conference. He authored seventeen poetry collections and two short story collections and received numerous literary awards, including the Robert Frost Fellowship, the New England Poetry Club Golden Rose Award, and the North Carolina Literature Award.

Edward Falco's most recent book is the poetry collection *Wolf Moon Blood Moon* (Louisiana State University Press, 2018). His novel *Transcendent Gardening* is forthcoming from C&R Press, and his poetry collection *X in the Tickseed* is forthcoming from Louisiana State University Press. He teaches in the MFA Program in Creative Writing at Virginia Tech.

Lawrence Ferlinghetti, a prominent voice of the wide-open poetry movement, wrote poetry, translation, fiction, theater, art criticism, film narration, and essays. In 1953, after receiving his BA from UNC–Chapel Hill, he opened the City Lights bookstore in San Francisco. Prominent works include *Coney Island of the Mind* (New Directions, 1958), *Pictures of the Gone World* (City Lights, 1955), and *Love in the Days of Rage* (E. P. Dutton, 1988).

Alice Fulton's new poetry collection, *Coloratura on a Silence Found in Many Expressive Systems*, was published in 2022 by W. W. Norton. She has received an American Academy of Arts and Letters Award in Literature, the Bobbitt National Prize for Poetry, and fellowships from the MacArthur Foundation, the National Endowment for the Arts, and the Guggenheim Foundation.

Marianne Gingher retired from UNC–Chapel Hill in 2021 after teaching creative writing for more than forty years. A former Doris Betts Term Professor and the recipient of numerous teaching awards, she has published both fiction and nonfiction. She also writes and performs the occasional puppet play.

Albert Goldbarth has been publishing notable collections of poetry for fifty years. Two of his collections have received the National Book Critics Circle Award. His most recent are *Other Worlds* (University of Pittsburgh Press, 2021) and *Everybody* (Lynx House, 2022). He lives in Wichita, Kansas.

Sharon Hashimoto, who was born in Seattle and is a lifelong resident of Washington state, is a poet and fiction writer. She is a Sansei (third-generation Japanese American) with paternal ties to Hawai'i. Her MFA is from the University of Washington. She was a William Raney Scholar for poetry at the Bread Loaf Writers' Conference. Her poems and stories have appeared in *Shenandoah, North American Review, Tampa Review, Crab Orchard Review, Poetry*, and others. For twenty-nine years, she taught at Highline College in Des Moines, Washington. In 1990, she was awarded a National Endowment for the Arts award in poetry. She is at work on a novel.

Ha Jin has published many books of fiction and poetry and nonfiction. His most recent book is a novel, *A Song Everlasting* (Pantheon, 2021). He has received the National Book Award, two PEN/Faulkner Awards, and the PEN/Hemingway Award. He teaches fiction writing and literature at Boston University.

Karen An-hwei Lee is the author of *Duress* (Cascade, 2022), *Rose Is a Verb: Neo-Georgics* (Slant, 2021), *Phyla of Joy* (Tupelo, 2012), *Ardor* (Tupelo, 2008), and *In Medias Res* (Sarabande, 2004), winner of the Norma Farber First Book Award. She has authored two novels, *Sonata in K* (Ellipsis, 2017) and *The Maze of Transparencies* (Ellipsis, 2019). The recipient of a National Endowment for the Arts grant, she currently lives in greater Chicago.

Denise Levertov (1923–97) was a British-born American poet. She wrote and published twenty books of poetry, criticism, and translations. She also edited several anthologies. Among her many awards and honors, she received the Shelley Memorial Award, the Robert Frost Medal, the Lenore Marshall Prize, the Lannan Award, a grant from the National Institute of Arts and Letters, and a Guggenheim Fellowship.

Lisa Lewis's most recent collections of poetry include *The Body Double* (*Georgetown Review* Press, 2016), *Taxonomy of the Missing* (Word Works, 2018), and a chapbook titled *The Borrowing Days* (Emrys Press, 2021). She directs the creative writing program at Oklahoma State University and serves as editor of the *Cimarron Review*.

Frannie Lindsay's sixth book of poems, *The Snow's Wife*, was published by Cavankerry Press in 2020. She has received the May Swenson Award, the Perugia Award, the Washington Prize, the Benjamin Saltman Award, and the Missouri Review Prize. Her poems have appeared in *Best American Poetry 2014*, the *Yale Review*, *Field*, *American Poetry Review*, *Plume*, the *Atlantic Monthly*, and many other journals. She has been granted fellowships by the Massachusetts Cultural Council and the National Endowment for the Arts. She currently teaches poetry workshops on crafting grief and trauma. She is also a classical pianist.

Nathaniel Mackey is the author of numerous books and chapbooks of poetry, most recently *Double Trio*, a boxed set of three books: *Tej Bet, So's Notice*, and *Nerve Church* (New Directions, 2021). His honors include the National Book Award and the Bollingen Prize. He teaches at Duke University.

Jill McCorkle is the author of seven novels and four story collections. Her latest novel is *Hieroglyphics* (Algonquin, 2020). Her work has appeared in numerous periodicals and four of her short stories have been selected for *Best American Short Stories*. She lives in Hillsborough, North Carolina.

Michael McFee has published seventeen books; his tenth full-length collection of poetry, *A Long Time to Be Gone*, came out from Carnegie Mellon University Press in 2022. He is the Doris Betts Term Professor of English in the Creative Writing Program at UNC–Chapel Hill, where he has taught since 1990.

Heather McHugh writes, "I live on the Olympic Peninsula, & come to terms with where I am, these days, by taking thousands of photos of it. Recent poems of mine can be found in a chapbook called *Feeler*, from Sarabande, or the larger collection (from Copper Canyon) titled *Muddy Matterhorn*. Or just visit heathermchugh.com."

Kathleen McNamara's short fiction and essays have appeared in *North American Review*, *Witness*, the *Columbia Journal*, *Redivider*, *Nimrod*, *This Side of the Divide: New Lore of the American West* (Baobab, 2023), and elsewhere. She lives in central Arizona with her husband and their two sons.

Faith Merino is a Stegner Fellow at Stanford, with an MFA in fiction from UC Davis. Her novel *Cormorant Lake* (Blackstone, 2021) was longlisted for the Center for Fiction's First Novel Award. She lives in Sacramento with her husband, sons, and animal friends.

Matthew Moore is the author of *The Reckoning of Jeanne d'Antietam* (University of Nevada Press, 2023), winner of the 2021 Betsy Joiner Flanagan Award in Poetry. He is the translator of Tomaž Šalamun's *Opera Buffa* (Black Ocean, 2022). He was born in Illinois in 1985.

Robert Morgan is the author of several books of poems, including *Terroir* (Penguin, 2011) and *Dark Energy* (Penguin, 2015). He has published ten books of fiction, including the *New York Times* bestseller *Gap Creek* (Algonquin, 1999) and, most recently, *Chasing the North Star* (Workman, 2016) and *As Rain Turns to Snow and Other Stories* (Broadstone, 2017). His works of nonfiction include *Lions of the West* (Shannon Ravenel, 2011) and the national bestseller *Boone: A Biography* (Shannon Ravenel, 2007). The recipient of awards from the Guggenheim Foundation and the American Academy of Arts and Letters, he is currently Kappa Alpha Professor of English at Cornell University.

Alicia Mountain is the author of *Four in Hand* (BOA Editions, 2023) and *High Ground Coward* (University of Iowa Press, 2018), the latter of which won the Iowa Poetry Prize. She teaches in the Writer's Foundry MFA program at St. Joseph's University in Brooklyn.

Joyce Carol Oates is the author most recently of the novel *Breathe* (Ecco, 2021) and the poetry collection *American Melancholy* (Ecco, 2021). She is a member of the American Academy of Arts and Letters and the 2020 recipient of the Cino Del Duca award, and has been a longtime resident of Princeton, New Jersey.

Gloria Oden was born in Yonkers, New York, on October 30, 1923. She was a poet, editor, and professor of English. She was nominated for the Pulitzer Prize in 1979 for her poetry collection *Resurrections* (Olivant, 1978). She was the author of *The Naked Frame: A Love Poem and Sonnets* (Exposition, 1952), *The Tie That Binds* (Olivant, 1980), and *Appearances* (Saru, 2004). Oden lived in Cantonsville, Maryland, and passed away on December 16, 2011.

Adriana Páramo is a Colombian anthropologist and author of three nonfiction books, *Looking for Esperanza* (Benu, 2012), *My Mother's Funeral* (CavanKerry, 2013), and *Unsent Letters to My Mother* (Floricanto, 2020). She teaches creative writing in the low-residency MFA program at Fairfield University. She writes from the Emirate of Qatar, where, oddly enough, she works as a fitness and yoga instructor.

Ron Rash is the author of seven novels, six collections of stories, and five books of poems. He teaches at Western Carolina University.

Kalamu ya Salaam is a New Orleans writer, filmmaker, and educator. He is the moderator of neo•griot, an information blog for Black writers and supporters of our literature worldwide, and the founder of WordBand, the NOMMO Literary Society, and Runagate Press. Salaam has written seven books of poetry. His play *The Breath of Life* was honored by Louisiana State University, and *BLK Love Song #1* won a Best of Fringe Award from the *Manchester Evening News* in England. A respected music writer and critic, he is the arts and entertainment editor for the *New Orleans Tribune* and is a regular contributor to *Wavelength*, the *Louisiana Weekly*, and the *New Orleans Music Magazine*.

James Salter authored numerous books, including the novels *All That Is* (Knopf, 2013), *Solo Faces* (North Point, 1988), *Light Years* (Random House, 1975), *A Sport and a Pastime* (Doubleday, 1967), *The Arm of Flesh* (revised as *Cassada* [Counter-point, 2001]), and *The Hunters* (Counterpoint, 1997); the memoirs *Gods of Tin* (Counterpoint, 2005) and *Burning the Days* (Random House, 1997), the collections *Dusk and Other Stories* (North Point, 1989), which won the 1989 PEN/Faulkner Award, and *Last Night* (Vintage, 2006), which won the Rea Award for the Short Story and the PEN/Malamud Award; and *Life Is Meals: A Food Lover's Book of Days* (Knopf, 2006), written with his wife, Kay Salter. He died in 2015.

Jane Satterfield is the recipient of awards in poetry from the National Endowment for the Arts, the Maryland Arts Council, *Bellingham Review*, Ledbury Poetry Festival, *Mslexia*, and more. Her most recent book is *Apocalypse Mix* (Autumn House, 2016), awarded the Autumn House Poetry Prize, selected by David St. John. Visit her at https://janesatterfield.org.

Alan Shapiro's new poetry collection, *Proceed to Check Out*, was published in 2022 by the University of Chicago Press.

Evie Shockley is the author of *the new black* (Wesleyan University Press, 2011), *semiautomatic* (Wesleyan University Press, 2017), and *suddenly we* (Wesleyan University Press, 2023). Her honors include two Hurston/Wright Legacy Awards, the Holmes National Poetry Prize, and a Lannan Literary Award, among others. She is the Zora Neale Hurston Professor of English at Rutgers University.

Jessica Q. Stark is the author of *Buffalo Girl* (BOA Editions, 2023), *Savage Pageant* (Birds, LLC, 2020), and four poetry chapbooks, including *INNANET* (Offending Adam, 2021). She is a poetry editor at *AGNI* and an assistant professor of creative writing at the University of North Florida.

Terese Svoboda, author of twenty-one books of poetry, fiction, biography, memoir, and translation, has won the Guggenheim, the Bobst Prize in fiction, the Iowa Poetry Prize, a National Endowment for the Humanities translation grant, the Graywolf Nonfiction Prize, a Jerome Foundation video prize, the O. Henry Award for the short story, and a Pushcart Prize.

Lee Upton's most recent book is *The Day Every Day Is* (Saturnalia, 2023). Her poetry has appeared widely, including in three editions of *Best American Poetry*. Her comic novel, *Tabitha, Get Up*, is forthcoming in May 2024.

David Wagoner was a leading poet of the Pacific Northwest and the author of ten acclaimed novels and twenty-four poetry collections. He was the recipient of numerous literary awards, including the Ruth Lilly Poetry Prize, two Pushcart Prizes, and the Academy of Arts and Letters Award, and was nominated twice for the National Book Award. Wagoner died in late 2021 at age ninety-five.

G. C. Waldrep's most recent books are *The Earliest Witnesses* (Tupelo/Carcanet, 2021) and *feast gently* (Tupelo, 2018), winner of the William Carlos Williams Award from the Poetry Society of America. His recent work has appeared in *American Poetry Review, Poetry, Paris Review, New England Review, Yale Review, Colorado Review, The Nation, New American Writing, Conjunctions*, and other journals. Waldrep lives in Lewisburg, Pennsylvania, where he teaches at Bucknell University.

Daniel Wallace is the author of six novels and one book of nonfiction, titled *This Isn't Going to End Well* (Algonquin, 2023). His first novel, *Big Fish* (Pandher, 1998), was converted into a film by Tim Burton and a Broadway musical. He teaches in the Creative Writing Program at UNC–Chapel Hill.

Ross White is a teaching assistant professor at UNC–Chapel Hill, where he teaches poetry writing, editing and publishing, podcasting, and grammar. His collections include *Valley of Want* (Unicorn, 2022), *Charm Offensive* (Eyewear, 2023), and *How We Came Upon the Colony* (Unicorn, 2014).

Felicia Zamora is the author of six poetry collections, including *I Always Carry My Bones* (University of Iowa Press, 2021), winner of the Iowa Poetry Prize. Her poems have appeared in *Boston Review, Guernica, Orion, The Nation*, and others. She is an assistant professor of poetry at the University of Cincinnati and associate poetry editor for *Colorado Review*.

PERMISSIONS ACKNOWLEDGMENTS

....

Rilla Askew, "Irrevocable Acts," from *Strange Business* (Norman: University of Oklahoma Press). Copyright © 1992 by Rilla Askew. Reprinted with the permission of the author.

Wendell Berry, "The Brothers," from the *Carolina Quarterly* (1956). Later revised by the author and included in *Nathan Coulter: A Novel*. Copyright © 1956, 1960, 2008 by Wendell Berry. Reprinted with the permission of The Permissions Company, LLC, on behalf of Counterpoint Press, counterpointpress.com.

Adam Day, "His Dementia," from *Model of a City in Civil War* (Louisville, KY: Sarabande Books). Copyright © 2015 by Adam Day. Reprinted with the permission of The Permissions Company, LLC, on behalf of Sarabande Books, www.sarabandebooks.org.

Edward Falco, "Night Drives," from *In the Park of Culture* (Notre Dame, IN: University of Notre Dame Press). Copyright © 2005 by Edward Falco. Reprinted with the permission of the author.

Denise Levertov, "Anamnesis at the Faultline," from *Sands of the Well* (New York: New Directions Publishing). Copyright © 1994, 1995, 1996 by Denise Levertov. Reprinted with the permission of New Directions Publishing Corp.

Nathaniel Mackey, "Song of the Andoumboulou: 245," from *Double Trio* (New York: New Directions Publishing). Copyright © 2021 by Nathaniel Mackey. Reprinted by permission of New Directions Publishing Corp.

Jill McCorkle, "from *Carolina Moon*," from *Carolina Moon* (Chapel Hill, NC: Algonquin Books). Copyright © 1996 by Jill McCorkle. Reprinted by permission of Algonquin Books, an imprint of Hachette Book Group, Inc.

Michael McFee, "Pearly Gates," from *Colander* (Pittsburgh: Carnegie Mellon University Press). Copyright © 1996 by Michael McFee. Reprinted with permission of the author.

Alicia Mountain, "Haymaker Barnburner," and "Glaring Pattern Baldness" from *High Ground Coward* (Iowa City: University of Iowa Press). Copyright © 2018 by Alicia Mountain. Reprinted with the permission of University of Iowa Press.

Joyce Carol Oates, "Lovers' Bodies," from *Angel Fire* (Baton Rouge: Louisiana State University Press). Copyright © 1973 by Joyce Carol Oates. Reprinted with the permission of the author.

Ron Rash, "Junk Car in Snow," from *Waking* (Spartanburg, SC: Hub City Press). Copyright © 2011 by Ron Rash. Reprinted with the permission of the publisher, Hub City Press. All rights reserved.